James Martin

The Collection

with 300 classic recipes

James Martin

The Collection

with 300 classic recipes

Photographs by
Jean Cazals and
Simon Wheeler

MITCHELL BEAZLEY

THE COLLECTION
by James Martin

First published in Great Britain in 2008 by Mitchell Beazley,
an imprint of Octopus Publishing Group Ltd.
2–4 Heron Quays, London E14 4JP
An Hachette Livre UK Company
www.octopusbooks.co.uk

Distributed in the U.S. and Canada by Octopus Books USA:
c/o Hachette Book Group USA, 237 Park Avenue
New York NY 10017

The recipes in this book are taken from the following James
Martin titles: *Eating In with James Martin*, *James Martin's
Great British Dinners*, *James Martin's Easy British Food*,
James Martin's Great British Winter Cookbook, and
Delicious! The Deli Cookbook.

The publishers will be grateful for any information that will
assist them in keeping future editions up to date. Although all
reasonable care has been taken in the preparation of this
book, neither the publishers nor the author can accept any
liability for any consequence arising from the use thereof, or
the information contained therein.

The author has asserted his moral rights.

ISBN: 978 1 84533 460 4

Set in Helvetica Neue LT and LubalinGraph LT.

Color reproduction in China by Sang Choy.

Printed and bound in China by Toppan Printing Company Ltd.

Commissioning Editor Rebecca Spry
Art Director Tim Foster
Project Editor Leanne Bryan
Editor Susan Fleming
Indexer Diana Lecore
Executive Art Editor Yasia Williams-Leedham
Designer Nicky Collings
Prop Stylists Isabel De Cordova, Sue Rowlands
Food Stylists Lisa Harrison, Bethany Heald,
  Katherine Ibbs, Chris Start, Karen Taylor, Linda Tubby
Photography Jean Cazals and Simon Wheeler
Production Manager Peter Hunt

contents

introduction

I'm probably best known for cooking British food, which isn't all that surprising because it's been a major part of my life since I was a kid. My love of British foods developed as I watched my mother, grandmother, and aunt cooking. Many of their dishes are included in this book, and you can't get more traditional than that.

If I grew up enjoying my grandmother's sponge cakes, my mother's roast beef, and my grandad's poached haddock, I also grew up with dishes that we have adopted from abroad. Many of them are definitely "British" now: I'm talking about dishes like kedgeree, moussaka, burgers, and chicken tikka masala. They all taste fantastic, and so I've included them, too.

I've also added to my collection of British dishes over the years, due to my work as a chef: through cooking at the Hotel du Vin and on the *Ocean Village* cruise ships; through speedy invention on the television program *Ready Steady Cook* and presenting *Saturday Kitchen*; through researching British desserts for *Sweet Baby James*; and through traveling around the country meeting new people and tasting dishes for *The Great British Village Show*.

None of these recipes is difficult; in fact, I've simplified the original in many cases. Although I trained as a chef, I'm not against taking shortcuts in cooking, and I will happily use store-bought stocks, ice creams, and pastries. (But I've given recipes for many of these, so you can choose.)

Purist foodies may turn their noses up at some of the dishes here, but I don't care. I've been eating quiche and pizza, for instance, since my teens, and to me they're as much part of my experience of British food as apple pie and bacon rolls. This book is my all-singing, all-dancing (well, I did reach the semifinals of the television dance competition *Strictly Come Dancing* in 2005!) collection of foods that we celebrate in Britain, and I hope you enjoy them as much as I do.

breakfasts

I once presented a show on asparagus and was lucky enough to visit a farm in Sussex, England. The season for English asparagus normally runs from May to June, for about six weeks. The most amazing thing I found at the farm was that it seemed like you could see the asparagus stalks growing; the farmer told me it was common to finish picking the field one day and then to go back to start picking the same field again almost immediately because the asparagus grows so quickly.

Asparagus Spears with Poached Egg and Tarragon Butter

SERVES 4

20–30 asparagus spears, trimmed

salt, to taste

1 tbsp white wine vinegar

4 free-range eggs

7 tbsp butter

juice of 2 lemons

2 tbsp chopped fresh tarragon

4 slices brioche, toasted

Steam the asparagus over plenty of boiling water for 3–5 minutes, depending on the thickness of the spears.

Bring a pan of salted water to a boil and add the vinegar. Whisk to make a whirlpool. Once it's settled crack an egg in the middle. Simmer for 2–3 minutes, remove, and keep warm. Repeat with the other eggs.

Melt the butter in a pan and stir in the lemon juice and tarragon. Pile the spears of asparagus onto each toasted brioche. Top with a poached egg and spoon the butter sauce over it.

My Dad's Cheese on Toast
My father taught me this recipe—it's real cheese on toast. This has to be one of the first culinary skills people master when they leave home!

SERVES 4

4 slices brown bread, toasted

2 tbsp butter, softened

2 cups grated cheddar

3 tbsp heavy cream

a dash of Worcestershire sauce

a dash of Tabasco sauce (optional)

salt and pepper, to taste

Preheat the broiler to its highest setting.

Spread the toast with the butter.

Put the cheese in a bowl and add the cream, Worcestershire sauce, Tabasco (if using), and seasoning. Mix well. Spoon the mixture onto the buttered toasts.

Place the toast under the broiler, and then heat until the cheese starts to bubble on the top and turns golden brown. Remove and eat immediately.

Oatcakes
I suppose the main reason why oats are thought to be Scottish is that they are the country's most successful cereal crop. There's a saying that Scottish housewives are born with a rolling pin under their arms; it's not to whack men with, but because of their love for baking. You can use finer flour for a lighter oatcake, if you like.

MAKES 16 OATCAKES

scant 1¹/₄ cups medium fine oats

a pinch of salt

2 tbsp butter, melted

3 tbsp water

all-purpose flour, for dusting

Preheat the oven to 350°F/180°C. Place the oats and salt in a bowl and stir in the melted butter. Mix in enough water to create a firm, pliable dough.

Sprinkle the work surface with flour and knead the dough for a few minutes. Roll out the dough until it is about ¹/₈ inch thick and cut out large round cakes. On each one, mark out six to eight segments on the surface, but not all the way through. Bake in the oven for 8–10 minutes, until golden brown. Serve with any cheese you like—as long as it's British!

I'm lucky enough to have a local farmer deliver fresh eggs to me each day. But when doing my research for this book, I learned a simple thing that we take for granted—that the standard British egg has not always been British. In 1900, the country imported two billion fresh eggs from as far away as Eastern Europe, so they can't have been that fresh, after all, can they?

Plain and Sweet Omelettes

SERVES 1–2

PLAIN OMELETTE

3 free-range eggs

salt and pepper, to taste

2 tbsp unsalted butter

SWEET OMELETTE

3 free-range eggs

2 tbsp unsalted butter

3¹/₂ oz (100g) fresh raspberries

3 tbsp fresh raspberry coulis

confectioners' sugar, for sprinkling

Beat the eggs lightly with some salt and pepper (leave out the seasoning if you're making a sweet omelet).

Heat an 8 inch (20 cm) omelet pan. the pan, then add the butter. When it melts, swirl it around the pan to coat the bottom. Add the eggs and shake the pan to spread them out evenly. Use a fork to draw the edges of the egg toward the center, allowing any uncooked egg to run to the sides. Continue until the egg is neatly set but still soft, with a little liquid on top. Remove from the heat.

If you're making a sweet omelet, now add the raspberries to one-half of the omelet, then flip the opposite side over it. Turn the omelet out of the pan onto a plate. Serve with the coulis and a sprinkling of confectioners' sugar.

Yes, I know people are going to say it's an omelet Arnold Bennett, but who cares? I made this while filming in Whitby in northern England. I got the haddock from a store called Fortune's, which is mainly famous for smoked kippers, but the haddock was wonderful. I used fresh farm eggs and cream—English, of course—and it was one of the nicest dishes I've ever made.

Smoked Haddock Omelette

SERVES 2

11/4 cups milk

3 bay leaves

2 slices onion

6 black peppercorns

10 oz (280 g) undyed smoked haddock fillet

6 free-range eggs

salt and pepper, to taste

11/2 tbsp unsalted butter

1/4 cup heavy cream

2 tbsp freshly grated Parmesan

Mix the milk with 1¼ cups of water, pour it into a large shallow pan, and bring to a boil. Add the bay leaves, onion, and peppercorns, and bring back to a boil. Add the smoked haddock, bring back to a simmer, and poach for about 3–4 minutes, until the fish is cooked. Lift the fish out onto a plate and let stand until cool, then break into flakes, discarding any skin and bones. Preheat the broiler to high.

Whisk the eggs and season. Heat a 9–10 inch (23–25 cm) nonstick skillet over a medium heat, then add the butter and swirl it around to coat the bottom and sides of the pan. Pour in the eggs and, as they start to set, drag the back of a fork over the bottom of the pan, lifting up little folds of egg to allow the uncooked egg to run underneath.

When the omelet is set underneath but still moist on top, sprinkle over the flaked smoked haddock. Pour the cream over, add the Parmesan, and broil the omelet until lightly golden. Slide onto a warmed plate, and serve with a crisp green salad.

Kedgeree

My father used to cook the best kedgeree, always for breakfast. The shrimp are optional, but the curry powder is a must to kick-start the flavor. A little chopped green chile will give it the same kick if you don't have any curry powder.

SERVES 4

3 cups milk

1 lb 2 oz (500 g) undyed smoked haddock

3 tbsp butter

1 onion, finely chopped

generous 3/4 cup long-grain rice

1 tsp medium curry powder

1 handful frozen cooked shrimp, defrosted

salt and pepper, to taste

3 soft-boiled, free-range eggs, shelled and quartered

2 tbsp chopped, fresh flat-leaf parsley

Put the milk in a pan and bring to a boil. Add the haddock, making sure it is covered by milk, and simmer for 2 minutes. Remove from the heat and let cool slightly. Flake the fish and pick off any bones and skin. Reserve the milk.

In a heavy pan, melt 2 tablespoons of the butter and sauté the onion for 2–3 minutes. Add the rice and curry powder, then the milk. Stir well. Bring to a gentle simmer and cook for 20–25 minutes, until the rice is cooked. Add a little more milk if it begins to dry out.

When the rice is cooked, add the haddock, then the shrimp. Be careful when stirring not to break up the haddock too much. Season and put in a serving dish. Arrange the soft-boiled eggs around the edge, sprinkle with the parsley, and top with the remaining butter.

Chive Blinis with Smoked Salmon and Crème Fraîche

Perhaps not so traditionally British, but this is the first dish I remember making at catering college. It is a must for any canapé tray. It's sometimes made more fancy with a spoonful of caviar, but it's at its best when freshly made and served with sliced Scottish smoked salmon and some thick, creamy crème fraîche.

SERVES 4

BLINIS
5 free-range egg whites

1¼ cups all-purpose flour

scant 1 cup milk

1 free-range egg, beaten

1 free-range egg yolk

1 tsp baking soda

salt and pepper, to taste

TO COOK AND SERVE
butter, for cooking

7 oz (200 g) smoked salmon

½ cup thick crème fraîche or sour cream

2 tbsp finely chopped fresh chives

Whisk the egg whites until stiff.

Mix together the remaining blini ingredients, then carefully fold the egg whites into the mixture.

Put a teaspoonful of the mixture onto a very hot, lightly buttered, heavy skillet and cook in a little butter for approximately 2–3 minutes on each side, until golden brown. When bubbling, flip over with a spatula. Repeat with the remainder of the mixture.

Cut the smoked salmon into small strips. Arrange a squiggly shape of salmon on each blini and add a teaspoon of crème fraiche and a sprinkling of finely chopped chives.

I remember cooking this at college and wondering why we spent a whole day learning how to poach an egg. Now I know, as I have asked everybody I have interviewed since then to do it, and probably 50 percent of them make a mess of it. Why? Because most of them are too busy thinking about the next fancy garnish to go on their plate, and not about what is really important. Good cooking is all about getting the basics right, and doing them well, before progressing. To the British chef Delia Smith, you are correct about that, and I thank you.

Eggs Benedict with Smoked Haddock

SERVES 4

4 thick, undyed smoked haddock fillets, 3 1/2 oz (100 g) each, cooked (*see* page 15)

1 tbsp white wine vinegar

4 free-range eggs

TO SERVE AND GARNISH

1 quantity Hollandaise Sauce (*see* page 238)

2 English muffins

a few coarsely crushed black peppercorns

a few chopped fresh chives

Make the Hollandaise sauce and keep it warm, off the heat, over a pan of warm water.

Cook the smoked haddock as described on page 15. Lift the haddock out onto a plate, peel off the skin, discard any bones, and keep warm.

Bring about 2 inches (5 cm) of water to a boil in a medium-size pan, add the vinegar, and reduce it to a gentle simmer. Break the eggs into the pan one at a time, and poach for 3 minutes each.

Meanwhile, slice the muffins in half and toast them until lightly browned. Lift the poached eggs out of the water with a slotted spoon and drain briefly on paper towels.

To serve, place the muffin halves onto four warmed plates and top with the haddock and poached eggs. Spoon over the hollandaise sauce and garnish with a sprinkling of black pepper and chives.

Scrambled Eggs with Chilli and Crisp Streaky Bacon on Toast

Scrambled egg is so simple to make, but still people overcook it and end up with rubbery, gelatinized stuff on toast. To prevent this, add heavy cream halfway through the cooking while you whisk everything together in the pan.

SERVES 4

12 bacon strips

4 tbsp unsalted butter

6 free-range medium eggs, beaten

salt and pepper, to taste

1/3 cup heavy cream

TO SERVE

4 pieces sliced bread, toasted and buttered

1 green chile, seeded and finely diced

Heat a sauté pan on a medium heat. Add the bacon with half the butter, and cook until crisp and golden brown, a few minutes only. Remove from the pan and keep warm.

Wipe the pan and return to the heat with the remaining butter. Season the eggs well with salt and pepper, then pour into the pan. Quickly mix the eggs with a whisk and, when halfway cooked, add the cream, whisking all the time.

Just as the eggs are beginning to set, remove from the heat, and season again. Spoon onto the toast, with a scattering of chopped chile on top and bacon on the side. Serve immediately.

Gammon with Pineapple Salsa

This is an up-to-date ham and pineapple, but do you know where I think the best ham and pineapple can be tasted in the UK? In truckers' roadside cafés. Gammon with a broiled, canned pineapple ring, HP Sauce, and fries may not be the lowest cholesterol dish in the world, but it tastes fantastic!

SERVES 4

4 thick slices ham

6 pineapple rings, fresh or canned with natural juice, chopped

juice of 2 limes

1 red chile, seeded and chopped

1 tbsp roughly chopped fresh mint

2 tbsp olive oil

salt and pepper, to taste

Broil or fry the slices of ham until cooked.

Mix the remaining ingredients together for the salsa. Serve the ham with French fries, potato wedges, or vegetables and a generous of serving of salsa on the side.

Smoked Bacon Welsh Rarebit

You can make loads of this cheese mixture at the same time, and it can sit in the refrigerator for a week. Then, any time of day or night you want a quick snack, it's so easy to use. But serve your rarebit with the Tomato and Apple Chutney on page 370, and it becomes a very serious dish indeed.

SERVES 4–6

12 slices good bacon

4–6 thin slices white bread

RAREBIT

13 oz (375 g) strong cheddar cheese

75ml (2¹/₂ fl oz) milk

generous ¹/₃ cup heavy cream

**1 free-range egg plus
1 free-range egg yolk**

¹/₂ tbsp mustard powder

3 tbsp all-purpose flour

¹/₂ cup fresh white bread crumbs

a dash of Worcestershire sauce

a dash of Tabasco sauce

salt and pepper, to taste

To make the rarebit, grate the cheese into a pan with the milk and cream, and gently warm until the cheese has melted. Do not boil. Let cool slightly. Preheat the broiler.

Add the egg and egg yolk, mustard, flour, bread crumbs, and a dash of both Worcestershire and Tabasco sauces to the cheese mixture. Season, mix well, and let cool.

Broil the bacon until cooked, then broil the bread on only one side. Place the bread, unbroiled-side up, into an ovenproof dish, and top with the bacon. Pour the rarebit mixture over the bacon and bread, return to the broiler, and let color.

Remove from the broiler and cool a bit before serving with the Tomato and Apple Chutney on page 370.

Hot Stilton Rarebit

Rarebits or rabbits are centuries old, and were traditionally served before or instead of a dessert. You can use leftovers from cans of beer, but don't replace the beer with milk as some recipes suggest; this ruins the taste.

SERVES 4

2 tbsp butter

3 free-range egg yolks

1 tsp English mustard

1/3 cup ale or lager

a dash of Tabasco sauce

a dash of Worcestershire sauce

salt and pepper, to taste

2 cups grated Stilton cheese

4 slices toast

Preheat the broiler to its highest setting.

Melt the butter over a low heat, then remove from the heat and let cool slightly. Mix in the egg yolks, mustard, ale or lager, and the Tabasco and Worcestershire sauces. Season well with salt and pepper, and fold in the cheese.

Place on the toast (either on its own or with sliced tomatoes or flat-leaf parsley leaves underneath), and broil until brown on the top.

Sausage and Ketchup Sarnie

Use good-quality sausages; if you use cheap, poor-quality sausages your sandwich won't taste as nice!

SERVES 2

1 lb (450 g) sausages

4 slices bread

TO SERVE

Ketchup (bought or homemade, *see* page 241)

Broil or fry the sausages until cooked.

Spread the ketchup on 2 slices of bread, then top each of these slices with sausages and another slice of bread.

If there were one meal I could request before I died, it would be my grandmother's bacon roll. She's no longer with us, but if I could make a bacon roll as well as she could, I would be a very rich man.

Bacon Buttie

SERVES 2

approx. 1 oz (30 g) dripping

8 slices smoked bacon

4 slices bread (bloomer or pain de campagne)

3 tbsp butter

2 ripe tomatoes, sliced

black pepper, to taste

Warm a large pan on the stovetop and add the dripping. Separate the bacon and add to the pan—watch out for the fat spitting out of the pan.

While the bacon is cooking, toast the bread, either on a grill or under the broiler. When the bacon is nice and crispy, remove from the pan. Add the butter to the pan and melt.

Dip the bread into the pan and then place onto the plates and build up the sandwich with the bacon and sliced fresh tomatoes. Pour over the rest of the juices from the pan, grind over some pepper, top with the other slice of bread, and serve.

I remember hating bees from the moment, when I was a kid, that my father decided it was a good idea to visit a local honey farm in the North Yorkshire moors. The heather-flavored honey was great, but what of those mad people who, daily, had to face what seemed like certain death to collect it? Since then, I have tried to avoid going anywhere near bees again. This recipe is a tribute to all you beekeepers. Oh, and by the way, I think you're all crazy!

Pancakes with Honeycomb

SERVES 2–3

PANCAKES

1 large free-range egg

a pinch of salt

3/4 cup all-purpose flour

11/4 cups cold milk

2 tbsp melted butter, plus extra for cooking

HONEYCOMB BUTTER

7 tbsp unsalted butter, softened

3 oz (85 g) honeycomb

2 tbsp honey

Make the pancakes by mixing together the egg, salt, and flour and then slowly whisking in the milk. Just before cooking, mix in the melted butter.

Heat a heavy saucepan. Add a small pat of butter and place a spoonful of the batter in the center of the pan. Swirl the pan to coat the bottom with the pancake.

Place the pan back on the heat to cook the bottom of the pancake. Once the bottom is cooked, either flip the pancake over or use a spatula to turn it, then cook the other side. Continue making pancakes until all the batter is used. Keep the pancakes warm.

To make the honeycomb butter, place all the ingredients in a food processor and blend until smooth. This will keep in a covered container in the refrigerator.

Serve two to three pancakes per portion topped with a spoonful or so of the fragrant butter.

Hot cross buns are traditionally baked for Good Friday and are thought to originate from pagan times, but they are far too good to eat only at Easter. Here is a great way to use them as a nice breakfast or dessert (not forgetting, of course, the "true" way to eat them—toasted with butter—but I don't need to tell you that!).

Blueberry Sauce for Hot Cross Buns

SERVES 2

generous 1 cup milk

1 heaping tbsp superfine sugar

2 free-range eggs

a pat of butter

2 hot cross buns (bought or homemade, *see* page 363)

BLUEBERRY SAUCE

10 1/2 oz (300 g) blueberries (or strawberries)

1/3 cup superfine sugar

a splash of port or orange juice

TO SERVE

honeyed cream, crème fraîche, clotted cream, or ice cream

Put the milk and sugar into a bowl and, using a whisk, beat in the eggs. Reserve to one side.

Prepare the blueberry sauce by mixing together all the ingredients, crushing the berries lightly to allow the juices to run.

Heat the butter in a pan. Slice the hot cross buns in half, dip into the eggy mixture, and cook in the butter for about 2 minutes on each side.

Remove the buns from the pan and place on a serving plate. Pile the blueberry sauce on top of the bottom half of each bun, top with 2 spoonfuls of cream or ice cream, then add the lid of the bun. Serve immediately.

soups

Watercress is near to my heart. I am lucky enough to live in a part of England where watercress is famous. Hampshire, in particular Alresford, is the home of the famous "watercress line" that used to deliver freshly cut watercress from the beds to London. Sadly, this doesn't happen any more—instead, the cress travels by road. But the line does still exist and, for a small fee, you can travel a stretch of it in the original steam train and coach. Watercress is grown in beds fed by spring water from underground. It needs a constant flow of this water to grow, and is available most of the year.

Watercress Soup

SERVES 4–6

1 onion, sliced

2 cloves garlic, chopped

2 tbsp butter

5 cups chicken stock

1 lb (450 g) Estima potatoes, peeled and diced

2 bunches watercress

freshly grated nutmeg (optional)

scant 1 cup heavy cream

salt and pepper, to taste

bread croutons, to garnish (optional)

In a heavy saucepan, sauté the onion and garlic in the butter until softened but not colored.

Add the stock and potatoes and bring to a boil. Simmer for 15–20 minutes, until the potatoes are cooked.

Chop up the watercress (leaves and stalks) and add to the soup with the freshly grated nutmeg, if using.

Simmer for 2–3 minutes before blending in a food processor in batches, adding the cream as you go.

Return to the pan to heat through gently and season with salt and pepper. Garnish with bread croutons—baked or fried—if you like.

Rich Onion Soup with Cheese Toasts French

in inspiration, but now a real favorite in other countries. The start of this recipe is most important. The knack of making a good onion soup is first coloring the onions well, because this will give the finished dish flavor and a deep color. No gravy browning—that's cheating!

SERVES 6

5 onions, thinly sliced

3 cloves garlic, thinly sliced

3/4 oz (20 g) duck fat

1 1/4 cups red wine

5 cups fresh beef stock

1/4 cup brandy

generous 1/3 cup good balsamic vinegar

salt and pepper, to taste

1/4 cup chopped fresh flat-leaf parsley, finely chopped

4 tbsp unsalted butter

CHEESE TOAST

8 thick slices white bread

2 1/2 cups grated Gruyère cheese

Sauté the onion and garlic in a large pan in the duck fat for about 20–30 minutes, coloring very well.

Stir before adding the red wine and stock. Bring to a boil and simmer for about 10 minutes. Add the brandy and balsamic vinegar and simmer for another 20 minutes.

Preheat the broiler. Toast the bread on both sides, top with the grated cheese, and place under the broiler to melt.

Season the soup well with salt and pepper and add the chopped parsley. Pour into soup bowls. Top with the grilled cheese toast and a knob of butter.

Leek, Potato and Stilton Soup

A classic soup with that most classic of all British ingredients: Stilton, the king of cheeses. Stilton has conquered the world, but is still exclusively made in seven dairies in the counties of Leicestershire, Nottinghamshire, and Derbyshire. The best Stilton is made in the summer, with summer milk, which gives it a creamy yellow color. It is usually sold at Christmas time. When buying it, look for evenly distributed veins and a good contrast between the blue veins and the creamy cheese.

SERVES 4

1 chicken stock cube

2¹/₂ cups hot water

generous ¹/₃ cup white wine

1 medium leek, split, washed, and thinly sliced

1 shallot, finely chopped

2 cloves garlic, finely chopped

1 large baking potato, peeled and finely chopped

4¹/₂ oz (125 g) strong Stilton checse

¹/₂ cup heavy cream

salt and pepper, to taste

1 package storebought croutons

1 tbsp chopped fresh parsley

Place the stock cube, water, and wine in a pan and bring to a boil. Add the leek to the pan with the shallot, garlic, and potato. Cover and cook for 10 minutes.

Add the Stilton and cook for 4–5 minutes to melt the cheese. Add the cream, salt and pepper, and blend.

Warm the croutons. Serve the soup hot, sprinkled with the parsley, and offer the warmed croutons separately.

I made this soup while filming in York. It's a nice twist to an old English favorite, almond soup. The vegetables came from a man called John Mannion, who is an old friend of the family. I remember going to his stall in York Market (and his store nearby) as a kid with my grandmother and watching her squeeze all the fruit first before buying them. What's great now is that most of the market stalls are selling a mixture of new and traditional fruit and vegetables. I wonder what my grandmother would have thought of garlic and ginger grown in Yorkshire! Probably nothing, as they were never her thing, but she could make a great broccoli soup, and this is as near as I can get to it.

Broccoli and Almond Soup

SERVES 4

2 tbsp butter

2 cloves garlic, crushed

1 large white onion, diced

1 large potato, peeled
and diced

5 tbsp white wine

3 cups vegetable stock

2 heads broccoli, cut into
small florets

2/3 cup heavy cream

3/4 cup slivered almonds, toasted

2–3 sprigs fresh parsley,
finely chopped

salt and pepper, to taste

Heat a large saucepan and add the butter. Once foaming, add the garlic and onion, and sweat without coloring for a few minutes. Next add the potato, white wine, and stock. Bring to a boil and simmer for 5 minutes to get the potato cooking.

Add the broccoli to the pan and continue to cook for another 6–8 minutes. Add the cream, half the almonds, and all the parsley. Bring to a boil, remove from the heat, and let cool slightly.

Blend in a food processor, then return the liquid to the pan. Bring to a boil and season with salt and pepper.

To serve, spoon the soup into bowls or mugs and top with the remaining toasted almonds. You could also add a little partly whipped heavy cream.

A twist on our traditional tomato soup. Roasting vegetables for soups, as I've done here and in the Butternut Squash and Lime Soup with Pine Nuts and Herb Oil on page 38, makes the soup taste even better. Serve with thick slices of crusty bread.

Roast Tomato and Cumin Soup

SERVES 6–8

2 3/4 lb (1.25 kg) ripe tomatoes

6 tbsp olive oil

2 medium onions, roughly chopped

3 cloves garlic, roughly chopped

1 large fresh red chile pepper, seeded and chopped

2 tbsp cumin seeds, roasted and ground

2 1/4 cups tomato sauce

salt and pepper, to taste

Preheat the oven to 325°F/170°C.

Slice the tomatoes in half and place them on a large, heavy baking sheet. Sprinkle over 2 tablespoons of the olive oil and roast for about 1 hour, or until the tomatoes are dehydrated and have caramelized. Remove the tomatoes from the baking sheet and set aside.

Place the onion, garlic, and chile in a large saucepan with the remaining olive oil. Cook over a low heat, stirring occasionally, until the onion is soft and translucent, about 10 minutes. Add the cumin and cook for another 5 minutes. Add the roasted tomatoes and the tomato sauce and cook for 10 minutes.

Puree the mixture in a food processor or blender.

To serve, transfer the mixture back into a saucepan and reheat gently until warm. Taste and add salt and pepper as desired. Ladle into warm bowls. Serve with some charred ciabatta.

One-minute Chilled Tomato Soup

This soup takes only a minute because the ice chills it instantly. I use plum tomatoes only if they are good ones. But if you are unsure about the tomatoes' quality, use a 14-ounce (400 g) can of plum tomatoes.

SERVES 4

6 plum tomatoes, quartered

2 cloves garlic, roughly chopped

1 small red onion, roughly chopped

1/4 cup white wine

1/4 cup water

1 tsp tomato puree

5 ice cubes

1/3 cup fresh basil leaves

salt and pepper, to taste

olive oil

Put the tomatoes, garlic, and onion in a food processor or blender. Then add the wine, water, tomato puree, ice cubes, fresh basil, a lot of black pepper, and a pinch of salt.

Place the lid on securely and blend for about 30 seconds, until all the ingredients are mixed together well. There may be some funny noises from the machine, but that's only the ice being ground up.

Remove and serve in chilled bowls, drizzled with a little olive oil, with some hot French bread and butter. You can garnish it with some ripped-up fresh basil leaves, if you like.

Sweetcorn and Crab Soup

This may be taking its place in a British cookbook, but the idea came from one of the Indian chefs in my restaurant.

SERVES 6

1 large white onion

9 oz (250 g) potatoes, peeled

curry powder, to taste

2 1/2 tbsp unsalted butter

5 cups chicken stock

a handful of fresh basil leaves

1 1/4 cups heavy cream

salt and pepper, to taste

1 lb (450 g) frozen corn kernels

meat from 2 freshly cooked crabs

olive oil

Dice the onion and potatoes. In a large, heavy pan, sweat them with the curry powder in the butter until soft. Pour in the stock, stir, and bring to a boil, then simmer until the potato is tender, about 15 minutes.

Meanwhile, blend most of the basil in a blender until finely chopped. Add a generous 1 cup of the heavy cream and mix. Season and chill.

Add the corn to the soup, simmer for 3 minutes, then add the crabmeat and remove from the heat. Puree while still hot, then return to the pan, add the remaining cream, and simmer for 3 minutes. Season again. Spoon into bowls. Garnish with a little basil cream and olive oil and a basil leaf.

Not long ago I tried to grow squash in the garden and was amazed by all the different kinds available. The one we are most familiar with must be the common butternut, and since growing these I've become an even bigger fan. This soup is different to the norm; I roast the squash first because I think it tastes much better.

Butternut Squash and Lime Soup with Pine Nuts and Herb Oil

SERVES 6–8

1 butternut squash, about 2¹/₄ lb (1 kg)

2 tbsp honey

extra virgin olive oil

1 white onion, chopped

2 cloves garlic, chopped

²/₃ cup white wine

generous 2 cups chicken stock

¹/₄ cup pine nuts

²/₃ cup heavy cream

finely grated zest and juice of 3 limes

salt and pepper, to taste

¹/₄ cup crème fraîche or sour cream

¹/₄ cup fresh basil, torn

HERB OIL

¹/₄ cup fresh basil

1 cup fresh chervil

generous ¹/₄ cup olive oil

Preheat the oven to 400°F/200°C.

Cut the squash in half, scoop out the seeds, then peel it and dice the flesh into 1 inch (2.5 cm) chunks. Place in a large baking sheet with the honey and a little olive oil. Roast for 30–40 minutes.

Meanwhile, sauté the onion and garlic in a little olive oil to soften, then add the wine and stock. Bring to a boil and simmer for 3–4 minutes.

Sauté the pine nuts in a little olive oil until golden brown. Remove and reserve.

To make the herb oil, chop the basil and chervil and place in a blender with the olive oil. Blend to a fine puree. Season and reserve.

Remove the squash from the oven and place it in a blender with the stock mixture, cream, lime juice, and lime zest, and blend. Season well. Return to the pan and reheat and check the seasoning.

Pour into individual bowls, and top with a dollop of crème fraîche. Drizzle with the pureed herb oil, pine nuts, and the basil. Serve.

I thought this dish up in Prince Charles's Duchy Estate in Cornwall, where I stumbled across a farm store while filming for a television show. It had over 30 different types of squash! I bought a pumpkin, which I roasted when I got home and made into a great, inexpensive, vegetable soup.

Puff Pastry Crusted Pumpkin and Rosemary Soup

SERVES 6

1 small pumpkin, about 2¼ lb (1 kg), peeled, seeded, and diced into 1 inch (2.5 cm) chunks

1 white onion, chopped

2 cloves garlic, chopped

2 tbsp honey

3 fresh rosemary sprigs

extra virgin olive oil

generous 2 cups chicken stock

generous ⅓ cup white wine

⅔ cup heavy cream

juice of 1 lemon

salt and pepper, to taste

TOPPING

7 oz (200 g) puff pastry sheets

1 free-range egg yolk, beaten

Preheat the oven to 400°F/200°C.

Place the pumpkin, onion, and garlic in a large baking tray with the honey, rosemary sprigs, and a little olive oil. Roast for 25–30 minutes, until the pumpkin is cooked and golden brown. Keep basting the pumpkin because the honey may stick to the bottom of the tray. Remove from the oven.

Heat the stock and wine on the stovetop. Place into a blender with the pumpkin mixture, cream, and lemon juice, and blend until smooth. Check the seasoning, and reserve.

On a slightly floured work surface, spread out the pastry sheets and, either using four large ovenproof soup dishes or four smaller deep dishes, cut the pastry into four circles, ¾inches (2 cm) bigger than the rim of each dish.

Fill the dishes no more than three-quarters full with soup and brush the edges of the dishes with the beaten egg yolk. Place the pastry on top and crimp it down onto the egg to seal. Use any of the leftovers to make a small pumpkin-shaped piece on the top.

Brush the pastry with the egg and bake for 15 minutes, until golden brown on the top. Serve piping hot.

This inexpensive soup has great strong flavors, but be careful; a common mistake is to use too much saffron, because it takes a while to get the right color and flavor. The soup goes well with the caramelized onions, which I like to make loads of at a time— I also use them in sandwiches and with cheese, especially cheddar.

Mussel and Saffron Soup with Caramelized Onions

SERVES 6

50 mussels, scrubbed and bearded (discard any that do not close when tapped)

5 tbsp dry white wine

1 tbsp olive oil

2 tsp minced garlic

a pinch of crushed red pepper flakes

1/2 small onion, chopped

1 tsp tomato puree

scant 1 cup heavy cream, whipped

2 1/2 cups fresh chicken stock

1 tsp saffron strands

1 tbsp chopped fresh chives

salt and pepper, to taste

CARAMELIZED ONIONS

2 tbsp unsalted butter

2 onions, halved and thinly sliced

First caramelize the onions. Melt the butter in a medium sauté pan over a low heat. Add the onions and sauté until caramel brown, about 30 minutes, stirring occasionally.

To make the soup, combine the mussels and wine in a large, heavy pot over a high heat. Cover and cook, shaking the pot occasionally, until the mussels open, about 4–5 minutes. Discard any mussels that do not open. Drain, reserving the mussel liquor. Shell 40 of the mussels. Strain the reserved mussel liquor through a fine strainer.

In a large saucepan over a medium heat, heat the olive oil and sauté the garlic and pepper flakes until the garlic is light brown. Add the chopped onion and sauté until tender, about 5 minutes. Add the reserved mussel liquor, the tomato puree, cream, and stock. Bring to a boil and skim off any foam that develops.

Lower the heat, add the saffron, and simmer for 5 minutes. Add the shelled mussels and the chives, and season with salt and pepper. Liquidize.

To serve, place a spoonful of caramelized onions in the center of each bowl and scatter a few mussels around in their shells. Then pour the soup over the lot.

Pea Soup

I was brought up on this, and I love it! My grandmother used to put chunks of leftover ham with the bone in this soup, which adds extra flavor. I like it with fresh mint leaves thrown in at the end. But soups can be easily overcooked and none more so than this: the last thing you want is a wrinkly bullet in the bottom of your soup bowl.

SERVES 6–8

1 bunch scallions or young green-stemmed onions, chopped

2 cloves garlic, chopped

2 tbsp unsalted butter

1 lb 5 oz (600 g) shelled young peas

1¹/₂ lb (675 g) leftover cooked/ boiled ham, roughly chopped

2¹/₂ cups fresh chicken stock

generous 1 cup heavy cream (optional)

salt and pepper, to taste

1 fresh mint sprig (8–12 leaves), chopped

Sauté the onion and garlic in the butter in a covered pan for 5 minutes, without coloring.

Add the peas, ham, and stock, and bring to a boil. If using the cream, add now and simmer until the peas are tender, about 10 minutes.

Season to taste, and liquidize if you like, adding another 2 tablespoons of butter. But why bother blending? I think it looks and tastes so much better when you can see the parts of the food you're eating (and without the extra cream). Serve sprinkled with the mint.

salads, terrines & pâtés

Salad of Chargrilled Leeks and Red Onions with Mozzarella

The thing I love most about this dish is the dressing; I sometimes serve it with plain Bibb lettuce and some croutons or, even better, warm French beans and seared tuna or salmon. You can change this salad totally by adding smoked chicken or plainly cooked chicken. You can also use a mild British cheese instead of the mozzarella.

SERVES 4

a pinch of superfine sugar

salt and pepper, to taste

24 young leeks, trimmed

2 red onions, cut into wedges

2 x 7 oz (200 g) mozzarella balls, cut into 4 slices each

DRESSING

4 tbsp tarragon vinegar

1 tsp Dijon mustard

1 tbsp chopped fresh tarragon

1/4 cup extra virgin olive oil

1 tomato, seeded and finely diced

1 tbsp fine capers, rinsed and drained

1 tbsp pitted green olives, finely chopped

1 hard-boiled, free-range egg, shelled and finely chopped

Make the dressing first. Combine all the ingredients and let stand for an hour or so for the flavors to come together.

Bring a large pan of water to a boil with the sugar and a little salt. Throw in the leeks, return to a boil, and cook gently for 2–3 minutes. Drain them well and dry on a cloth.

Grill the leeks and onions on a hot, ridged, cast-iron grill pan. When they are tender and slightly blackened, remove from the heat and season with salt and pepper.

Toss the leeks and onions in most of the dressing, then divide between four plates. Arrange two slices of mozzarella over each portion, sprinkle with the remaining dressing, and serve.

Stilton and Red Onion Salad

This is another one of those dishes I did in my first year at college, and I remember it because it's so simple. So once more, it's very 1970s, I suppose.... but then again I did eat it a lot in Berni Inns. Stilton, to my mind, needs a strong, robust flavor to accompany it, and red onion fits the bill for this salad.

SERVES 4 AS
A STARTER

4 red onions

2 tbsp olive oil

2 tbsp peanut oil

2 tbsp balsamic vinegar

a squeeze of lemon juice

salt and pepper, to taste

10 very thin slices baguette

8–12 oz (225–350 g) mixed
green leaves

4 oz (115 g) Stilton cheese,
broken into pieces

DRESSING

3 tbsp port

2 tbsp Dijon mustard

2 tbsp red wine vinegar

4 tbsp walnut oil

4 tbsp peanut oil

Cut each onion into six wedges, keeping the root of the onion in place to prevent it from falling apart. Bring a pan of water to a simmer, add the cut onions, and cook for 2 minutes.

Warm together the oils, balsamic vinegar, and lemon juice. Drain the onions and add them to the oil/vinegar mix. Remove from the heat, season with some salt and pepper, and let the onions marinate at room temperature, turning every so often to ensure an even flavor. The onions will be at their best after an hour or so.

Preheat the oven to 400°F/200°C. To make the dressing, boil and reduce the port by half and cool. Mix the mustard with the red wine vinegar. Whisk together the oils and pour slowly onto the mustard- and- vinegar mixture, while continuing to whisk vigorously. Once all has been added, whisk in the reduced port and season with salt and pepper.

Crisp up the sliced bread by drizzling with a little extra oil and baking for 5–10 minutes.

To serve, separate the red onion wedges, and remove from the marinade. Mix with the green leaves and Stilton. Add some of the red wine/port dressing to bind. Place on a plate, trickle over some more of the dressing, and place the crispy toasts on top.

Seared Salmon with Sesame Watercress Salad

This is a modern twist to a recipe that uses two great British ingredients: salmon and watercress.

SERVES 2

2 x 7 oz (200 g) salmon fillets (no skin or bone), cut on a slant

olive oil

salt and pepper, to taste

1 3/4 oz (50 g) watercress

2 tbsp sesame seeds, toasted

WATERCRESS DRESSING

1 3/4 oz 50g (50 g) watercress, blanched

2 tbsp rice wine vinegar

1/2 cup canola oil

Make the dressing first. Blend together all the ingredients in a food processor and let stand to one side for the flavors to infuse.

Heat a cast-iron grill or skillet until very hot and brush the salmon on both sides with a little oil. Season and then cook on both sides for 3–4 minutes.

While the fish is cooking, place the watercress on the plate, then put the cooked salmon in the middle.

Sprinkle the toasted sesame seeds over the top, drizzle with the watercress dressing, and serve immediately.

This salad is great: charred eggplant (which we Brits have come to love) served warm with roast loin of lamb. I put watercress and cilantro in the salad with red onions, but scallions will work well, too. The lamb comes from the best end, which has been removed from the bone and trimmed down.

Lamb, Aubergine and Watercress Salad

SERVES 6

1 lb 5 oz (600 g) lamb loin, trimmed of fat and silver skin

olive oil

salt and pepper, to taste

2 small eggplants, cut into 5/8 inch (1.5 cm) slices

BALSAMIC VINAIGRETTE

4 tbsp balsamic vinegar

1 clove garlic, finely chopped

a pinch of superfine sugar

1/2 cup olive oil

leaves from 2 fresh thyme sprigs

WATERCRESS SALAD

3 1/2 oz (100 g) watercress, stems removed

1 oz (25 g) fresh cilantro, leaves picked

1 red chile, seeded and cut into strips

1 red onion, halved and sliced

rind of 1/2 salted lemon or preserved lemon, cut into strips

Preheat the oven to 425°F/220°C.

Brush the lamb with olive oil and season with salt and pepper. Heat a skillet over a high heat and seal the lamb on all sides until browned. Transfer the lamb to a baking sheet and roast for 6–8 minutes for medium. Set aside to rest for 5 minutes before slicing.

Preheat a broiler, or ridged cast-iron grill pan to a high heat. Lightly brush the eggplant with olive oil and cook for 5–8 minutes, or until tender and browned. Keep warm.

Meanwhile, to make the balsamic vinaigrette, whisk all the ingredients together until combined. Season to taste with salt and pepper.

To make the salad, combine the watercress, cilantro, chile, onion, and lemon rind. Add enough balsamic vinaigrette to moisten it.

To serve, place two to three slices of eggplant on each serving plate. Slice the lamb loin into disks, about 1/4 inch (5 mm) thick. Arrange the salad over the eggplant, and the lamb on top. Finish with another light drizzle of balsamic vinaigrette.

Egg and Bacon Salad

Here is an easy salad that can be served on its own or as an appetizer. You can, of course, poach the eggs as a change, or use pancetta instead of bacon. When doing the latter, though, cook the pancetta on a baking sheet until crispy. This will stop the pancetta from sticking to the broiler pan while cooking.

SERVES 4

4 slices thickly-sliced white bread, crusts removed

4 soft-boiled, free-range eggs (boiled from room temperature for 5 minutes in simmering water)

6 slices thickly-sliced bacon

4 Bibb lettuces, leaves separated, rinsed, and drained

salt and pepper, to taste

4 scallions, washed and finely shredded

3 tbsp red wine vinegar

2 tbsp each of olive and peanut oil, mixed

Cut the slices of bread into 1/2 inch (1 cm) dice. Shell the boiled eggs, and cut into quarters.

The bacon can now be pan-fried until crispy in a nonstick pan with no oil. Any fat content will be released into the pan from the bacon. This will also happen if broiling. Whichever method you choose, keep the bacon fat for frying the bread. Once cooked, remove the bacon from the pan and keep warm.

Add the bread dice to the bacon fat, and cook until golden and crispy. You might need a little extra oil to achieve a golden color.

Season the lettuce leaves with salt and pepper. It's best, whenever making salads, to sprinkle salt around the bowl and not directly onto the leaves. This prevents the salt from falling onto wet leaves and sticking in lumps.

Chop the bacon into chunky strips, and mix into the leaves with the scallions and fried bread. Mix together the red wine vinegar and the oils and spoon over the leaves, adding just enough to coat.

Arrange in a large bowl as one large salad. You can season the soft-boiled egg quarters with salt and pepper and place them among the leaves. Serve immediately.

Bacon and Bean Salad

The dressing is the key to this delicious salad. Its texture is like that of a Caesar salad, but less creamy and heavy. It's a nuisance to remove the shells of fava beans, but it will be worth it. You'll need about 7 oz (200 g) fresh or frozen large beans to end up with 3 1/2 oz (100 g) here.

SERVES 4

8 slices bacon or 10 slices Parma ham

1 3/4 oz (50 g) fresh white bread, crusts removed, cubed

a knob of unsalted butter

5 1/2 oz (150 g) mixed red and white chicory and arugula

3 1/2 oz (100 g) cooked green beans

3 1/2 oz (100 g) podded, blanched and peeled fava beans

1/8 oz (5 g) fresh flat-leaf parsley, picked and washed

extra virgin olive oil

Parmesan shavings (optional)

DRESSING

2 slices white bread, crusts removed

4 tbsp milk

juice and finely grated zest of 1 lemon

2 cloves garlic

scant 1 1/2 cups fresh shelled walnuts

2/3 cup extra virgin olive oil

salt and pepper, to taste

To make the dressing, tear the bread into the blender and moisten with the milk. Add the lemon zest and juice, garlic, and walnuts and blend to a paste. Add, and blend in, the olive oil and some salt and pepper to taste.

Broil the bacon or Parma ham until crisp. Sauté the cubed bread in a little butter until golden brown.

Place the salad greens and the beans into a bowl. Add the dressing and some salt and pepper and mix.

Place a portion of the salad on each plate and top with the crispy bacon, the parsley, and croutons. Drizzle with the olive oil and top with the Parmesan shavings (if using).

Good sausages are used as the base of this simple terrine. Play around with the flavors by using beef or game sausages instead of pork. I've used plum sauce, because this combines with the orange segments to create a sweet-and-sour flavor. When making terrines, don't overcook them or they will break up while being sliced.

Pork Terrine with Apricots and Pistachios

SERVES 8–12

olive oil

9 oz (250 g) bacon slices

2 lb (900 g) or 14–15 large sausages (Lincolnshire are best)

10 fresh sage leaves, chopped

1¹/₂ tbsp chopped fresh flat-leaf parsley

¹/₂ cup chopped dried apricots

¹/₂ cup roughly chopped, shelled pistachio nuts

salt and pepper, to taste

SALAD

2 oranges, peeled and segmented

2oz (55 g) wild arugula leaves

1 large potato, peeled, cooked and diced

8 tbsp plum sauce (make your own, or buy the Chinese stuff from the supermarket)

3 tbsp olive oil

Preheat the oven to 350°F/180°C. Take a terrine dish, 12–14 inches (30–35 cm) long, 4 inches (10 cm) wide, and 3¹/₂–4 inches (9–10 cm) deep, and brush it with olive oil. Line the dish with bacon, leaving 2–2¹/₂ inches (5–6 cm) overlapping the edge of the terrine.

Make the filling by removing all the meat from the sausage skins (discard these). Add the sage, parsley, chopped apricots, and pistachio nuts and mix well with plenty of seasoning.

Pile the meat mixture into the terrine mold and press down well. Fold over the bacon and cover with either the lid or with foil, and place in a bain-marie filled halfway with hot water. Cook in the oven for 60 minutes. Remove from the oven, cover with foil, and press down with a weight. Cool, then place in the refrigerator.

When ready to serve, make the salad by mixing the orange segments, arugula and potato together in a bowl. Mix the plum sauce with the olive oil and season to taste.

Cut the terrine into slices and serve in the center of the plates with the salad to one side and the dressing spooned over the top.

Yorkshire Ham Terrine with Spiced Pickle

Scott's Butchers in York is still the best place to buy Yorkshire pork products, but if you visit you have to line up. Last time I was there it was obviously pension day, because the place was like a bingo hall on a jackpot night!

SERVES 10

3 ham knuckles

4 bay leaves

6 black peppercorns

1 large onion, halved

1 medium leek, halved

1 medium carrot, halved

extra virgin olive oil

6–8 thin slices York ham, or other cooked sliced ham

2 shallots, finely chopped

1 clove garlic, chopped

salt and pepper, to taste

$1/3$ cup finely chopped fresh parsley leaves

a pinch of ground allspice

2 gelatin leaves, soaked in cold water for 5 minutes

$3/4$ cup mixed salad greens and herbs, such as chervil and wild arugula

PINEAPPLE CONDIMENT

1 clove garlic, crushed

1 tsp grain mustard

5 tbsp white wine vinegar

a good pinch of turmeric powder

$3/4$ cup raw brown sugar

1 medium pineapple, skinned, cored, and finely chopped

DRESSING

4 tbsp each of grain mustard, extra virgin olive oil, and cider vinegar

Put the ham knuckles, bay leaves, peppercorns, onion, leek, and carrot in a large saucepan. Cover with cold water, bring to a boil and simmer, covered, for 3 hours, until the meat is tender.

Meanwhile, grease a 8 x 3 $1/4$-inch (20 x 8 cm) terrine mold with olive oil. Line with plastic wrap, then with the sliced York ham.

When the ham knuckles are nearly cooked, heat a little olive oil in a small pan and gently sauté the shallots and garlic.

Remove the cooked ham knuckles from the pan, reserving the stock, and let cool slightly. While warm, remove the meat in pieces from the bone. Place in a small bowl with the shallot and garlic, some salt and pepper, and the parsley. Mix well, then pack into the terrine mold.

Strain the ham stock. Taste and, if it is too salty, dilute with water. Pour 2$1/4$ cups into a pan and add the allspice. Warm gently and add the soaked gelatin; let stand for 2–3 minutes so the gelatin can dissolve before stirring. Pour into the terrine and overlap the edges of the ham. Cover with plastic wrap; the terrine needs to be solid and "packed". Put a uniform weight on the terrine to press it down (I use a brick) and let stand overnight in the refrigerator.

To make the condiment, put all the ingredients together in a pan except for the pineapple. Simmer for 3 minutes, then add the pineapple and cook for an additional 3 minutes. Put into sterilized jars (*see* page 368 for sterilizing instructions) and cool.

To make the mustard seed dressing, whisk all the ingredients together, then use some of it to dress the salad greens at the last minute.

To serve, turn out the terrine and remove the plastic wrap. Using a sharp knife, cut into $3/4$ inch (2 cm) slices and place a slice in the center of each plate. On each plate, spoon a pile of pineapple condiment, placing a few dressed leaves on, too. Grind over a little black pepper, and serve.

Chicken and Ham Terrine

This is one of the dishes I put on the menu at The Bistro onboard *Ocean Village*, and I love it. But as with most terrines and pâtés, I think it should be served with a fruit condiment or caramelized onions, or something else to break up the taste.

SERVES 10–12

16–20 slices bacon (depending on the size of the terrine)

10 1/2 oz (300 g) ground chicken

10 1/2 oz (300 g) ground pork

2 1/2 cups heavy cream

1 free-range egg, beaten

scant 1/2 cup Armagnac

3 tbsp each of chopped fresh parsley and chives

2 tbsp chopped fresh tarragon

salt and pepper, to taste

2 tbsp butter

2 shallots, finely chopped

10 1/2 oz (300 g) chicken breast, cut into 1/4-inch (5-mm) strips

8 oz (225 g) sliced cooked ham

5 oz (140 g) chicken livers, cleaned

TO GARNISH

Pear Chutney (*see* page 370)

mixed dressed salad greens

First, line a terrine dish measuring 11 x 6 1/2 x 2 1/2 inches (28 x 16 x 6 cm) with bacon, allowing the slices to overlap the mold at the sides by a few inches.

Put the chicken and pork into a bowl, and work the mixture with a wooden spatula. Stir in the cream, egg, Armagnac, and chopped herbs. Season with salt and pepper to taste.

Heat the butter in a small saucepan and sauté the shallots for 2–3 minutes. Cool and add to the meat mixture.

Spread half the mixture over the bottom of the terrine, then make a layer with some of the sliced chicken breast, then some of the sliced ham, and fill with some of the remaining ground mixture. Continue with two or three layers of the ham, ground mixture, and chicken breast, with a layer of the chicken livers running though the middle of the terrine. Finally, fold the bacon over the terrine from the sides and either cover with a lid or cover with foil.

Preheat the oven to 400°F/200°C.

Place the terrine in a roasting pan, and fill the tray halfway with warm water. Cook in the oven for 1 hour. Remove from the oven and place a weighted board (maximum weight 1 lb 2 oz/500 g) on the terrine to compress it gently until it has cooled completely.

Serve in thick slices with pear chutney and dressed salad greens.

Duck Liver Pâté

I hated liver as a kid, as most kids do. The only two dishes my grandad would cook were calf's liver and poached haddock. I used to watch him with his Brylcreemed slicked-back hair as he pan-fried his slice of liver with precision. He never failed to try to get me to eat some as I ran out of the door in horror. I now know I was missing out on something great.

SERVES 14–16

2 1/4 lb (1 kg) organic duck livers, left whole, but all green and thready parts removed

Cognac

2 cloves garlic, finely chopped

a handful of fresh basil leaves

salt and pepper, to taste

1 1/2 cups unsalted butter

GARNISH

whole-wheat bread, sliced and toasted, or Melba toast

Pear Chutney (*see* page 370)

mixed salad greens, dressed

Place the livers in a single layer in a heatproof dish, and scatter over some Cognac. It should not cover them, but they need to wallow in it for several hours. Turn them over so both sides absorb the alcohol. Throw the garlic, all but 2 of the basil leaves (torn and minus the stalks), and some salt and pepper into the brew just before poaching.

Gently poach the livers, turning them over after a couple of minutes, and continue to stew until they are cooked on the outside but pink within, about 3–4 minutes. Do not overcook them or you will end up with a drab, brown, crumbly result.

Tip the contents of the dish straight into your blender with 1 cup of the softened butter, and blend until smooth. Check the seasoning, then scrape into a large terrine dish and let cool.

Meanwhile, clarify the remaining butter. Gently melt it, and pour into another container, leaving behind all the curdlike sediment. Cool a little.

Pour the buttercup-colored clear liquid butter over the surface of the pâté, place the reserved basil leaves in the center, and put it into the refrigerator until it is set.

Using a hot knife, slice the terrine. Serve with a slice of toast, a spoonful of chutney, and some dressed mixed salad greens.

grills
& fry-ups

Rib-eye Steak with Caesar Salad

Rib-eye steak has only really become popular in Britain over the past ten years, but it is such a great piece of meat. It comes from the end of the sirloin part of the beef that the rib joint is attached to (where you get the rib joint for roasting from). I love steak and salad, and Caesar salad works particularly well in this case. The recipe for the dressing was invented by a chef I used to work with—cheers, Adam!

SERVES 4

4 rib-eye steaks, about 8 oz (225 g) each

salt and pepper, to taste

olive oil

CAESAR SALAD

2 romaine lettuce

2 thick slices white bread, cubed

2 tbsp butter

4 cloves garlic

2/3 cup white wine

4 free-range egg yolks

2 anchovy fillets

1 1/4 cups freshly grated Parmesan cheese

1 1/4 cups vegetable oil

1 tbsp Dijon mustard

To start the salad, separate the lettuce leaves, and wash and dry well, then tear into chunky pieces. Place in a serving bowl. Gently cook the bread cubes in the butter in a skillet until golden brown.

To start the Caesar dressing, peel the garlic and place in a pan with the wine. Bring to a boil and cook for about 5 minutes, until the cloves are soft. Using a hand blender, blend the wine and garlic together with the egg yolks, anchovy fillets, and cheese, adding the oil slowly to stop the mix from splitting. (This shouldn't happen, because the cheese should make the mix blend together more easily.) Add the mustard and seasoning to taste.

Preheat a skillet on the stovetop. Season the steaks with salt and pepper, and cook in a little olive oil. If you want medium, cook the steaks for about 3–4 minutes on both sides. Once cooked, remove the steaks from the pan and place them on the plate while you return to the salad.

To serve, throw the bread cubes into the bowl with the lettuce, add the dressing, and mix together well. Season, place on plates alongside the steaks, and munch away.

Rib-eye Steak with Herbs and Mustard served with Honeyed Oven Chips

Nothing beats sirloin steak, deep-fried onion rings, peas, and baked potatoes or fries. This is just a more up-to-date version of our classic steak and fries. It uses rib-eye steak that is now, thankfully, found in most stores and butchers.

SERVES 4

4 rib-eye steaks, about 8 oz (225 g) each

olive oil

salt and pepper, to taste

8 tbsp Dijon mustard

4 1/2 oz (125 g) chopped herbs, such as parsley, cilantro, basil, thyme, and chervil

1 lemon, quartered

HONEYED OVEN FRIES

1 lb 2 oz (500 g) waxy potatoes, peeled

4 tbsp honey

1 tsp fresh thyme, chopped

1 clove garlic, chopped

4 tbsp olive oil

Preheat the oven to 400°F/200°C.

For the fries, cut the potatoes into large, fry-size pieces. Mix together the honey, thyme, and garlic in a bowl. Whisk in the olive oil and use the mixture to coat the potatoes well.

Season the fries and place on a baking sheet in the oven for 35–45 minutes.

Meanwhile, heat a ridged, cast-iron grill pan until it is very hot. Brush the steaks with a little olive oil and season with salt and pepper. Seal on the pan and cook to taste, probably about 3–4 minutes on both sides.

Once cooked, brush the steaks with mustard and dip into the herbs. Slice each steak into four to six slices, arrange on a plate, and serve with fries and a lemon quarter.

Fillet Steak with Stilton Rarebit

Rarebits are usually associated with toast—and, in one celebrated chef's recipe, with smoked fish—but the combination here of Stilton cheese, beer, and beef is great. It's a dish I created at the Hotel du Vin and Bistro; there, I served the steak on toast with a liver pâté. This is a simpler version.

SERVES 4

4 beef tenderloin steaks, 7 oz (200 g)

salt and pepper, to taste

3 tbsp olive oil

1³/₄ cups red wine

2¹/₂ cups fresh beef stock

1¹/₂ tbsp cold butter, diced

2 tbsp pesto

RAREBIT

2 free-range egg yolks

1 tsp mustard

2 tbsp fresh bread crumbs

a dash of Worcestershire sauce

a dash of Tabasco sauce

generous ¹/₃ cup milk

generous ¹/₃ cup beer

4 oz (115 g) Stilton cheese

Season the steaks well and place in a hot skillet with the olive oil. Cook on both sides for a total of about 5–6 minutes, then remove from the skillet and keep warm. (This is for a medium steak; if you prefer it cooked more or less than this, cook to the degree you prefer because no additional cooking is necessary.)

Keep the skillet on high heat and add the wine. Boil to reduce by half, then add the beef stock and continue to reduce.

For the rarebit, place the egg yolks, mustard, and bread crumbs in a bowl along with the Worcestershire and Tabasco sauce. Then stir in the milk and beer, and season well with salt and pepper. Grate the Stilton cheese, and fold in as well. Mix everything together until it has formed a very thick paste.

Preheat the broiler to a high heat. Top the steaks with the rarebit and place under the broiler until golden brown on the top. Remove from the broiler and place on the four plates.

Season the reduced sauce and add the butter to give it a nice glaze. To finish, add the pesto to the sauce, then pour it around the steaks and serve.

Classic Beef Burgers with Soft Onions

Use good-quality ground meat so you can serve the burgers pink. Prepare them in advance so they can firm up in the refrigerator before frying. If you barbecue them, seal them in a pan first.

SERVES 4

2 lb (900 g) ground beef

salt and pepper, to taste

3 white onions, thinly sliced

2¹/₂ tbsp unsalted butter

olive oil

TO SERVE

4 burger buns

1 head Bibb lettuce, leaves separated

2 medium tomatoes, sliced

Place the meat in a bowl and season. Divide the meat into four equal-size portions and mold them with your hands into burger shapes. Place the burgers on a tray or plate, cover with plastic wrap and let stand in the refrigerator.

When you want to eat the burgers, sauté the onions in a pan in the butter until golden brown, about 10–15 minutes.

Heat a little olive oil in a ridged, cast-iron grill or sauté pan and fry the burgers, depending how you like them. You need 3 minutes each side for medium. Serve the burgers in the buns with a couple of lettuce leaves, some sliced tomato, and some soft onion.

Beef Burgers with Bacon

Although hamburgers are usually thought of as American, so many British people have grown up eating them, either from frozen, bought from a burger chain, or—best of all—homemade, that they have attained British status.

SERVES 4

1¹/₂ lb (675 g) ground beef

1 tsp French mustard

salt and pepper, to taste

1 shallot, finely diced

1 clove garlic, finely diced

1 tbsp chopped fresh flat-leaf parsley

1 free-range egg

TO COOK AND SERVE

1 tbsp olive oil

2 tbsp butter

4 slices bacon

lettuce leaves, shredded

4 burger buns

Combine all of the burger ingredients in a large bowl. Form into four oval-shaped patties.

Sauté the patties in a hot pan in the olive oil and butter for 3–4 minutes on each side. While sautéing, broil the bacon until cooked through.

Place the salad leaves in your bun and put the burger and then bacon on top of the leaves.

Everybody loves burgers, from burned to a cinder by the old man who once a year takes over the cooking on the barbecue, to the "drive-thru" eaten from in-between your legs as you drive off to the next meeting. But there's one thing that gets me going, and it's those pretentious chefs who put down burgers in favor of a tenderloin.

The Best Cheeseburger

SERVES 4

2 shallots, chopped

a splash of olive oil

1¹/₂ lb (675 g) beef tenderloin

4 tbsp chopped pickles

2 tbsp heavy cream

¹/₂ tsp Dijon mustard

a splash of Worcestershire sauce

salt and pepper, to taste

1 ball mozzarella cheese, drained and cut into 4 slices

Sauté the chopped shallots quickly in the oil to take off the rawness, then let cool.

Ground the beef into a bowl through the fine plate of a meat grinder. Add the shallots, pickles, cream, mustard, and Worcestershire sauce. Beat well together and season to taste with salt and pepper.

Using a little oil on your hands, shape the mixture into four even-sized burger shapes. Then, using the palm of your other hand, mould the burger into a bowl shape and place a slice of the mozzarella in the middle. Fold over the meat to enclose it, then reshape into a burger. Leave in the fridge to firm up for at least 30 minutes.

Preheat the grill, then cook the burgers medium-rare, about 4 minutes on each side. Season well.

Kids love to make this recipe because it's a lot of fun to do. It's even better if you have buy a sausage-making machine. If you can't find one, you can use a piping bag, although it's more work. Get sausage skins—at least 2 feet (60 cm) in length—from your local butcher; you can find synthetic ones now as well.

Cumberland Sausage

SERVES 4–6

1 lb (450 g) boned, skinned shoulder of pork

6 oz (175 g) pork fat

4 slices smoked bacon

1 tsp each of grated nutmeg and mace

1/2 cup fresh white bread crumbs, soaked in 8 tbsp hot water

salt and pepper, to taste

Cut the pork, fat, and bacon into strips, and put first through the coarse blade of a grinding machine, then through the medium blade. Add the spices, then the soaked, squeezed bread crumbs. Mix well together with your hands, then add salt and plenty of pepper.

Rinse the salt from the sausage skins. Ease one end of a piece of skin onto the cold tap of the faucet. Run cold water gently through the skin to make sure there are no splits or large holes. Turn off the water, remove the skin and ease it on to the long spout of the sausage-making attachment. Screw the whole thing onto the grinding machine with a coarse blade in position.

Feed the pork sausage meat through the grinding machine again and, as it comes through, slide the skin gently off the attachment and coil it onto a large plate. Let stand in the refrigerator until next day.

When ready to cook, preheat the oven to 350°F/180°C. Prick the sausage, place on a greased baking sheet, then bake for 30–45 minutes. Alternatively, cook the coil in a pan on top of the stove in a little oil—the oven is easier. The sausage coil is enough for four on its own, or six as part of a meal.

The fact that a blood sausage is made from pig's blood mixed with oatmeal, suet, and onion may not appeal to you, but I consider it one of the best of British tastes (where it is known as black pudding and served at breakfast). Try to buy your blood sausage from good butchers' stores, because it is usually made fresh on the premises. These have much more flavour and taste than the commercial, branded blood sausages. I believe blood sausages should be sliced and pan-fried. The cooking time is important as well as the heat of the pan, and you don't need much fat. A cooked slice of blood sausage should be slightly crisp on the edges but moist in the center.

Black Pudding with Caramelized Apple and Cider

SERVES 2

1 Golden Delicious apple

4 tbsp butter

1 tbsp superfine sugar

6 oz (175 g) blood sausage, cut into 1/2 inch (1 cm) slices

1/4 cup cider

salt and pepper, to taste

Place two skillets on the stove and heat to a high heat while you prepare the apple. Core the apple whole, then cut it in half and slice each half into five slices.

Divide the butter between the two pans, and put the sugar in one of them. Place the blood sausage into the non-sugared pan, reduce the heat, and cook for 2–3 minutes, turning occasionally.

When the sugar and butter in the other pan have started to turn golden brown, add the apple slices. Turn up the heat and quickly caramelize the apple: about 3 minutes. Pour in the cider to deglaze the pan, stirring well, and season quickly with salt and pepper.

To serve, either put the apple mixture and the blood sausage into separate bowls or plates for the two of you to help yourselves from, or arrange the blood sausage on the two plates with the apple on top.

Corned beef and Spam were the basis of so much food we ate as kids, but they're not deemed trendy any more. Or are they? I cook corned beef hash to remind me of what my aunt used to cook for me. Served with salad, it is a satisfying snack that can be eaten at any time of the day. It's good for breakfast, perhaps topped with a fried egg. It can also be made into little patties—when the mix might need to be bound with an egg. In the United States, corned beef hash is served with Ketchup (see page 241) or a chili sauce.

Corned Beef Hash

SERVES 4

2 onions, chopped

1 tbsp fresh thyme leaves

2 tbsp butter

1 tsp yeast extract

1 1/2 cups beef stock

2/3 cup red wine

13 oz (375 g) corned beef

2 tbsp chopped fresh
flat-leaf parsley

salt and pepper, to taste

FILLING

9 oz (250 g) potatoes, peeled

milk, for mashing potatoes

2 tbsp butter

scant 1/2 cup cheddar cheese

1/2 cup fresh bread crumbs

Preheat the oven to 400°F/200°C.

For the filling, boil the potatoes in plenty of simmering, salted water. When they are just cooked, remove from the heat and cool in cold water. Drain, dice, and reserve.

In a large skillet, sauté the onions and thyme in the butter for about 3 minutes. Add the yeast extract, stock, and red wine and reduce by half. Add the corned beef, parsley and and some salt and pepper and cook for 5–10 minutes, breaking the beef up with a fork.

Season the cooled potatoes and mash them thoroughly with some milk and the butter.

Place the corned beef mixture into an ovenproof dish and top with the mashed potatoes. Mix the grated cheese together with the bread crumbs. Sprinkle the mixture over the mashed potatoes and bake for 20 minutes to cook through and brown the top.

Serve with a dressed green salad.

I like calf's liver with onions, but what I really remember is the tripe and onions I had when I was a kid. It's hard to find now. There is one place that still does good tripe and onions, and that's a café in Leeds city center vegetable market. It tastes great, but what's even better is that the café is full of old men telling stories of the old days. A fabulous place.

Pan-fried Calf's Liver with Bacon and Onions

SERVES 4

8 medium onions, sliced

6 tbsp butter

8 slices smoked bacon

scant 1/2 cup Madeira, plus extra for deglazing

3 1/2 cups beef or chicken stock

salt and pepper, to taste

1 1/2 lb (675 g) calf's liver, thinly sliced

TO SERVE
Mashed Potatoes (*see* page 222)

Preheat the broiler to high. Sauté the onions in 2 tablespoons of the butter until well caramelized. This will take about 15 minutes. While the onions are cooking, cook the bacon under the broiler.

Once the onion is ready, add the Madeira and stock and reduce by half, until you have a rich sauce. Check the seasoning and reserve.

Heat a skillet on a high heat and add a pat of the remaining butter. Cook the liver in batches to keep the pan really hot. Season while in the skillet. The liver will only take about 1–2 minutes to cook on each side, and should be nice and pink in the middle.

Remove the liver from the skillet and deglaze the skillet with a little more Madeira, then add the reduced onion sauce as well, and season.

To serve, place the mashed potatoes on the plate, top with the liver, and spoon over the sauce. Top with the crispy bacon.

Meatballs with Tomato Sauce

A grown-up version of a kid's delight. I remember hating meatballs as a child. My grandmother used to cook them all the time, but they were truly awful, always from a can and never heated through, and served with a mound of overcooked rice. My sister and I used to be made to sit through this ordeal, and we weren't allowed to leave the table until we had finished. I used to hide mine, anywhere and everywhere I could…But these are infinitely more delicious!

SERVES 4

2 shallots, chopped

1 clove garlic, chopped

olive oil

1 lb (450 g) beef tenderloin

2 tsp Dijon mustard

1/2 cup heavy cream

salt and pepper, to taste

BASIC TOMATO SAUCE

3 lb 5oz (1.5 kg) ripe and meaty tomatoes

4 tbsp olive oil

1 medium onion, very finely sliced

1 clove garlic, coarsely chopped

1 tbsp chopped fresh oregano

10 small fresh basil leaves, shredded

For the tomato sauce, plunge the tomatoes into boiling water for 1 minute to loosen the skin. Remove the skin, and cut the tomatoes in half. Discard the inner liquid and seeds. Coarsely chop the remaining flesh.

Heat the oil in a pan and sauté the onion for 5 minutes. Add the garlic and sauté for another minute. Add the tomatoes and bring to a boil, then add the oregano, reduce the heat, and simmer for 30–40 minutes. Halfway through, add the basil leaves.

When the sauce has finished cooking, add some salt to taste, and liquidize. Keep warm. (The sauce keeps for a few days in the refrigerator, but is best if eaten when freshly made.)

Meanwhile, to make the meatballs, sauté the shallots and garlic quickly in a little oil to take off the rawness, then let cool. Grind the beef through the fine plate of a meat grinder into a bowl. Add the shallots, garlic, mustard, Worcestershire sauce, and cream. Beat well together, then season to taste with salt and pepper.

Using a little oil on your hands, shape the mixture into eight to ten even-size shapes about the size of a golf ball. Let stand for 10 minutes, covered, in the refrigerator to firm up.

Preheat a pan on the stove and add a little olive oil. Cook the meatballs until golden brown all over, and serve with the warm tomato sauce.

pies
& tarts

Masham, which is near Thirsk, has two breweries: Theakstons and the Black Sheep Brewery. It was once also home to one of the largest sheep markets in the country, which was held in the town's market square. That trade has now gone, but the breweries are still going strong. Run by Paul Theakston, the Black Sheep Brewery is open to the public and is well worth a visit. Their strongest beer is Riggwelter; the words "rigged" and "welted" in old Yorkshire slang would suggest to a farmer that one of his sheep is upside down. Trust me, a few glasses of this stuff, and you'd be rigged, too!

Beef and Black Sheep Ale Pie

SERVES 4

2 lb (900 g) braising beef, diced

scant 1/4 cup all-purpose flour

salt and pepper, to taste

butter

2 white onions, sliced

2 cloves garlic, sliced

2 medium carrots, sliced

5 oz (140 g) button mushrooms, wiped

2 sprigs fresh thyme

1 bay leaf

1 3/4 cups Black Sheep Ale

2 1/4 cups fresh beef stock

1 free-range egg, beaten, for egg wash

10 1/2 oz (300 g) package puff pastry, thawed if frozen

Preheat the oven to 350°F/180°C, and place a large casserole dish over a medium heat on the stove.

While the dish is heating, place the meat in a bowl, and add the flour and seasoning, turning to coat. When the dish is hot, melt about 1 tablespoon of the butter. Add the meat in batches, adding more butter if necessary, and seal until golden brown all over.

Once browned, add the vegetables, herbs and liquids to the meat and bring to a simmer on the stove. Cover with a lid or some foil, and either gently simmer on top of the stove for 1 1/2 hours or (what I would do) cook it in the oven for 1 1/4 hours. Once the meat is tender, season and turn into an ovenproof oven-to-table pie plate. Increase the oven temperature to 400°F/200°C.

Brush the beaten egg along the edges of the dish and top with the puff pastry. Pinch the edges of the dish so that the pastry will stick to it, and trim off any remaining pieces of pastry from around the edge. Use the pastry trimmings to make leaves, berries, and a decorative rope to go along the outside. Make holes in the top for steam to escape. Brush the pastry all over with the remaining egg wash, and place the pie plate on a baking sheet. Bake for 30–40 minutes, until the pastry is golden brown on the top. (Use a baking sheet, as the mixture inside the pie plate can sometimes bubble out and make a huge mess on the bottom of your oven.)

Steak and Kidney Pie

Great pub food is one of the joys of where I live, and steak and kidney pie is one of my favorites. There are so many variations of this classic. Some say it should have oysters, beer, or stout in the mix, but I think this one is the nicest I've cooked. Besides, would you want me to give you a recipe with beef, kidneys, and oysters topped with pastry? I don't think so. Although purists say this pie should be made with a regular pie pastry, I feel puff pastry makes a much better topping.

SERVES 4

10 1/2 oz (300 g) package puff pastry, thawed if frozen

1 free-range egg and 1 extra free-range egg yolk, beaten together

FILLING

2 tbsp beef dripping or vegetable oil

1 lb 9 oz (700 g) braising beef, diced

7 oz (200 g) lamb's kidney, diced

2 medium onions, diced

8 button mushrooms, halved

scant 1/4 cup all-purpose flour

1/2 tbsp tomato paste

3 cups beef stock

2/3 cup red wine

salt and pepper, to taste

2 tbsp chopped fresh parsley

a dash of Worcestershire sauce

Heat the dripping or vegetable oil in a large skillet, and heat the beef in batches to seal until well colored. Browning the meat is important, because it gives the pie a really deep, golden color.

Brown the kidney in the same skillet, then add the onions and mushrooms and cook for 3–4 minutes.

Return all the meat to the skillet, then sprinkle the flour over to coat the meat and vegetables. Add the tomato paste, stock, and red wine to the pan, stir well, and bring to a boil. Turn the heat down and simmer for 1 1/2 hours without a lid on. If the liquid is evaporating too much, add a little more stock.

Shortly before the end of the cooking time, preheat the oven to 425°F/220°C.

Add some salt and pepper, the parsley, and Worcestershire sauce to the filling. Let cool slightly.

Place the cooked meat mixture into a pie plate. Roll out the pastry to 1/4 inch (5 mm) thick, and 2 inches (5 cm) larger than the plate you are using. Cut a strip of pastry to fit around the edge of the pie plate, and stick it down using a little water. Brush the top with beaten egg.

Using the rolling pin, lift the pastry and place it over the top of the pie plate. Trim and crimp the edges with your fingers and thumb. Brush all over the surface with the beaten egg and decorate with any pastry trimmings. Brush any decorations with beaten egg. Bake for 30–40 minutes. I love this with either mash potatoes, peas, or carrots or—forget the waistline—have all three!

Cornish Pasty

You can find all kinds of recipes for Cornish "pasties" in Britain, but the simple ones are the best. This pastry dish was never invented to achieve stars in restaurants. It is what it is: a good gut filler (even better warm, of course). I have kept this recipe very simple and made it with packaged pastry, but you can make your own pastry if you want.

SERVES 2

1 lb 2 oz (500 g) packaged flaky pie dough

1 free-range egg, beaten, to glaze

FILLING

9 oz (250 g) sirloin or top round steak

1 cup chopped onions,

$2/3$ cup chopped turnip

2 medium potatoes, peeled and thinly sliced

salt and pepper, to taste

a pinch of dried thyme

To make the filling, remove the fat from the lean meat, and cut the meat into rough cubes. Mix together with the vegetables, salt, pepper, and thyme.

Preheat the oven to 350°F/180°C.

Roll out the dough and cut it into two large dinner-plate circles. Divide the steak mixture between the two, putting it down the middle. Brush the rim of the dough with beaten egg. Fold over the dough, to make a half circle, or bring up the two sides to meet over the top of the filling, and pinch them together into a scalloped crest going right over the top of the pasty. Make two holes on top, so that the steam can escape.

Place the pasties on a baking sheet and brush them with beaten egg. Bake for 40 minutes. Serve hot or cold.

Even in Britain, cottage pie is always mixed up with shepherd's pie. But think about it: how many shepherds do you see looking after beef cattle?

Cottage Pie

SERVES 4–6

1¹/₂ lb (675 g) ground beef

salt and pepper, to taste

2 tbsp olive oil

butter

3 onions, finely chopped

3 carrots, cut into ¹/₂ inch (1 cm) dice

4 celery stalks, cut into ¹/₂ inch (1 cm) dice

¹/₂ tsp cinnamon

¹/₂ tsp chopped fresh rosemary

1 tbsp tomato paste

1 tbsp ketchup

2 tsp Worcestershire sauce

²/₃ cup red wine

scant ¹/₄ cup all-purpose flour

scant 1 cup beef stock

2 lb (900 g) Mashed Potatoes (*see* page 222)

Season the ground beef with salt and pepper, and fry in the oil in a hot skillet. For the best results, fry in batches. As one lot is fried and colored, pour off from the pan and drain in a colander.

In another large saucepan, melt a pat of butter. Add the vegetables and season with salt, pepper, and cinnamon, then add the rosemary. Cook for 5–6 minutes, until beginning to soften. Add the beef, tomato paste, ketchup, and Worcestershire sauce, and stir into the mix. Add the red wine in three parts and turn the heat up, reducing each time. Sprinkle the flour into the pan and cook for 2–3 minutes.

Pour in the beef stock, bring to a soft simmer, cover, and gently cook for about 1–1¹/₂ hours on top of the stove. During the cooking time, the sauce may become too thick; if so, add a little water to loosen. However, remember that the mash will spread on top, so don't let the sauce become too thin.

Make the mashed potatoes during the last 30 minutes of the cooking time. Reduce the quantities of the butter and cream given in the recipe on page 222 to create a slightly firmer topping.

Once the beef mixture is ready, spoon into a suitable ovenproof serving dish. The mashed potatoes can now be spooned or piped on top, brushed with a little butter, and finished in a very hot oven or under the broiler to become golden. Another method is to allow the beef to become cold in the dish before covering with the potato. This can now be refrigerated until needed, then reheated at 400°F/200°C for 35–40 minutes.

Shepherd's Pie

I think you might have got the idea by now. *This* is the pie that uses lamb…I've put cheese on the mashed potato topping for extra flavor.

SERVES 4

1 onion, cut into chunks

1/2 cup rutabaga, cut
into chunks

4 medium carrots, cut
into chunks

1/2 tsp cinnamon

1 tsp chopped fresh thyme

1 tbsp chopped fresh
flat-leaf parsley

1/4 cup all-purpose flour

12 oz (350 g) ground lamb

salt and pepper, to taste

1 tbsp tomato paste

scant 2 cups vegetable stock

TOPPING

2 lb (900 g) russet potatoes

generous 1/4 cup heavy cream

1/4 cup semiskimmed milk

1/3 cup grated cheddar cheese

1/4 cup) freshly grated Parmesan
cheese

Preheat the oven to 275°F/140°C.

Place the onion, rutabaga, and carrots into the bowl of a food processor. Add the cinnamon, herbs, and flour and blend everything until it is finely chopped, but not puréed. Place in a casserole dish, add the lamb, and season well.

Heat the tomato paste and stock together to boiling point. Stir this into the casserole and mix together well. Place the casserole over a gentle heat and bring it to simmering point. Cover with the lid and place it in the oven for 2 hours.

About 30 minutes before the end of the cooking time, peel the potatoes, cut them into chunks, and put them into a pan of cold water. Bring to a boil and simmer for 20 minutes, or until tender.

Drain the potatoes thoroughly, then mash them well. Add the cream, milk, and some salt and pepper. Continue to beat the potatoes until they are light and fluffy.

Take the casserole out of the oven and turn the temperature up to 400°F/200°C.

Transfer the meat to a shallow dish and cover it evenly with the mashed potato. Cover the potatoes with grated cheddar cheese and sprinkle with the grated Parmesan cheese.

Place the pie in the oven for 15 minutes, or until the top is golden and crusty.

Chicken and Leek Pie

This is a tasty pie, making good use of the underrated leek. Serve with a green vegetable, such as broccoli.

SERVES 4

8 oz (225 g) package flaky pie dough or puff pastry

1 free-range egg, beaten

FILLING

4 chicken breasts (without skin or wing bone)

olive oil

9 oz (250 g) shallots

2 leeks, washed

2 tbsp unsalted butter

1¼ cups crème fraîche or sour cream

⅔ cup chicken stock

salt and pepper, to taste

Preheat the oven to 400°F/200°C.

Seal the chicken breasts in a hot pan in a little oil or charbroil on both sides. Set aside to rest.

Pan-fry the shallots in a little oil, then bake in the preheated oven for 10 minutes. Chop the leeks and pan-fry in the butter until soft.

Heat the crème fraîche and stock together and season with salt and pepper. Cut the chicken into fork-size pieces and add to the stock mixture. Simmer for 5 minutes, then add the leeks and shallots. Put into a suitably sized pie plate.

Roll out the dough and cut a strip to go around the rim of the pie plate. Top the pie with the piece of dough and crimp the edges to seal. Decorate if you like, and brush with the beaten egg

Bake in the oven for 30 minutes.

This pie tastes fantastic, and while it is cooking your kitchen will be filled with the most mouthwatering aromas. It is my belief that, no matter where you are, you can judge how good a butcher is by his pork pie. Although the main spice in a pork pie is usually pepper, other spices, such as mace, cinnamon, nutmeg, coriander, and ginger, can also be added. You can make this as one large pie or two smaller ones (as in the photograph).

Pork Pie

MAKES 1 X 6–8 INCH
(15–20 CM) PIE

DOUGH

1 cup lard

$2/3$ cup water

$3^1/4$ cups all-purpose flour, plus extra for dusting

a good pinch of salt

butter, for greasing

1 free-range egg, lightly beaten

FILLING

2 lb (900 g) lean ground pork or diced pork shoulder

2 medium onions, diced

2 pinches freshly grated nutmeg

salt and pepper, to taste

scant $1/2$ cup dry white wine

$1^1/4$ cups chicken stock

Make the dough by bringing the lard and water to a boil in a pan. Sift the flour into a food processor and add the salt. While the processor is on, pour the hot water and lard onto the flour and blend until you have a smooth dough. When finished, turn the dough out into a large bowl and let cool slightly.

Grease a 6–8 inch (15–20 cm) pie mold with butter. On a lightly floured surface, roll out two-thirds of the dough and line the pie plate, leaving an overhang. Don't worry if it's a bit like working with clay; it will be worth it in the end. Place in the refrigerator to set. Keep the remaining dough covered and warm.

Preheat the oven to 350°F/180°C. To make the filling, mix the pork with the onions and season with nutmeg, salt, and pepper. Add the wine and mix. Pile the filling into the pastry shell.

On a lightly floured surface, roll out the remaining dough, using a little extra flour if it's sticky. Put it on top of the pie, then trim and crimp the edges with your thumbs. Brush the top with some of the beaten egg.

Bake in the oven for 40 minutes. Carefully remove from the plate and brush the edges with the lightly beaten egg again. Return to the oven for an additional 20–30 minutes to set the sides and cook through.

Remove from the oven and let cool. Warm the chicken stock, then make a little hole in the top of the pie. Pour as much stock as the pie will take in through the hole. Chill to set.

Toad in the Hole

Well, if I can't make Yorkshire puddings I shouldn't be writing this book. I'm going to give you some top tips. Make the batter well in advance, so it can rest, and make sure the dish is hot before you add the batter to it. When in the oven, keep the door closed for at least 20 minutes. So there you go: good luck and happy rising of your Yorkshires! You can make large "toads" or individual ones (as in the photograph).

SERVES 6

6 sausages, such as Cumberland or Lancashire

olive oil

3 tbsp whole-grain mustard

2 tbsp beef dripping or vegetable oil

YORKSHIRE PUDDING

scant 1²/₃ cups all-purpose flour

4–5 medium free-range eggs

salt and pepper, to taste

2¹/₂ cups milk

1 tbsp chopped fresh, thyme leaves

First, make the Yorkshire pudding batter by placing the flour and all the eggs into a bowl with some salt and pepper. Whisk until smooth and stir in all the milk and the chopped thyme.

Cover and place in the refrigerator for at least 2 hours, or preferably overnight.

Preheat the oven to 425°F/220°C, and place a large tartlet pan in the oven to warm.

Sauté the sausages in a hot pan with a little oil to color them. Remove them from the pan and coat in the mustard. Remove the hot tray from the oven, add the dripping and heat again until very hot.

Put the sausages in the center of the tray and, while the tray is hot, pour in the batter.

Bake for 25–30 minutes, until risen and golden brown.

Sausage Rolls

Weddings and funerals are usually where we see the very worst of buffet food. It's a chef's pet hate: those rows on rows of cheap, store-bought sausage rolls, undercooked vol-au-vents filled with cold shrimp and mushrooms, Scotch eggs, pickled eggs, warm ham, undressed salad, overcooked dry chipolatas on toothpicks, and cheap smoked salmon. However, these delicious homemade sausage rolls might just surprise you!

MAKES 15–20

1 lb (450 g) sausage meat (either from your butcher or use linked sausages and take the meat out of the skins)

1 onion, finely chopped or grated

finely grated zest of 1/2 lemon

1 heaped tsp each of chopped fresh thyme and sage

salt and pepper, to taste

freshly grated nutmeg

8 oz (225 g) package puff pastry, thawed if frozen

all-purpose flour, for dusting

1 free-range egg yolk, mixed with 2 tsp milk

Preheat the oven to 400°F/200°C.

Mix together the sausage meat, onion, lemon zest, and chopped herbs. Season with the salt, pepper, and nutmeg. This can now be refrigerated to firm while the pastry is being rolled.

Roll the pastry thinly (1/8 inch/3 mm) on a floured surface, then cut into three long strips approximately 4 inches (10 cm) wide.

The sausage meat can now be molded, using your hands, into three long sausages, preferably 1 inch (2.5 cm) thick. If the meat is too moist, dust with flour.

Sit each "sausage" on a pastry strip, 3/4–1 1/4 inches (2–3 cm) from the edge of the pastry. Brush the pastry along the other side, close to the sausage, with the egg yolk and milk mixture. Fold the pastry over the meat, rolling it as you do so. When the pastry meets, leave a small overlap before cutting away any excess. Once rolled all along, lift them carefully, making sure that the seal is on the bottom when put down. Cut each strip into 2-inch (5-cm) sausage rolls.

These can now be transferred to a greased baking sheet. The sausage rolls can be left as they are, or you can make three to four cuts with scissors along the top. Brush each with the remaining egg yolk before baking for 20–30 minutes.

Once baked golden and crispy, remove from the oven and serve warm.

This is one of the first dishes that I cooked as a young chef at Castle Howard, when I was about eight or nine. It reminds me of the garden fêtes and village shows, where wars were waged between grandmothers, aunts and the Women's Institute!: rolling pins at dawn over the best sponge cake in the show!

Quiche Lorraine

SERVES 4

DOUGH

1¼ cups all-purpose flour, plus extra for dusting

salt, to taste

5½ tbsp butter, plus extra for greasing

water

FILLING

generous 2 cups grated cheddar cheese

4 tomatoes, sliced (optional)

7 oz (200 g) bacon, rind removed and chopped

5 free-range eggs, beaten

scant ½ cup milk

generous ¾ cup heavy cream

salt and pepper, to taste

2 sprigs fresh thyme

Sift the flour together with a pinch of salt in a large bowl. Rub in the butter until you have a soft bread-crumb texture. Add enough water to make the crumb mixture come together to form a firm dough, and then rest it in the refrigerator for 30 minutes.

Roll out the dough on a lightly floured surface and line a 8½-inch (22-cm) well-buttered flan dish. Don't cut off the edges of the dough yet. Chill again.

Preheat the oven to 375°F/190°C.

Remove the pastry shell from the refrigerator and line the bottom of the pastry with parchment paper and then fill it with dried beans. Place on a baking sheet and bake for 20 minutes. Remove the beans and parchment and return to the oven for another 5 minutes to cook the bottom.

Reduce the temperature of the oven to 325°F/160°C.

Sprinkle the cheese into the pastry bottom and add the sliced tomatoes if you are using them. Pan-fry the bacon pieces until crisp and sprinkle them over the top.

Combine the eggs with the milk and cream in a bowl and season well with salt and pepper. Pour over the bacon and cheese. Sprinkle the thyme over the top and trim the edges of the pastry. Bake for 30–40 minutes, or until set.

Remove from the oven and let set. Trim the pastry edges to get a perfect edge (top chef tip), then serve in wedges.

I love to make classic dishes easy—and this one really is simple. Tarte tatin is originally French, but over the years the British have stolen it, and now it's ours, too!

Shallot Tarte Tatin

SERVES 4

12 oz (350 g) shallots

olive oil

generous 1/2 cup superfine sugar

2 tbsp unsalted butter

salt and pepper, to taste

7 oz200 g (200 g) package puff pastry, thawed if frozen

TO SERVE

8 oz (225 g) goat's cheese

8 tbsp honey

truffle oil

generous 1 cup wild arugula leaves

Preheat the oven to 400°F/200°C.

Roast the shallots with a little olive oil for 20 minutes.

In a clean, nonstick ovenproof pan, melt the sugar to a caramel. Add the butter and mix with the caramel. While hot, pour the mixture into four 3-inch (7.5-cm) nonstick tartlet pans. Add the roasted shallots until each tartlet is full and a tight fit. Season with salt and pepper.

Cut the puff pastry into four circles about 1/2 inch (1 cm) bigger than the tartlets. Place the pastry on top of the shallots, and tuck in the edges down the side of the tartlets to seal in the shallots. Place the pans in the oven and bake for 15 minutes, until the pastry is cooked.

Meanwhile, preheat the broiler to medium. With a sharp knife, cut the goat cheese into 1/2 inch (1 cm) slices.

Turn the tartlets out, while piping hot, onto a baking sheet, pastry down. Top with slices of goat cheese and place under the broiler for a few minutes to brown.

Meanwhile, mix the honey and a little truffle oil together. Place a tartlet on each plate and garnish with the arugula dressed with the honey and truffle oil.

Red Onion and Crème Fraîche Tarts

I use red onions for these instead of Spanish white onions because they require much less cooking and because they start off red, but instantly turn a dark, deep, rich caramel when you add balsamic. I serve this in my restaurant on the ship, and it always proves popular. I've planted red onions in my garden and always look forward to the new season.

SERVES 4

9 oz (250 g) package puff pastry thawed if frozen

1 small free-range egg, beaten

salt and pepper, to taste

2 tbsp balsamic vinegar

scant 1/2 cup olive oil, plus extra for drizzling

4 1/2 cups fresh arugula leaves

FILLING

3 large red onions, thinly sliced

6 cloves garlic, crushed

4 fresh thyme sprigs

2 tbsp unsalted butter

generous 1/2 cup whole-fat crème fraîche or sour cream

Preheat the oven to 425°F/220°C. Roll the puff pastry out until it is half as thick as it was when it was opened (about 1/8 inch/3 mm thick, or as thin as you dare) and cut into four round circles the size of a side plate. Using a sharp knife, cut a small, framelike edge around the whole pastry and lay this, in pieces, around the outer edge of the tarts. Alternatively, make 1 large rectangular tart, as in the photograph.

Break the egg into a bowl and whisk with a fork. Brush the pastry circles or rectangle around the edges. Prick with a fork before baking for 15–20 minutes, until the pastry is cooked.

For the filling, in a large pan fry the onions, garlic, and thyme in the butter for 15 minutes, until well caramelized. Season well. Remove the cooked shell/s from the oven and spread with the crème fraiche, then top with the caramelized onions, drizzle with olive oil, and return to the oven for a few minutes, until cooked.

In a bowl, mix the balsamic vinegar with the olive oil and some salt and pepper. Combine the arugula with the dressing.

Remove the tart/s from the oven and place on a serving plate. Drizzle with a little olive oil and serve with a small pile of the dressed arugula in the middle of the tart.

Asparagus has a very short season in Britain: only about six to eight weeks in May and June. It's best eaten with melted butter, using your fingers, but is also great in a tart, cooked with a Quiche Lorraine filling.

Asparagus Tart

SERVES 4

14 oz (400 g) package flaky pie dough, thawed if frozen (or 1 1/2 times the quantity on page 94)

a little flour, for dusting

1/2 tbsp butter

FILLING

4 free-range eggs

1 free-range egg yolk

1 shallot, finely chopped

1 3/4 cups crème fraîche or sour cream

salt and pepper, to taste

2 tbsp chopped fresh flat-leaf parsley

generous 3/4 cup grated Gruyère cheese

14 oz (400 g) asparagus, blanched and cold, halved lengthwise

Roll out the dough on a lightly floured surface and line a 10 inch (25 cm) well-buttered tart pan. Let the excess to hang over the edge. Chill for 30 minutes.

Preheat the oven to 375°F/190°C.

Remove the pastry shell from the refrigerator. Line the bottom of the pastry with parchment paper and fill with dried beans. Place on a baking sheet and bake blind for 20 minutes.

Remove the beans and parchment from the pastry shell and return to the oven for another 5 minutes to cook the bottom.

Reduce the temperature of the oven to 325°F/160°C.

For the filling, beat the eggs, egg yolk, and shallot together with the crème fraîche and season well. Fold in the parsley and half the cheese and spoon the mixture onto the bottom of the tart. Top with the asparagus and cover with the remaining cheese.

Trim the pastry around the edges. Bake for another 30 minutes, until set, and serve warm.

roasts

What can I say about roast beef that hasn't been said already? The picture says it all. I was brought up on this every week, and it's one of the best things we produce in Britain. When I was about 14, I went to work in two two-star Michelin restaurants in France and got treated like a skivvy for ten weeks, because both head chefs thought all we cooked in Britain was roast beef and Yorkshire pudding. Roast beef; they don't know what they're missing.

Peppered Roast Beef

SERVES 8

1¹/₂ – 2 lb (675–900 g) tenderloin or rib of beef on the bone

2–3 tbsp black peppercorns, finely crushed

salt

cooking fat or oil

1 large sprig fresh rosemary

Preheat the oven to 425°F/220°C. Roll the beef in the crushed peppercorns until completely covered. Season with salt.

Heat some oil in a hot roasting pan, then add the meat to seal. Remove from the heat and tuck the rosemary underneath the meat or place it on top. Roast in the oven—a joint of this size will take between 25 and 40 minutes to cook, but this depends on how you would like to eat it. Cooking for 20 minutes will keep it rare; 30 minutes, medium; and 40 minutes, medium-to-well-done.

Once cooked, let the meat rest for 15–20 minutes before carving. This will relax the meat, and it will become even more tender.

Roast Sirloin of Beef

Roast beef with Yorkshire pudding is the best meal in the world, period. But then I am Yorkshire born and Yorkshire bred: strong in the arm and really good at making Yorkshire puddings!

SERVES 8

5–6 lb (2.25–2.7 kg/3 ribs) tenderloin of beef on the bone

1 onion, quartered

1 tbsp all-purpose flour

salt and pepper, to taste

TO SERVE
Yorkshire Pudding (*see* page 132)

Preheat the oven to 475°F/240°C.

Place the beef upright in a roasting pan, tucking in the onions by the side.

Dust the flour liberally over the surface of the beef. Season with some salt and pepper. This floury surface will help to make the fat very crusty, while the onion will caramelize to give the gravy a rich color and flavor.

Place the joint in the oven. After 20 minutes, turn the temperature down to 375°F/190°C, and continue to cook for 30 minutes for rare beef, plus 45 minutes for medium-rare or 60 minutes for well-done.

While the meat is cooking, baste with the juices at least three times. To check if the beef is cooked to your liking, insert a thin skewer and press out some of the juices; the red, pink, or clear color will indicate to what stage the beef is cooked.

Remove the cooked beef to a board for carving and let it rest for at least 30 minutes before serving. During this time, you can make the Yorkshire pudding. Pour any juices that are released from the beef into the gravy.

Roast Loin of Pork with Five Vegetables

This is a must for a Sunday lunch: roast loin of pork with crackling, roast potatoes, a quartet of other vegetables, and gravy.

SERVES 4

4–4¹/₂ lb (1.8–2 kg) loin of pork with the skin on

2 tbsp white wine vinegar

1 tbsp sea salt

1 tbsp chopped fresh thyme

vegetable oil, lard or dripping

salt and pepper, to taste

3 cups cauliflower florets

4 medium carrots, chopped

7 oz (200 g) green beans, trimmed

1¹/₃ cups broccoli florets

2 tbsp yeast extract

²/₃ cup red wine

1¹/₄ cups chicken stock

3¹/₂ tbsp

TO SERVE
Roast Potatoes (*see* page 221)

Preheat the oven to 350°F/180°C.

Score the skin of the pork 12–15 times with a sharp knife. Rub the vinegar over the skin, then mix together the sea salt and thyme and rub into the skin.

Place in a roasting pan with some fat and roast in the oven for about 2 hours, basting every 15 minutes or so.

While the meat is in the oven, precook the vegetables separately in plenty of boiling salted water. Begin with the cauliflower, then remove and plunge into cold water. Do the same with the carrots, beans, and broccoli—in this order. Once they are all cooked and cooled, set aside until needed. Blanch and roast the potatoes as described on page 221, but for an hour instead of 50 minutes.

Once the meat is cooked, remove from the pan and let rest. Pour off the excess fat.

To make the gravy, place the oven pan on the stove and add the yeast extract, red wine and stock. Boil to reduce by about half, stirring. Add half the butter and some seasoning before passing through a strainer. Keep warm until needed.

To serve, put the roast potatoes in a serving dish. Reheat the vegetables in boiling salted water, tip into a serving dish, and dot with the remaining butter. Remove the crackling, break into pieces, and carve the meat. Pour the gravy into a pitcher.

Roast Pork

Even cold roast pork with cold apple sauce is fantastic, let alone straight from the oven just roasted. How many of you are tempted to taste a thick slice while you're carving? All, if you're like me. And I can never walk past one of those hog roasts without grabbing a floury roll filled with sliced meat and stuffing. Delicious!

SERVES 6

4 lb (1.8 kg) boned and rolled shoulder or loin of pork

salt and pepper, to taste

bones from the joint (optional)

1–2 tsp yeast extract

scant 1/2 cup red wine

scant 1 1/4 cups gravy, made from gravy granules

1 tsp cornstarch mixed with a little cold water

TO SERVE
Roast Potatoes (*see* page 221)

Put your joint of pork on a rack set over a dish or small roasting pan, and let it stand somewhere cool and airy for a few hours, so the skin can dry off. Preheat your oven to the highest possible setting.

Season the cut faces of the pork with salt and pepper, but leave the skin untouched. Place the pork, skin-side up, in a large roasting pan—on the bones, if you have them. Roast for 20 minutes, then lower the oven temperature to 350°F/180°C, and continue to roast for 30 minutes per 1 pound (450 g)—so, for example, a 4 pound (1.8 kg) joint will take another 2 hours—basting every 15 minutes or so.

Blanch and roast the potatoes as described on page 221, but for an hour instead of 50 minutes. Reserve the cooking water for the gravy.

Remove the pork from the oven, transfer to a tray, and let rest.

For the gravy, pour off the excess fat from the roasting pan and put the pan over a medium heat. Add 2½ cups of the reserved potato cooking water and scrape the bottom of the pan with a wooden spoon to loosen all the caramelized juices. Add the yeast extract, red wine, and liquid gravy. Bring to a boil, and boil for a few minutes. Thicken with the cornstarch (you may not need it all—just enough to get a good consistency). Strain into a warmed sauceboat, and adjust the seasoning if necessary.

To carve, cut and remove the strings. Slide a knife under the crackling, lift it off, and break it into pieces. Carve the pork across into thin slices, and arrange them on a warmed serving plate with the crackling and roast potatoes. Serve with the gravy and some vegetables.

Pot-roasted Shoulder of Pork with Chilli and Beer

Good pork is so hard to find nowadays. Supermarkets seem to sell pork that has been bred to run the 100 yards rather than for flavor. Why have our tastes changed? We seem to want pork with no fat on it. I visit the man I consider to be the best pork producer in the country, Martin Martindale, who is based in Hampshire and sells his pork at local farmers' markets. Get there early though—before me! No Carl Lewis pigs here, this is the best-tasting pork I've ever had.

SERVES 8

6–7 lb (2.7–3.25 kg) small, whole boned shoulder of pork, with the skin on

10 cloves garlic, crushed

salt and pepper, to taste

juice of 3 lemons

4 tbsp dried red chiles

3 tbsp olive oil

1¼ cups beer

SALSA VERDE

4 scallions

1¼ oz (30g) mixed fresh herbs (chervil, basil, mint, and parsley)

1 heaping tbsp chopped capers

1 tbsp chopped pickles

juice of 1½ lemons

2 tbsp extra virgin olive oil

Preheat the oven to 230°C/450°F/gas mark 8.

Using a small sharp knife, score the whole skin of the shoulder of pork with deep cuts about 5mm (¼ in) wide.

Mix the garlic with the salt, pepper, lemon juice, chillies and oil. Rub and push this mixture into and over the skin and on all the surfaces of the meat.

Place the shoulder on a rack in a roasting tin and pour the bottle of beer into the base. Roast for 45 minutes, or until the skin begins to crackle and turn brown. Baste the shoulder once or twice while cooking, turn the oven down to 180°C/350°F/gas mark 4 and leave the meat to pot-roast for 3–4 hours.

The shoulder is ready when it is completely soft under the crisp skin. You can tell by pushing with your finger: the meat will give way and might even split.

To make the salsa verde, chop spring onions and herbs finely, then mix with the chopped capers and pickles and the lemon juice and oil. Season well.

Serve each person with some of the crisp skin, meat cut from different parts of the shoulder, and a spoonful of the salsa verde. I think this is best served cold with hot new potatoes.

Sugar and Mustard-glazed Gammon

I remember when I was a kid my grandmother used to take me to Scott's Butchers in York (which has some fantastic pork and great pork pies, by the way). They'd always give her a free ham bone for the dog: a 6-inch (15-cm)-high Yorkshire terrier. It's a wonder the thing wasn't the size of a horse! However, it did live to a ripe old age. I was always told that, originally, York hams took their flavor from smoke from the oak sawdust that was around when they were building York Cathedral. This recipe doesn't go to that extreme, but it's a must for any buffet party.

SERVES 20–26

11–13 lb (5–6 kg) whole ham

3 tbsp English mustard

30 cloves

4 tbsp raw brown sugar

6 tbsp honey

Soak the ham in a sinkful of cold water overnight. (Ask your supplier how long you should soak it, because ham pieces vary.)

Preheat the oven to 325°F/160°C.

Remove the ham from the water and pat dry. Put into a large baking pan and cover with foil. Put in the oven for about 3$^{1}/_{2}$ – 4$^{1}/_{2}$ hours, or about 20 minutes per 1 pound (450 g), depending on the size of your joint.

Half an hour before the end of the cooking time, remove the joint from the oven and turn the temperature up to 425°F/220°C.

Remove the foil and peel off the skin, being careful not to burn yourself (rubber gloves can help here).

Using a sharp knife, score the fat in a crisscross pattern all over the ham. Rub the ham with mustard and stud with the cloves, then sprinkle with the sugar.

Drizzle with honey and return to the oven for about 20–30 minutes, until golden brown and well glazed. Keep basting with the juices in the pan and let cool before serving.

I remember lining up at Scott's Butchers as a kid with my grandmother and aunt. Armed with their handbags and pensions every Thursday, they would wait for dry-cured, smoked bacon and York ham. Sadly, they don't do York ham anymore, but if you're in York it's worth going to the store, on Petergate, to experience one of the greatest pork suppliers there is.

Honey-glazed Ham with Spiced Apple Sauce

SERVES 4–6

7¹/₂ lb (3.5 kg) boiled ham, cooled

¹/₃ cup honey

1 tbsp English mustard

finely grated zest and juice of 1 orange

20 cloves

TO SERVE

Spiced Apple Sauce (*see* page 234)

Preheat the oven to 425°F/220°C.

Score the ham fat diagonally at 1 inch (2.5 cm) intervals, first in one direction, then another, to produce a diamond pattern.

Mix the honey, mustard, orange zest, and enough orange juice to make a spreadable mixture. Smear this glaze over the ham. Stud the ham with the cloves at the points of the diamond shapes. Bake for 30 minutes, or until cooked through.

Serve the ham in slices, hot or cold, with the Spiced Apple Sauce.

Roast Leg of Lamb

I first tried this garlic, rosemary, and anchovy combination with lamb while working at Antony Worrall Thompson's restaurant in the late 1980s. I was hooked; it's to die for. You might consider combining anchovies with meat curious, but somehow the anchovies make the meat meatier!

SERVES 4

1 leg of lamb

6 cloves garlic, cut into slivers

3 large sprigs fresh rosemary

2³/₄ oz (75 g) can anchovy fillets in oil

olive oil

Preheat the oven to 350°F/180°C.

Make small cuts all over the meat and insert a sliver of garlic, a small piece of rosemary, and half an anchovy fillet into each cut until all the ingredients are used up.

Drizzle with a little olive oil and roast in the oven, allowing 20 minutes per 1 pound (450 g) for meat that is pink in the center, 25 minutes if you prefer it more well-done.

Once the joint is cooked to your liking, remove and let to rest before you carve the meat.

Lavender Roast Leg of Lamb

Using lavender instead of rosemary contributes a subtly different flavor to your lamb.

SERVES 4

1 leg of lamb, about 5 lb (2.25 kg)

1 bulb garlic, cloves peeled

2³/₄ oz (75 g) can anchovy fillets in oil!

tiny sprigs of fresh lavender

salt and pepper, to taste

about 2 tbsp lavender honey or lavender mustard

LAVENDER HONEY GLAZE

scant ¹/₂ cup lavender honey

scant ¹/₂ cup olive oil

Preheat the oven to 350°F/180°C. Using a sharp knife, prick the leg of lamb all over about 20 times and about ³/₄ inch (2 cm) deep. Cut the garlic into thin strips and place one slice of garlic and one-third of an anchovy fillet into each hole. Pick a sprig of lavender and place this into the holes, too. Continue until all the holes are full.

Place the joint in a roasting pan. Season with salt and pepper, and drizzle with lavender honey or spread with lavender mustard. Roast in the oven for 1 hour 20 minutes for a 5 pound (2.25 kg) leg of lamb, basting occasionally.

Warm the honey for the glaze in a small pan, then, with a hand blender on a high speed, blend in the oil as you pour it in to create a warm glaze. Pour over the lamb, and return to the oven to cook for another 20 minutes.

When the lamb is cooked, let it rest for 15 minutes before carving.

Yeah, yeah, before we start: Corn-fed and organic chickens do have a better flavour than the normal fare, but my grandmother didn't use them, nor did my mom or my aunt, so they should have no place in this book. (Come to think of it, we had chickens that my dad used to breed in our yard at home.) Stuffing the chicken under the skin creates flavor and helps keep the meat nice and moist.

Roast Chicken with Tapenade

SERVES 4

4 1/2 lb (2 kg) chicken

6 oz (175 g) tapenade, store-bought or made as below

1 lemon, halved

1 bulb garlic, halved

salt and pepper, to taste

extra virgin olive oil

TAPENADE

1 cup black olives, pitted

1 clove garlic

1 onion

3 tbsp capers

6 anchovy fillets

a small bunch of fresh flat-leaf parsley

juice of 1 lemon

extra virgin olive oil

Preheat the oven to 375°F/190°C.

To make the tapenade, finely chop the olives, garlic, onion, capers, anchovy fillets, and parsley. Mix in the lemon juice and enough oil to make a pastelike texture. Season well with salt and pepper.

Starting at the neck end of the chicken, push your fingertips between the skin and flesh to form a pocket. Spoon the tapenade between the flesh and skin, and pat down so that it spreads evenly.

Place the chicken in a roasting pan, squeeze over the lemon juice, and then place the lemon halves around. Place the garlic into the body cavity. Season and drizzle with oil.

Roast in the oven for about 70–80 minutes, basting the skin every 10 minutes with its own juices. Push a skewer into the thigh at the thickest point. If the juices run clear, it is done; if not, give it another 5 minutes then test again.

Serve slices of chicken with a spoonful of tapenade on the side.

Roast Chicken with Lemon and Bacon

Roast chicken is everyone's favorite, and this is a simple recipe given an extra little kick of flavor by the lemon and bacon.

SERVES 4

3 lb (1.3 kg) chicken

olive oil

salt and pepper, to taste

a pat of butter

6 slices bacon

2 lemons

Preheat the oven to 400°F/200°C. Brush the bird all over with olive oil and season generously. Put the pat of butter inside the bird, and place the bacon over the breast part of the chicken. Place in an roasting pan.

Cut the lemons in half and squeeze the juice over the bird. Place the lemon halves around the chicken, then drizzle everything with a little more olive oil.

Roast in the oven for 20 minutes per 1 pound (450 g), basting frequently. Push a skewer into the thigh at the thickest point. If the juices run clear, it is done; if not, give it another 5 minutes, then test again.

Let the cooked bird stand in a warm place for 15 minutes before carving. This standing time is vital. The bird finishes cooking while the juices are recovered and absorbed back into the meat, making every slice moist.

Spiced Pot-roasted Chicken
A twist to make the standard roast chicken taste a little different.

SERVES 4

4¹/₂ lb (2 kg) chicken

4¹/₂ tbsp butter

8 tbsp dark soy sauce

6 tbsp honey

2 cinnamon sticks

4 cloves garlic, halved

2 star anise

¹/₂ cup dry sherry

1¹/₂ cups chicken stock

Preheat the oven to 400°F/200°C.

Wipe the chicken. Melt the butter in a casserole dish, add the chicken, and brown the bird on all sides. Sit breast-side up in the casserole and pour over the soy sauce and honey. Add the cinnamon, garlic, and star anise to the base of the pan and pour in the sherry and stock.

Place the casserole on the stove and bring to a simmer. Then cover the dish loosely with foil and put into the preheated oven. Cook for about 80 minutes, uncovering and basting with the juices every now and then. Push a skewer into the thigh at the thickest point. If the juices run clear, it is done; if not, give it another 5 minutes, then test again.

When cooked, remove the chicken and let rest in a warm place. Strain the juices into a clean pan and boil to reduce.

Serve the chicken, cut into pieces rather than carved, with the reduced juices, some rice, and a salad.

Here's a quick-and-easy turkey recipe that all the family will love! The stuffing beneath the skin keeps the flesh nice and moist.

Roast Turkey Stuffed with Cream Cheese and Herbs

SERVES 10–12

10 lb (4.5 kg) turkey, giblets removed

1 bunch fresh parsley, stalks removed

generous 1 cup cream cheese

1 bunch fresh cilantro, stalks removed

4 tbsp olive oil

salt and pepper, to taste

Preheat the oven to 350°F/180°C.

Place the turkey on a board and carefully lift the skin up at the neck. Work your hand under it to ease it away from the breast completely.

Process the parsley in a blender until chopped. Add the cream cheese and gradually add the cilantro, blending between each addition until smooth. Finally, add 1 tablespoon of the olive oil and blend well. Alternatively, chop the herbs as finely as you can and mix with the cream cheese and 1 tablespoon olive oil.

Press the cream mixture into the space between the breast and the skin of the turkey. Pull the skin back into place over the cheese mixture, press to reshape, and smooth over.

Place the turkey in a roasting pan and drizzle with the rest of the olive oil. Season well with salt and pepper, and roast for 18 minutes per 1 pound (450 g), or until the juices run clear when the thickest part of the leg is pierced with a knife. Baste the turkey with the pan juices after 45 minutes.

Cover with foil and let stand for at least 20 minutes before carving.

Roast Turkey with Orange

The most common mistake people make when they roast turkey is the timing, especially at Christmas. With the kids running around and the gravy boiling over, you tend to forget about it! Calculate 18 minutes per 1 pound (450 g). Let the turkey rest well before you carve it, and never use an electric carving knife, because this will rip the meat and make it tough.

SERVES 10–12

10–12 lb (4.5–5.4 kg) turkey, giblets removed

2 oranges

24 large fresh rosemary sprigs

4 tbsp unsalted butter, at room temperature

salt and pepper, to taste

22 bacon slices

GRAVY

2¹/₂ cups chicken stock or water

1¹/₄ cups white wine or water

3 tbsp all-purpose flour

2 tsp Dijon mustard

Preheat the oven to 375°F/190°C. Wash the turkey inside and out and dry well with paper towels. Quarter 1 orange and put the quarters in the cavity with 2 rosemary sprigs. If you are stuffing the turkey (see page 129), put the stuffing in the only neck-end, pushing it up toward the breast (don't pull the neck skin too tightly, because the stuffing expands during cooking). Secure the neck end with skewers crosswise, then tie the turkey legs together at the top of the drumsticks for a good shape.

Weigh the turkey and calculate the cooking time at 18 minutes per 1 pound (450 g). Grease a large roasting pan with a little butter. Put the turkey in the pan. Melt the remaining butter. Halve the remaining orange and squeeze one-half over the turkey, then mix the remaining juice with the melted butter. Brush some of this butter over the turkey skin and season (keep the rest for basting later). Cover the turkey with foil and roast for the calculated time. Brush it every hour with the orange-butter mixture. An hour before the end of the cooking time, remove the foil. If you want, you can turn the oven up a bit higher. The turkey is ready if the juices run clear when the thickest part of the leg is pierced with a knife.

For each rosemary and bacon spike, lay a bacon slice on the work surface with a rosemary sprig on top. Wrap the bacon around the sprig and lay it on a baking sheet with the seam underneath.

Remove the turkey from the oven and transfer it to a platter, tightly cover with foil, and let to rest for up to 30 minutes before carving, leaving the oven on. Put the bacon and rosemary spikes in the oven 20 minutes before you are ready to serve, and cook until the bacon is crisp.

While the turkey is resting, pour off all but 6 tablespoons of the juices from the roasting pan into a large pitcher and let them settle. When the fat has risen to the surface, spoon it off and make the darker juices underneath up to 2¹/₂ cups with water or stock, then add the wine. Heat the juices in the roasting pan on the stove. Stir in the flour, scraping up the parts from the bottom of the pan, and cook, stirring, to a nutty brown. Slowly pour in the liquid, then bring to a boil and keep stirring until thickened. Season with the mustard and salt and pepper.

Serve the bird with the spikes, roast potatoes, and whatever else you want.

While doing some of the photography for this book, I went shooting at Jody Schekter's farm up the road from me. It was a great day and, as usual, the number of birds we said we shot was different to the number we took home. Typical men, I know! If you buy a brace of birds, or a cock and a hen, remember hens are smaller so will need to be removed from the oven before the cocks.

Pot-roast Pheasant with Cider and Calvados

SERVES 4

4 tbsp butter

2 pheasants, cleaned

salt and pepper, to taste

1 onion, finely chopped

3 oz (85 g) bacon, cut into strips

1 stick celery stalk, chopped

1 carrot, chopped

4 sprigs fresh sage

2 Granny Smith apples, peeled, cored, and cut into large chunks

1/4 cup Calvados

21/4 cups hard cider

11/4 cups chicken stock

11/4 cups heavy cream

BAKED APPLES

4 apples, peeled and cored

2 tbsp butter, melted

1 tbsp light brown sugar

TO SERVE

kale, blanched

deep-fried sage leaves

8 slices crispy, cooked pancetta

Preheat the oven to 375°F/190°C. Melt the butter in a large nonstick casserole pot. Season the pheasants with salt and pepper. Place the pheasants into the casserole pot and brown over a medium heat until pale golden on all sides. Remove from the pot and set aside.

Add the onion, bacon, celery, carrot, and sage sprigs to the pot and cook over a medium heat until the onion is soft and translucent and the bacon is crispy. Carefully pour off any excess fat from the bacon.

Return the pheasants to the pot and scatter over the apples. Pour over most of the Calvados and set alight. Once the flames have died down, add 11/4 cups of the cider and the chicken stock. Bring to a simmer, cover, and place in the oven for about 20 minutes, until the birds are cooked through.

For the baked apples, place the apples on a baking sheet that has been brushed with a little butter and sprinkle with the sugar. Bake for about half an hour, basting the apples a few times during cooking.

Remove the pheasants from the pot and place on a cutting board. Remove the thighs and breasts and set aside to keep warm. Chop the birds into four pieces and place them back in the pot with the vegetables and the remaining cider. Bring to a boil and simmer gently for 5 minutes.

Strain the sauce into a bowl through a fine-meshed strainer. Pour the strained sauce back into the pot and add a splash of Calvados. Reduce by half. Add the cream and simmer for another 5 minutes, or until the sauce is creamy and slightly thickened. Return the pheasant breasts and thighs to the pot to warm through and become coated in the sauce.

Remove the baked apples from the oven. Serve the pheasant on a bed of kale with a baked apple. Garnish with deep-fried sage leaves and crispy pancetta.

Mother's Pheasant with Wild Garlic Leaves, Shallots and Bacon

Wild garlic is found in damp woods and shady roads; it has white flowers and dark green leaves which are like a cross between dock and dandelion. If you can't find it, use 1 pound (450 g) spinach with two cloves of garlic.

SERVES 4

2 large pheasants, cleaned

1 carrot

1/2 leek

1 onion

1³/4 cups red wine

4 cups fresh chicken stock

4 sprigs fresh thyme

salt and pepper, to taste

1 tbsp olive oil

16 slices streaky bacon

16 shallots

3 tbsp butter

8 handfuls freshly picked wild garlic leaves

Remove the breasts and legs from the pheasants and reserve.

Preheat the oven to 425°F/220°C. For the sauce, dice the carrot, leek, and three-quarters of the onion and place this and the pheasant carcasses in a roasting pan. Roast in the oven for about 1 hour until nice and brown. Leave the oven on.

Remove the birds and vegetables from the oven and place in a large pan with the red wine, stock, and half the fresh thyme. Bring to a boil and simmer gently without a lid so the liquor can reduce.

Season the pheasant legs and breasts with salt and pepper and seal in a hot pan in the olive oil. Put in an ovenproof dish in one layer and cover with the bacon. Add the shallots and remaining thyme to the dish. Place in the oven at the same heat, and roast for about 15 minutes.

Meanwhile, finely dice the remaining onion and cook in half the butter in a pan over a high heat for a few minutes. Throw in the garlic leaves and cook for only about 1 minute, until wilted. Remove from the heat.

Strain the sauce and continue to reduce over a high heat.

Remove the pheasant from the oven and let stand for about 5–10 minutes to rest. Add the remaining butter and some seasoning to the sauce.

Season the garlic leaves, place on the plates, and put the pheasant on top with the bacon, shallots, and thyme from the pan. Pour over the sauce and serve.

Honeyed Duck Confit with Crispy Seaweed and Creamy Mash

You can buy, or prepare yourself, plump, tender duck legs that have been cooked deliciously slowly in their own fat. Known as duck confit, they are ideal for many dishes.

SERVES 2

2 duck legs, confited in their own fat, homemade (see page 127) or from a can or jar

4 tbsp honey

3 tbsp olive oil

leaves stripped from 2–3 sprigs fresh thyme

10 1/2 oz (300 g) russet potatoes, peeled and chopped

salt and pepper, to taste

3 tbsp hot milk

a small pat of butter

scant 1/2 cup red wine

generous 1 cup fresh chicken stock

2 oz (55 g) crispy seaweed

Heat the oven to 350°F/180°C. Scrape the fat from the duck legs and place them in a roasting pan. (Don't waste the fat—it's wonderful for frying eggs or roasting potatoes.)

Whisk the honey and oil together and smear over the duck legs. Sprinkle over the thyme leaves. Roast the legs in the oven for about 20 minutes, spooning the honey glaze over the legs two to three times.

Meanwhile, boil the potatoes in a saucepan of lightly salted water for about 15 minutes, until just tender. Drain, then mash with a fork, gradually beating in the hot milk, butter, and plenty of seasoning.

Place the wine and stock in a saucepan, bring to a boil, and continue boiling until reduced by two-thirds. Season well.

Spoon the mashed potato onto the center of warmed serving plates, sprinkle the seaweed around the mash, and sit the duck legs on top. Scrape any meaty parts from the roasting pan and sprinkle over, then pour over the reduced red wine sauce and serve immediately.

I love 1970s food—the shrimp cocktail, the chicken in a basket, and *duck à l'orange*. It's fine to embrace the future, but don't ever forget the past. I cooked this recipe the other day for a dinner party, and it took the diners by storm. I gave them shrimp cocktail as an appetizer and a Black Forest gâteau for dessert. Serve with some extra orange slices, briefly caramelized in butter, if you like, and perhaps some shreds of candied orange zest.

Duck with Orange

SERVES 2

4 tsp honey

3 tbsp butter

2 duck breasts, 7 oz (200 g) each

salt and pepper, to taste

caramelized orange slices, to garnish (optional)

SAUCE

3 tbsp butter

1 heaping tbsp plain flour

2¹/₄ cups hot duck, game, or beef stock

2 Seville oranges, or 2 sweet oranges and 1 lemon

1 tbsp superfine sugar

4 tbsp port

Make the sauce first. Melt the butter in a small pan and let it turn a delicate golden brown color. Stir in the flour, cook for 2 minutes, then stir in the stock. Let simmer gently for at least 20 minutes—the longer the better. Meanwhile, preheat the oven to 400°F/200°C.

To cook the duck, melt the honey and butter together in a very hot pan, then place the duck in, skin-side down. Season well with salt and pepper, and color very well (until almost black) before turning over. Place on an baking sheet and bake for 8–10 minutes, until pink. Once cooked, remove from the oven and let rest. Reserve any juices from the pan for use in the sauce.

Meanwhile, remove the peel from the oranges, and cut it into matchstick strips. Simmer these in boiling water for 3 minutes, then drain and add to the simmering sauce. Add the juice of the oranges (and lemon, if used) to the sauce. Stir in some sugar to taste; start with a little, and add more if necessary. Finally, pour in the reserved meat juices from the duck, which should be well skimmed of fat, then the port.

Slice the duck breast, pour the sauce over it, and serve garnished with caramelized orange slices, if you like.

Honey-roast Duck Confit with Tomato Beans

I made this dish up while doing a dinner party in Scotland, and it's now a favorite. Canned beans and canned tomatoes can taste great heated together but this goes to another level.

SERVES 4

4 duck legs

salt and pepper, to taste

leaves from 2–3 fresh thyme sprigs

10 1/2 oz (300 g) duck fat

2 tbsp honey

TOMATO BEANS

4 tbsp extra-virgin olive oil

1 white onion, peeled and finely chopped

4 cloves garlic, finely chopped

scant 1/2 cup white wine

leaves from 2 fresh thyme sprigs

14 oz (400 g) canned chopped tomatoes

6 medium tomatoes

12 oz (350 g) canned flageolet beans, drained and rinsed

4 tbsp unsalted butter

3 tbsp chopped fresh parsley

RED WINE SAUCE

1/2 red onion, chopped

2 tbsp extra-virgin olive oil

3 cups fresh beef stock

1/3 bottle red wine

1/2 tbsp unsalted butter

To make the duck confit, weigh the duck legs, then put them in a small, shallow pan. Sprinkle with 2 teaspoons salt per kg 2 1/4 pounds (1 kg) and the fresh thyme leaves. Cover with plastic wrap and place in the refrigerator overnight.

The following day, remove the legs from the pan, wipe off the salt, and put the legs in a skillet with the duck fat. Cook slowly, covered, for about 2 1/2 hours, turning occasionally. Let cool in the fat.

When you are about half an hour from serving, preheat the oven to 350°F/180°C.

To make the beans, heat the olive oil in a pan and sauté the onion and garlic for a few minutes. Add the wine, thyme, and tomatoes, both canned and fresh, and bring to a simmer. After 15 minutes, add the beans and simmer for another 15 minutes. Season with salt and pepper, and add the butter and parsley to finish. Keep warm.

To make the red wine sauce, sauté the onion in the oil until it is softened, about 2 minutes, then add the stock and red wine. Bring to a boil, then simmer to reduce to a good sauce consistency. Pass through a strainer, add the butter, and keep warm to one side.

Meanwhile, scrape the fat from the duck legs and place in a roasting pan. Smear the honey over the duck legs, then roast for 20 minutes, until cooked through, spooning the honey glaze over the legs at least a couple of times during cooking.

To serve, place the beans on the plates and put the duck confit alongside. Spoon the sauce around.

I bought my first goose from a butcher's store in Malton called Derrick Fox, which used to have geese, turkey, rabbit, and pheasant hung up outside. Goose is fantastic, but you must get a good bird, otherwise it can be as tough as old boots. Serve the roast bird with a green vegetable, potatoes roasted in the goose fat, fried apple slices, and blood sausage.

Roast Goose with Stuffing

SERVES 6

10 lb (4.5 kg) goose with giblets (and any extra giblets you might get from your butcher if you ask nicely)

salt and pepper, to taste

2 1/2 cups chicken stock

a little cornstarch mixed in water

a little yeast extract

STUFFING

2 1/4 lb (1 kg) good-quality sausage meat

1 onion, chopped

1 clove garlic, smashed

1 medium free-range egg, beaten

freshly grated nutmeg

2 tbsp brandy

Preheat the oven to 425°F/220°C.

Prick the bird all over with a fork or needle, rub generously with salt and pepper, then roast on a rack over a deep pan, starting it loosely covered with foil, for 15 minutes per 1 pound (450 g). From time to time, remove fat from the roasting pan and reserve. Remove the foil 30 minutes before your calculated completion time to let the skin brown and crisp.

While the bird is roasting, make the gravy. Chop up the neck, gizzard, and heart, and simmer in the stock for about 2 hours, topping up with more stock or water as necessary. Strain. Boil to reduce a little if necessary, and thicken with the cornstarch. Season and add yeast extract to taste.

About 1 hour before the bird is due to come out of the oven, make the stuffing. In a large bowl, mix all the ingredients together well and then spoon the mixture into a large nonstick loaf pan. Put in the oven with the bird and leave it in there when you take the bird out.

When the goose is cooked through, let it stand for 20 minutes before attempting to carve it. Transfer it to a large cutting board and sever the legs. Cut off one breast in a single piece, then the other, reversing the bird to point the other way to make this easier. Cut through the legs at the ball-socket joint to separate them into drumsticks and thighs. Lay the breast pieces skin-side down and cut into slices across and down at a 45-degree angle. Arrange the slices on a warmed ovenproof dish. Cut slices off the legs and arrange them, skin-side up, around the breast meat. Detach the wings and cut them in half across the middle joint, slicing off what meat you can. Pick over the bird, removing any meat that is left. Just before serving, you can flash this carved meat under the broiler briefly. This will crisp up the skin as well.

Turn the stuffing out of its pan, and slice it like a meat loaf. Serve the goose accompanied by slices of the stuffing, and any other chosen accompaniments. Pass the hot gravy separately.

Sausage meat, Red Pepper and Apricot Stuffing Balls

I did these for a magazine article once, and people love them with turkey. They're so simple to prepare!

MAKES 16 BALLS

1 lb (450 g) good sausage meat (or good sausages removed from their casings)

2 tbsp ground almonds

2 roasted red peppers (canned or bottled), finely chopped

8 dried apricots, finely chopped

1 tsp mixed dried herbs

salt and pepper, to taste

olive oil

Place the sausage meat in a bowl. Add the ground almonds, red peppers, apricots, and herbs. Season with salt and pepper and mix well.

Roll into 16 balls and place on a greased baking sheet. Brush with olive oil and cook at 350°F/180°C for 30 minutes while the turkey (*see* page 119) is resting.

Chestnut Stuffing

Stuff this into the turkey as described on page 119, or bake in a separate loaf pan—or make into balls as here.

FOR A 10–12LB (4.5–5.4 KG) TURKEY

2 tbsp unsalted butter

1 large onion, finely chopped

5 juniper berries

2¼ lb (1 kg) good sausage meat (or good sausages removed from their casings)

7 oz (200 g) package cooked, peeled whole chestnuts, roughly chopped

2 medium free-range eggs

4 tbsp chopped fresh sage

2 tbsp chopped fresh parsley

2 cups fresh white bread crumbs

1/4 tsp ground allspice

salt and pepper, to taste

In a medium saucepan, melt the butter over a gentle heat, then add the onion and juniper berries. Cook for 5 minutes, without letting the onion color. Let cool. Remove and discard the juniper berries.

In a large bowl, mix the onion with the rest of the ingredients. To make sure you've got the seasoning right, fry a small piece of the stuffing before shaping, then taste and adjust as necessary. (You can make the stuffing to the end of this step a day ahead and keep in the refrigerator until ready to use. It can also be frozen.)

Shape into about 24 balls—this is easier with wet hands—and bake in a roasting tin at 350°F/180°C for 35–40 minutes, while the turkey (*see* page 119) is resting.

Just look at them bubbling away in the pan: a lovely mixture of sausage and bacon to garnish roast turkey, goose, or chicken. Both sausage and bacon will end up being nice and crisp and brown.

Sausage and Bacon Wraps with Sage and Honey

SERVES 4

8 bacon slices

16 cocktail sausages

16 small fresh sage leaves

2 tbsp honey

Preheat the oven to 350°F/180°C. Cut each of the bacon slices in half.

Roll up the sausages in the bacon with a small sage leaf. Secure with a wooden toothpick if you like (it's not entirely necessary), and arrange in a shallow pan. Drizzle with the honey.

Place in the oven and cook for 25–30 minutes. Turn over once or twice to brown evenly all over. Remove the toothpicks before serving, if necessary.

Yorkshire Pudding

Once again, this is my grandmother's recipe, which she used to serve with Rich Onion Gravy (*see* below). I love these with fois gras pâté in the center, served with the same gravy. This makes a great dinner party starter, and tastes fantastic.

SERVES 4

1²/₃ cups all-purpose flour

salt and pepper, to taste

4–5 medium free-range eggs

2¹/₂ cups milk

¹/₄ cup good dripping or vegetable oil

Place the flour and some seasoning in a bowl, and make a well in the middle. Add the eggs one by one, using a whisk, then whisk in the milk, mixing very well until the batter is smooth and there are no lumps. If possible, let stand in the refrigerator for at least an hour or, even better, overnight.

Preheat the oven to about 425°F/220°C. Divide the dripping or vegetable oil between four tartlet pan depressions (about 5 inches/13 cm in diameter) or use a muffin pan, and place in the oven to get very hot.

Carefully remove the pan from the oven and, with a ladle or from a pitcher, fill the pan with the batter and place back in the oven right away. Cook for about 20 minutes before opening the door to check—otherwise they will collapse. If undercooked, reduce the heat to 400°F/200°C, and cook for another 10–15 minutes.

Rich Onion Gravy

Some of my grandmother's recipes are over 100 years old and have been passed down through the Yorkshire generations. This gravy is the perfect accompaniment to Yorkshire Pudding.

SERVES 4

2 white onions, sliced

1 tbsp good dripping

generous 1 cup red wine

1³/₄ cups fresh beef stock

Cook the onions in a pan in the dripping for about 10 minutes, then add the wine and stock. Reduce until you have a nice thickened mixture: about another 10 minutes or so.

Season well. Serve with Yorkshire Pudding (*see* above).

stews, pots & spicy foods

How many people have eaten dumplings and thought they tasted like rubber bullets? Not if you follow this recipe! The secret to a good stew, I think, is sealing the meat well before adding the stock. This, if done properly, will give the stew increased flavor and a much better dark color.

Beef Stew and Dumplings

SERVES 4

4 tbsp olive oil

1 lb (450 g) braising beef, diced

2 3/4 oz (75 g) chicken livers, cut into chunks

2-3 celery stalks, diced

2 medium carrots, diced

1/2 leek, chopped

1 small red onion, diced

2 cloves garlic, crushed

2/3 cup good-quality red wine

2 1/4 cups fresh beef stock

4 canned anchovies, diced

salt and pepper, to taste

10 pearl onions

1 tbsp butter

8 sun-dried tomatoes, diced

10 new potatoes, cooked

4 tbsp fresh pesto

3 tbsp chopped, fresh flat-leaf parsley

4 tbsp torn, fresh basil

DUMPLINGS

scant 1 cup all-purpose flour

1 tsp baking powder

generous 1/4 cup lard

1 tbsp chopped, fresh flat-leaf parsley

Preheat the oven to 275°F/140°C.

Put two large pans on a high heat with one-third of the olive oil in each and, when hot, brown the beef and livers in one pan and the vegetables and garlic in the other. Cook both until they are nice and brown.

Place the contents of both pans into a casserole dish and deglaze the pans with the red wine and beef stock. Add the liquid to the stewing dish.

Add the anchovies, season with salt and pepper, and cook, with the lid on, in the oven for about 3 hours.

Meanwhile, make the dumplings. Sieve the flour, baking powder, and a pinch of salt together into a bowl. Mix in the lard and parsley and enough water to form a slightly thick dough. Placing a little flour on your hands, roll the dough into small balls, remembering that they will swell as they cook in the stew.

At the end of the stew's cooking time, sauté the pearl onions in the remaining oil and the butter, season with salt and pepper, and add to the stew with the sun-dried tomatoes and potatoes. Simmer for 5 minutes, then season well and add the pesto and herbs.

Remove the meat and vegetables from the liquid with a slotted spoon and keep warm in a dish, covered with foil, in the low oven.

Put the casserole over a high heat and, when bubbling, add the dumplings. Turn the heat down and poach gently for 20 minutes, because the dumplings will break up too much if you let them boil.

Serve the stew with the dumplings.

Beef Stroganoff

Thinly sliced beef in a rich onion, mushroom, and cream sauce, though Russian in origin, has become a classic, not just here in Britain but throughout Europe. Here, though, I've used ground beef; it's easier and less expensive—although it's a good idea to use good-quality meat for this recipe. Like the goulash opposite, this dish reminds me of my mother's food: food she placed in a big dish in the middle of the table with an even bigger bowl of pilaf rice.

SERVES 4

5 1/2 tbsp butter

1 tbsp olive oil

2 small onions, sliced

1 clove garlic, crushed

generous 3 cups sliced cremini mushrooms

8 oz (225 g) good-quality ground beef

1 tbsp paprika

1 tbsp French mustard

generous 1/4 cup heavy cream

salt and pepper, to taste

2 tbsp chopped, fresh flat-leaf parsley

TO SERVE

8 oz (225 g) fresh noodles, freshly cooked

a little butter

generous 1/4 cup sour cream

Heat a large skillet on the stove and add the butter and olive oil. Sauté the onions and garlic for about 5 minutes, until softened.

Add the sliced mushrooms, ground beef, and paprika. Cook on a high heat to seal the beef. After 5 minutes, add the mustard and pour in the heavy cream. Bring to a gentle simmer before adding some salt and pepper.

At this point, remove from the heat and add the chopped parsley.

Butter the freshly cooked noodles, pile them onto plates, then spoon on the stroganoff. Serve with a dollop of sour cream on the top.

Goulash

Goulash is Hungarian in origin, and was originally a beef soup. So why is this in a book on British food? Because, like dishes such as stroganoff and satay, it's a real classic that British people have been brought up with. Mom cooked this for me when I was a kid to get me used to spices and different flavors, the main spice here being paprika. Like all spices, paprika has a shelf life and an expiration date on the jar. The expiration date is not, as many of us might think, when the label has changed color in the sun....

SERVES 4

olive oil

1 lb 9 oz (700 g) braising steak, diced

3 tbsp all-purpose plain flour

1 large onion, thinly sliced

2 cloves garlic, finely chopped

1 green bell pepper, seeded and thinly sliced

1 red bell pepper, seeded and thinly sliced

2 tbsp tomato paste

2 tbsp paprika

2 large tomatoes, diced

generous 1/4 cup dry white wine

scant 1 1/4 cups fresh beef stock

2 tbsp fresh, chopped flat-leaf parsley

salt and pepper, to taste

2/3 cup sour cream

Preheat the oven to 325°F/160°C.

Heat a little olive oil in a heavy saucepan. Sprinkle the steak with the flour and brown well, in batches, in the hot pan. Set the sealed meat aside.

Sauté the onion, garlic, and peppers in the same pan in a little more oil. Return the beef to the pan with the tomato paste and paprika. Cook for about 2 minutes.

Add the tomatoes, white wine, and stock. Cook with a lid on in the oven for 1 1/2 hours. Alternatively, cook it on the stove on a gentle heat for about an hour, removing the lid after 45 minutes.

Before serving, add the chopped parsley and season well with salt and pepper. Stir in the sour cream.

PS: Thanks for the recipe, mom!

Ham, Potato, Leek and Herb Hotpot

This is based on my grandmother's recipe. For the stock, she used the end knuckle of hams left over from the butcher's slicer, and for the meat, the parts around the bones of a carved joint. Use good-quality ham, not the sliced, processed variety bought in a package. I use lots of herbs because the casserole should be like a thick stew. These thicken and flavor the sauce.

SERVES 4

1 cup butter

1 red onion, finely chopped

4 cloves garlic, finely chopped

2 small leeks, cleaned and sliced

scant 1 cup white wine

2¹/₄ cups fresh ham stock

1 lb (450 g) new potatoes, cooked

1¹/₄ lb (550 g) cooked ham, cut into chunks

salt and pepper, to taste

1 cup each of chopped fresh basil, parsley, chives and cilantro

Using about 4 tablespoons of the butter, sauté the onion, garlic, and leeks in a large pan, until soft.

Add the white wine, ham stock, potatoes, and ham and cook for 5–10 minutes, until everything is nice and hot.

Drain off the liquid, keeping the meat and vegetables warm. Gently simmer the liquid, adding the remaining butter a little at a time, whisking constantly to thicken the sauce. Do not boil.

Put all the ingredients back into the sauce and season. To finish, add all the chopped fresh herbs. Serve piping hot in bowls with some French bread.

Spicy Bean Stew with Sausages

Most adults and kids love this because it's so simple to make. Onions and garlic are used as a base, and good-quality sausages are the key. Cut them up into pieces, fry them all, add some canned beans and tomatoes, and stew down for about 15 minutes. Beautiful! I served this at a truckers' café once, but for breakfast, and 150 of them woofed it down!

SERVES 4

5 tbsp olive or vegetable oil

8 good free-range pork sausages

4 bacon slices, chopped

1 medium onion, chopped

2 cloves garlic, chopped

1 red chile, chopped (or more if it is really cold!)

1 tbsp brown sugar

28 oz (800 g) canned plum or chopped tomatoes

a dash of red or white wine (whatever is open)

(21 oz) (600 g) canned cannellini beans, drained and rinsed

10 oz (300 g) canned kidney beans, drained and rinsed

leaves from 1 small bunch fresh parsley, chopped

salt and pepper, to taste

Place a large, heavy saucepan on the stove and heat 3 tablespoons of the oil. Add the sausages and fry over a medium heat, turning them over until they are browned on the outside. Take them out of the pan and chop them into 1½ inch (4 cm) pieces. Set them aside on a plate.

Add the remaining oil to the pan, turn the heat down to low, add the bacon and onion, and fry gently for around 10 minutes, stirring from time to time so that they don't catch on the bottom. They will pick up all the lovely sausage remnants in the bottom of the pan.

Add the garlic and chile and fry for another couple of minutes, then add the brown sugar. Pour in the tomatoes, wine and 1¼ cups water, then stir in the sausage pieces along with the beans, and cook for 15–20 minutes over a low to medium heat.

Stir in the chopped parsley, salt and a lot of black pepper, and serve with some nice fresh crusty bread or mashed potato.

This lamb stew made with sliced potatoes should, I think, be on every British pub menu.

Traditional Lancashire Hot Pot

SERVES 4

2 lb (900 g) good-quality end and middle neck of British lamb, chopped into large bite-size pieces

1 tbsp vegetable oil

butter

4 lamb's kidneys, cored, skinned, and chopped small

3 medium onions, cut into 1/2 inch (1 cm) pieces

1 tbsp all-purpose flour

2 1/2 cups hot lamb stock

1/2 tsp Worcestershire sauce

salt and pepper, to taste

1 bay leaf

2 sprigs fresh thyme

2 lb (900 g) potatoes, peeled and cut into 3/4 inch (2 cm) slices

Preheat the oven to 325°F/160°C.

Trim the lamb of any excess fat. Heat the oil with a little butter in a large skillet until it is very hot, then brown the pieces of lamb two or three at a time. As they cook, put them into a casserole (1 3/4 quart/3.5 liter capacity). Brown the pieces of kidney, too, and tuck these in among the meat.

Sauté the onions, adding a little more butter to the pan if necessary, for about 10 minutes, until they turn brown at the edges. Stir in the flour to soak up the juices, and gradually add the hot stock and Worcestershire sauce, stirring or whisking until the flour and liquid are smoothly blended. Season with salt and pepper and bring to simmering point. Pour it over the meat in the casserole.

Add the bay leaf and thyme, then arrange the potato slices on top in an overlapping pattern. Season the potatoes and add a few pats of butter to the surface.

Cover with a tight-fitting lid and cook in the oven for 1 1/2 hours. You can remove the lid and brush the potatoes with a little more butter, then place under the broiler at the end of cooking time to make them crispy, if you like. Otherwise, turn the heat up during the last 15 minutes of cooking time in the oven and remove the lid. Remove the bay leaf and sprigs of thyme before serving.

Why do we now like moussaka so much in Britain? Probably because we first encountered it on vacation in Turkey or Greece, which is where I first tasted and fell in love with it. The traditional version would be cooked in a dish or a mold lined with cooked eggplant skins, and served either in the dish or turned out of the mold. Either way it's, fantastic: that hot, bubbling mass of lamb, eggplant, and cheese. Mmm, delicious.

Moussaka

SERVES 4–6

4 eggplants

olive oil

1/2 onion, chopped

2 cloves garlic, crushed

1 1/2 lb (675 g) ground lamb

3 plum tomatoes, diced

a good pinch of ground cumin

a good pinch of cinnamon

2/3 cup red wine

2 tbsp chopped fresh mint

2/3 cup chicken stock

scant 1 cup White Sauce (*see* page 154)

2 free-range eggs, beaten

a pinch of freshly grated nutmeg

salt and pepper, to taste

scant 1/2 cup grated mozzarella cheese

scant 1/2 cup grated cheddar cheese

Preheat the oven to 375°F/190°C.

Slice the eggplants, then cook them on both sides in a large pan with a little olive oil. Drain on paper towels.

To save on cleaning up, use the same pan with a little more olive oil to sauté the onion and garlic. After 5 minutes, turn the heat up and add the lamb to brown it. Add the tomatoes.

Add the cumin and cinnamon with the wine and sauté together to break up the tomatoes. Add the chopped mint and the stock in stages.

In an ovenproof dish, place the eggplants-and-lamb mixture in alternate layers, finishing with a layer of eggplant.

Combine the white sauce with the eggs, nutmeg, and some salt and pepper. Spoon over the top of the eggplants, then scatter with the grated cheeses.

Bake for 25–30 minutes to color the cheese and cook through.

This is a classic, thought to have originated in Russia, although I doubt it somehow. Wherever it comes from, we now look on it as our own. It has great flavor, and it's a very celebratory type of dish.

Chicken Kiev

SERVES 4

4 chicken breasts, with first joint of wing still attached

3 free-range eggs, beaten

scant 1 1/2 cups fine dried bread crumbs

vegetable oil, for deep-frying

1 lemon, quartered lengthwise

GARLIC BUTTER

3 cloves garlic, finely chopped

3 tbsp finely chopped, fresh flat-leaf parsley

1 tbsp finely chopped, fresh tarragon (optional)

generous 1/2 cup butter, softened

salt and pepper, to taste

1 tbsp lemon juice

To make the garlic butter, put the garlic, parsley, and tarragon (if using) in a blender with the butter. Season with salt, pepper, and lemon juice. Blend to a smooth paste. Roll the butter in foil or plastic wrap and put it in the refrigerator.

Remove the skin from the first chicken breast and wing, laying it skinned-side down. Detach the small fillet from the underside of the main fillet and cut this small fillet along its length and almost all the way through, folding it open like a book before flattening it by beating it gently with a rolling pin. Put 1 tablespoon of the chilled garlic butter in the middle of the small fillet and wrap the meat around it. Repeat with the three other small fillets, returning all four to the refrigerator once you've finished.

Cut open each of the larger fillets in the same way, place them between sheets of plastic wrap, and gently beat them with a rolling pin. Lay a small buttered fillet in the middle of each larger fillet and wrap the scallop around it.

Dip in beaten egg and then in bread crumbs. Repeat to create a double coating. At this point it is best to refrigerate them to let the butter harden again.

Heat a deep-fat fryer or a pan containing vegetable oil to high, and place the kievs in the hot oil, turning to allow 4–5 minutes' cooking time on each side. It is important to cook and handle the kievs gently to stop them from falling apart.

When the chicken is cooked and a golden brown color, remove and drain very well on paper towels.

Serve each kiev with a wedge of lemon and some salad.

When I was filming in an Indian restaurant in Birmingham this tasted so good I just had to get the recipe. The chef wouldn't cooperate at first but, after a night on the town and many beers, I got it in the end…at a cost, I might add, as my headache was unreal the day after.

Simple Lamb Curry

SERVES 4

2 tbsp vegetable oil

2 lb (900 g) boneless, rolled shoulder of lamb, trimmed and cut into 1 1/4 inch (3 cm) cubes

2 onions, roughly chopped

4 cloves garlic, crushed

1 tbsp grated fresh ginger

1 tbsp ground turmeric

1 1/2 tbsp garam masala

1 1/2 tbsp ground cumin

1 tbsp chili powder

1 tbsp all-purpose flour

6 large tomatoes, chopped

14 oz (400 g) canned coconut milk

2 1/2 cups chicken stock

9 oz (250 g) baby spinach leaves, stalks removed

scant 1 cup plain yogurt

salt and pepper, to taste

Heat 1 tablespoon of the oil in a large pan, add the lamb, and cook over a high heat to brown it quickly all over. Remove the lamb from the pan, place in a bowl, and reserve.

Add the remaining oil to the pan, together with the onions, garlic, and ginger, and cook gently for a few minutes until softened and golden brown. Add the spices and cook for a minute, then add the flour and mix well.

Add the tomatoes and coconut milk, and return the lamb to the pan. Add just enough of the chicken stock to cover the meat, and stir to release all the parts from the bottom of the pan. Cover and simmer gently for about 1 hour, until the lamb is tender, stirring occasionally.

Skim any excess fat off the surface. Stir in the spinach and cook for a few minutes until just wilted, then stir in the yogurt and season. Serve with plain, boiled basmati rice.

Coronation Chicken

A real classic that everyone must have tasted at some point, but there are loads of different recipes to choose from. I've found this one an easy and tasty way of making this dish.

SERVES 4–6

25g (1oz) butter

1/2 onion, finely chopped

3 tbsp curry paste

2 tbsp tomato paste

scant 1/4 cup red wine

juice of 1/2 lemon

4 tbsp apricot jam

1 1/4 cups mayonnaise

2/3 cup strained, plain yoghurt

salt and pepper, to taste

6 chicken breasts, cooked, skins removed

In a small pan, heat the butter and then add the onion and cook for 3–4 minutes, until softened. Add the curry paste, tomato paste, wine, and lemon juice. Simmer, uncovered, for about 5 minutes, until the sauce is reduced. Strain and cool.

Add the apricot jam to the mixture with the mayonnaise, yogurt, and salt and pepper to taste, and mix.

At this point you can leave the mixture like this, or do as I prefer to do: blend it until smooth. But I'll leave it up to you. However, I never did mind creating more cleaning up!

Cut the chicken into fork-size pieces. Spoon the sauce over the chicken and serve with bread or rice and a green salad.

Quick Chicken Tikka Masala

They say this is Britain's favorite dish—which is exactly why it is here!

SERVES 4

1-inch (2.5-cm) piece fresh ginger, finely chopped

1 tsp ground turmeric

2 cloves garlic, finely chopped

1 red chile, seeded and finely chopped

1 tbsp finely chopped, fresh cilantro leaves

juice of 2 limes

2 tbsp vegetable oil

salt and pepper, to taste

4 chicken breasts, skinned and sliced into strips

1 onion, finely chopped

1¼ cups heavy cream

juice of ½ lemon

In a large bowl, mix the ginger, turmeric, garlic, chile, half the cilantro, the lime juice, 1 tablespoon of the oil, salt, and pepper. Add the chicken slices and then stir well to make sure all the pieces are coated. Put in the refrigerator for 10–15 minutes.

Sauté the onion in a large pan with the remaining oil. Then add the chicken slices and all the marinade ingredients. Cook on a medium–high heat for 4–5 minutes.

Add the heavy cream and simmer gently for 3–4 minutes, until the meat is cooked through. Season and add lemon juice to taste, together with the remaining chopped cilantro.

Serve with naan and/or boiled rice, and a chilled beer.

pasta
& rice

Spaghetti Bolognese

This is, of course, Italian—but it is also one of Britain's most frequently cooked dishes. So, naturally, it has its place in this book—and rightly so, because the sauce is fantastic. To my mind it gets even better after a few days in the refrigerator before being reheated for a midnight snack.

SERVES 6

2 tbsp butter

8 slices bacon, diced

1 large onion, diced

1 large carrot, diced

3 cloves garlic, finely chopped

1 lb 2 oz (500 g) ground beef

2¹/₂ cups red wine

¹/₂ tbsp tomato paste

scant 1¹/₄ cups fresh beef stock

12 oz (400 g) canned tomatoes, or 6 fresh tomatoes, chopped

1 tbsp chopped, fresh flat-leaf parsley

a dash of Worcestershire sauce

salt and pepper, to taste

TO SERVE

11¹/₂ oz (325 g) spaghetti, freshly cooked

2 tbsp butter

Parmesan cheese, freshly grated

Heat a really large saucepan on the stove and add the butter.

Sauté the bacon, onion, carrot, and garlic for a few minutes, stirring all the time. Add the beef and cook for about 4 minutes to color well, before adding the wine and tomato paste. Simmer for about 5 minutes.

Add the stock and canned tomatoes (or fresh tomatoes if you are using them).

Simmer gently for 30–45 minutes before adding the parsley, Worcestershire sauce, and plenty of salt and pepper.

Serve with freshly cooked, buttered spaghetti and some freshly grated Parmesan (not the ready-grated stuff in a cardboard package!).

Macaroni Cheese

This is the simplest baked pasta dish of all. You can add sliced tomatoes to the mixture or put them on the top, and you can create new versions by experimenting with different types of cheese.

SERVES 4

12 oz (350 g) macaroni

salt and pepper, to taste

generous 3/4 cup grated cheddar cheese

2 tbsp fresh bread crumbs

a little butter

WHITE SAUCE

2 tbsp butter

2 tbsp all-purpose flour

1 1/4 cups heavy cream or milk

a little freshly grated nutmeg

Preheat the oven to 350°F/180°C.

Cook the macaroni in a large pan of boiling salted water for about 15 minutes. Drain well.

Meanwhile, to make the white sauce, melt the butter and then stir in the flour. Add the cream or milk gradually, stirring all the time, until you have a thick sauce. Season with salt, pepper, and freshly grated nutmeg.

Add most of the cheese to the sauce, saving some for the top.

Put the cooked macaroni into a 1-quart (1 liter) serving dish. Pour over the sauce. Top with the remaining cheese and the bread crumbs. Dot with butter and bake for 20 minutes, until golden brown.

Serve with crusty bread.

Wild garlic pesto

I made this recipe up while I was in Yorkshire at my mom's. Loads of wild garlic grows there, and you can smell it as you drive or walk past in the spring. The green leaves look similar to sorrel leaves. I have made pesto out of the pungent leaves here, but you can also add them to soups and stews, or cut them up into salads.

SERVES 4

1 lb (450 g) wild garlic leaves

scant 1/2 cup extra-virgin olive oil

salt and pepper, to taste

1/4 cup freshly grated Parmesan cheese

juice and grated zest of 1 lemon

Wash and dry the garlic leaves. Place in a pestle and mortar and crush down with the olive oil and some salt and pepper.

Finish by adding the Parmesan and the lemon juice and zest. Mix well and season again to taste. Serve with freshly cooked, buttered pasta.

Green Pea and Smoked Salmon Risotto

Risotto is unashamedly Italian, but it is a dish that has become very popular with the British. I'm using two great British ingredients in this one. Frozen or fresh, to be honest peas are good whatever they are, and I think they're one of the few vegetables that are great from the freezer. The only thing in this recipe is to watch the seasoning—in particular, the salt—as smoked salmon is quite often salty.

SERVES 4

2¹/₄ cups fresh fish stock

2¹/₄ cups fresh chicken stock

2 tbsp butter

1 shallot, chopped

1 clove garlic, chopped

9 oz (250 g) risotto rice (arborio or carnaroli)

¹/₄ cup white wine

3¹/₂ oz (100 g) mascarpone cheese

8 oz (225 g) smoked salmon, sliced into strips

scant 1¹/₂ cups frozen peas

scant 1 cup freshly grated Parmesan cheese

2 tbsp finely chopped, fresh flat-leaf parsley

salt and pepper, to taste

extra-virgin olive oil

Mix the two stocks and heat them in a pan on top of the stove.

Melt the butter in a separate pan and cook the shallot and garlic for a few minutes, but don't color. Add the rice to the pan and seal, stirring to coat it with butter, for about 30 seconds over a low heat.

Add the white wine to the pan and cook for another few seconds before adding the warm stocks, little by little, while stirring. Simmer for about 15–20 minutes, remembering to keep adding the stocks a little at a time, not all at once, until the rice is cooked but still has some bite.

Mix the mascarpone, salmon, peas, and Parmesan into the risotto with the parsley, and season well.

To serve, put the risotto in the center of warm plates. Top with a little extra grated Parmesan, and drizzle with a little extra olive oil.

Crab Risotto

This is one of my favorite recipes in the book—it tastes so good, and uses some of our wonderful crabs.

SERVES 4

1¼ cups fresh chicken stock

1¼ cups fresh fish stock

2 cloves garlic, finely chopped

2 shallots, finely chopped

2 tbsp butter

10 oz (280 g) risotto rice (arborio or carnaroli)

scant ½ cup white Muscat wine

2 green chiles, seeded and chopped

a pinch of curry powder

½ tbsp Thai green curry paste

1 stick lemongrass, crushed

3 kaffir lime leaves

2 tbsp mascarpone cheese

¼ cup heavy cream

¼ cup each of finely chopped, fresh flat-leaf parsley and cilantro

1 lb (450 g) fresh white and brown crab meat

1 cup freshly grated Parmesan cheese, plus extra for serving

juice of 1 lime

salt and pepper, to taste

chili oil

Heat the two stocks, mixed, in a pan on top of the stove.

Meanwhile, cook the garlic and shallots in the butter for about a minute. Add the rice, then the wine, with the green chiles, curry powder, curry paste, lemongrass, and lime leaves. Stir to coat the rice with fat.

Add the warm stock, a ladle at a time, while simmering and stirring. Stir, and keep adding stock, until the rice is cooked, which should take about 15–20 minutes.

Once the rice is cooked but still with a little bite, add the mascarpone, cream, chopped herbs, crab meat, and Parmesan. Adjust with more stock and cream if needed, then add the lime juice and season well.

Place the risotto in the center of the plates and top with a little chili oil and some extra Parmesan.

Leek and Haddock Risotto

You need the real Finnan haddock with its creamy golden flesh for this recipe, not the bright yellow, artificially dyed fish that masquerades as smoked fish. Good smoked haddock is naturally colored through the smoking process. The fish itself is plump and moist with a wonderful salty-sweet flavor from the simple, pure brine. I like to mix flakes of this fish into a leek risotto and, as a surprise, to toss in a few cubes of crisply fried blood sausage. Not only does it taste amazing, it looks so appealing. Try it for a light supper or an unusual appetizer.

SERVES 4

1 tbsp olive oil

6 oz (175 g) good-quality blood sausage, cut into thick slices, then into quarters

1 smoked Finnan haddock fillet, about 10 1/2 –14 oz (300–400 g)

2 tbsp butter

3 shallots, chopped

2 cloves garlic, crushed

scant 1/2 cup dry white wine

9 oz (250 g) risotto rice (arborio or carnaroli)

5 cups store-bought fresh fish or vegetable stock

2 medium leeks, thinly sliced

salt and pepper, to taste

2–3 tbsp mascarpone cheese or crème fraîche

freshly grated Parmesan cheese, to taste

chopped fresh parsley, to garnish

Heat the oil in a wide shallow pan, add the chunks of blood sausage, and fry quickly for 1–2 minutes, until crisp on the outside. Remove and set aside.

Skin the haddock and check carefully for any bones by running against the grain of the flesh with your fingertips. If you find any, pluck them out with your fingers or use a pair of tweezers. Cut the fish into 1/2 inch (1 cm) chunks and set aside.

Heat the butter in the wide shallow pan, add the shallots and garlic, and sauté for about 3 minutes, until softened. Pour in the wine, bring to a boil and cook until reduced by half, stirring frequently. Stir in the rice and cook for 1–2 minutes, until lightly toasted.

Heat the stock until simmering and add one-quarter to the rice. Simmer, uncovered, until the stock is absorbed, stirring frequently.

Add another quarter of the stock with the leeks and continue simmering until the liquid is absorbed, stirring occasionally. Add the fish, blood sausage, the remaining stock, and seasoning to taste. Continue simmering, stirring occasionally, until most of the stock is absorbed and the rice grains are plump and tender yet still retain a good "bite". The fish should be just cooked. The whole process should take 15–20 minutes.

Stir in the mascarpone or crème fraîche and Parmesan. Check the seasoning and serve immediately, sprinkled with chopped parsley.

Mussel and Artichoke Risotto

Both mussels and artichokes are warming wintry comfort foods, so this risotto is ideal for when you just want to curl up in front of an open fire. Cook the mussels first in a little wine and butter until they open, then pull out the meat from the shells.

SERVES 3–4

2 1/4 lb (1 kg) fresh mussels

3 cloves garlic, crushed

3 shallots or 1 onion, chopped

2/3 cup dry white wine

3 1/2 tbsp butter

2 tbsp olive oil

14 oz (400 g) Jerusalem artichokes, peeled and finely chopped

9 oz (250 g) risotto rice (arborio or carnaroli)

generous 3 cups store-bought fresh fish stock or chicken stock

2 tbsp mascarpone cheese

3 tbsp freshly grated Parmesan

1 tbsp chopped, fresh parsley

salt and pepper, to taste

Wash the mussels in cold water, then pull away the wispy "beards". Place the mussels in a large pan but discard any that remain open when tapped. Add 1 crushed clove garlic, 1 chopped shallot or one-third of the chopped onion, the wine, and half the butter.

Cover with a tight lid and cook over a medium heat for about 7 minutes. Uncover, strain the juices into a pitcher and set aside. When the mussels are cool enough to handle, pull the meat from the shells and set aside. Discard any mussels that have not opened.

Heat the oil in a skillet, add the remaining garlic and shallots or onion and the artichokes and gently sauté for about 5 minutes, until softened.

Stir in the rice and cook for 1–2 minutes, until lightly toasted, then pour in all the mussel juices. Bring to a boil, stirring, and cook for about 5 minutes, until the liquid is absorbed, stirring frequently.

Heat the stock until simmering and add one-quarter to the rice. Simmer, uncovered, until the stock is absorbed, stirring frequently. Add the remainder of the stock a ladleful at a time in the same way until all the stock is absorbed and the rice grains are plump and tender yet still retain a good "bite". This should take 15–20 minutes. You may not need all the stock.

Stir in the mussels, the remaining butter, the mascarpone, Parmesan, and parsley. Season well and serve piping hot and creamy.

As you might have guessed, I love blood sausage. Funnily enough, it goes very well with the delicate sweet flavor of scallops. They are used together here in a delicious risotto.

Scallop Risotto with Black Pudding

SERVES 4

4 cups fresh fish stock

2 tbsp butter

1 shallot, chopped

1 clove garlic, chopped

1 leek, washed and diced

9 oz (250 g) risotto rice (arborio or carnaroli)

1/4 cup dry white wine

generous 1/3 cup mascarpone cheese

scant 1 cup freshly grated Parmesan cheese

4 tbsp chopped fresh parsley

salt and pepper, to taste

1 tbsp olive oil

8 slices blood sausage

8 shelled scallops

Heat the stock in a large pan on the stove, but do not boil.

Melt the butter in a wide shallow pan, and cook the shallot, garlic, and leek without coloring.

Turn the heat down and add the rice, then stir to coat with butter. Add the wine and cook for a couple of minutes. Add the stock gradually, a little at a time, waiting until the last ladleful has been absorbed before adding the next. Simmer and cook for about 15–20 minutes, or until the rice is cooked but still retains a good "bite". Add the mascarpone and grated Parmesan to the risotto with the chopped parsley. Season well.

Meanwhile, heat the oil in a skillet. When it starts to smoke, add the blood sausage and cook for about 3–4 minutes. Turn over and add the scallops and cook for 1–2 minutes, turning once.

Remove the scallops, then the blood sausage. Season both, arrange next to the risotto on the plates, and serve.

This risotto uses my favorite British winter vegetable—beet. Served with salmon and cauliflower in a salad, or simply cooked in a risotto like this, it gives fantastic flavor and is a good way of introducing beet to those who think they don't like it. A friend of mine loves this risotto with a seared steak and salad.

Beetroot and Mascarpone Risotto

SERVES 4

6 raw beets, peeled and roughly chopped

2¼ cups fresh vegetable stock

2 cloves garlic, finely chopped

2 shallots, finely chopped

2 fresh thyme sprigs

2 tbsp unsalted butter

8 oz (225 g) risotto rice (arborio or carnaroli)

scant ½ cup white wine

3 tbsp mascarpone cheese

2 tbsp chopped fresh parsley

1 cup freshly grated Parmesan cheese

salt and pepper, to taste

Blend the beet in the food processor with half the stock and let stand to one side. Have the remaining stock warming in a pan on the stove.

Put the garlic, shallot, and thyme in a pan in the butter and sauté for about a minute. Add the rice and stir to coat with the butter. Add the wine and cook, stirring, until it evaporates.

Add a ladleful of beet stock and, stirring continuously, bring to a boil. Once this has been absorbed by the rice, add another ladleful and bring to a boil again. Keep going like this until all the beet stock is used up. Then continue the process with the hot vegetable stock. Simmer for about 15–20 minutes in all, stirring, until the rice is cooked but still has a little bite.

Once the rice is cooked, stir in the mascarpone, parsley, Parmesan, and salt and pepper. Serve hot.

fish

'Turbot and cabbage!' I hear you cry. But this works, like most fish, with savoy cabbage. This is not like the school cabbage that scared you when you were younger. It's trendy, that's what it is. Trendy. The mustard dressing recipe below will make more than you need for this recipe, but it will keep in the refrigerator for a week or so.

Turbot with Savoy Cabbage and Smoked Salmon

SERVES 4

1 small savoy cabbage, about 6 oz (175 g)

4 oz (115 g) smoked salmon

2 tbsp olive oil

salt and pepper, to taste

4 x thick turbot, halibut, or flounder fillet steaks, skin on but no bones, about 6–7 oz (175–200 g) each

4 tbsp butter

MUSTARD DRESSING

4 tsp Dijon mustard

2 tbsp white wine vinegar

1/4 cup walnut oil

1/2 cup peanut oil

For the dressing, whisk the mustard with the vinegar. Mix together the two oils and gradually add to the mustard, whisking all the time. Once everything is thoroughly mixed, season with salt and pepper.

Remove the dark outside leaves from the cabbage and cut the rest into quarters, then into 1/2 inch (1 cm) strips. Cut the slices of smoked salmon into pieces about the same size.

Heat a skillet and add the oil. Season the turbot fillets, place in the skillet, and add half the butter. Cook the fillets for about 3–4 minutes on either side, depending on their thickness, until cooked through.

At the same time, heat a pan and add 2–3 tablespoons of water and the remaining butter. Once the water and butter are boiling, add the cabbage. Season with salt and pepper, and keep turning in the pan. The cabbage will only take 1–2 minutes, and it's best eaten when just becoming tender but still with some texture. Add the smoked salmon to the cabbage, check for seasoning, and add 4 tablespoons of mustard dressing.

To serve, simply spoon the cabbage and smoked salmon at the top of the plates, and finish with the fried turbot on the side.

Brill with Peas, Pancetta and Sweet Potato Crisps

This is probably the most professional recipe in the book, but it tastes great. The most important thing is to use a great brill fillet—with thick white flesh with the skin still on—because this will help hold it together while cooking.

SERVES 4

4 x thick pieces brill, halibut, or flounder fillet, skin on, about 6–7 oz (175–200 g) each

olive oil

salt and pepper, to taste

1 cup warm Mashed Potatoes (*see* page 222)

8 slices pancetta, broiled until crisp

4 thin strips sweet potato, deep-fried

SAUCE

1³/₄ cups chicken stock

2 oz (55 g) pancetta, diced

2 tbsp unsalted butter

1 small onion, finely chopped

2 cloves garlic, crushed

2 tbsp horseradish cream

a dash of white wine

²/₃ cup heavy cream

3 cups frozen peas

a pinch of superfine sugar

Preheat the oven to 400°F/200°C.

Start the sauce by reducing the stock. Boil until you have about ¹/₄ cup.

Sauté the diced pancetta in the butter until crisp, then add the onion and garlic and soften without letting them color.

Add the horseradish, wine, and reduced stock and simmer for a few minutes. Add the cream, peas, and sugar, stir and season, and simmer for a few more minutes to heat the peas through.

Brush the brill fillets with olive oil, season and pan-fry for a minute on each side. Finish by cooking for 10 minutes in the oven, or until cooked.

Place the warm mash in the center of the plates with the brill. Put a slice of crisp pancetta and a sweet-potato chip on top, and spoon the sauce around.

Cod with Creamy Mashed Potatoes

Sadly, cod is becoming a rarity because of overfishing, but you can still find it at a price. Cook it carefully, please! I've made my normal mash much richer and creamier than usual here by adding heavy instead of light cream.

SERVES 2

1 tbsp olive oil

2 cod fillets, about 5 1/2 –7 oz (150–200 g) each

1 tbsp butter

CREAMY MASHED POTATOES

1 lb 5 oz (600 g) yukon gold or russet potatoes, quartered

salt and pepper, to taste

5 1/2 tbsp butter, softened

1/3 cup heavy cream

a little freshly grated nutmeg

Put the potatoes in a pan and cover with water. Add a good pinch of salt and bring to a boil. Cook for about 20–25 minutes.

Meanwhile, heat the oil in a pan and fry the cod, skin-side down, for about 5–7 minutes, until the flesh is about three-quarters cooked (it should feel springy). Turn over, add the butter, and turn off the heat—the fish will continue to cook in the residual heat of the pan.

Once the potatoes are cooked, drain and place back in the pan. Mash with a masher and add the butter and cream a little at a time; this will stop any lumps from appearing.

Season with salt, pepper, and nutmeg and serve with the cod.

As a kid I used to love lining up outside a takeout chain supplying fish and "chips", or fries, waiting to be served with the crisp, battered fish and floppy, buttered bread. Alas, that has all changed. I can now say without doubt that the best fish and chips on the planet are to be found at Trencher's in Whitby. Eat in or out, or do as I do and have one of each. Walk down the pier and sit on the seat at the end and, in the wind and cold, with your nose dripping onto the fish, munch away. That's how to eat fish and chips.

Deep-fried Cod

SERVES 2

vegetable oil, for deep-frying

a little all-purpose flour

salt and pepper, to taste

2 cod fillets, about 7 oz (200 g) each, boned (haddock if you prefer)

BATTER

1²/₃ cups self-raising flour, sifted

1¹/₄ cups lager

Heat the vegetable oil in the deep-fat fryer to 350°F180°C.

Lightly season some flour with some salt and pepper. Dip the cod fillets into the plain flour, shake off any excess and set aside.

To make the batter, place the sifted flour in a bowl and slowly whisk in the lager until very thick and slightly gluey in texture. Season with salt. Dip the cod fillets in, one at a time, to coat well with the batter. If the batter falls off, it is too thick.

Place the battered cod into the deep-fat fryer very slowly, literally a couple of inches at a time. If you drop the fish in, it will sink straight to the bottom and stick!

Let the fish cook for 4–5 minutes before turning over, and cook until golden brown. This should take 10–12 minutes in total.

Once the fish is cooked, drain on paper towels and season well. Serve with fries, peas, malt vinegar, and a wedge of lemon, if you like.

Pan-fried Bream with Honey-glazed Onions
Bream is wonderful with potatoes, but fantastic spiked with the onions.

SERVES 4

6 large onions

3 cloves garlic

5 1/2 tbsp butter

2 tbsp honey

a dash of white wine vinegar

salt and pepper, to taste

1 sprig fresh thyme

2 bay leaves

1 sprig fresh rosemary

4 bream fillets, about 5 1/2 – 7 oz (150–200 g) each

Preheat the oven to 350°F/180°C.

Slice the onions and garlic, and fry them together in 2 tablespoons of the butter for about 10 minutes, until well caramelized. Add the honey and vinegar and season with salt and pepper.

Place the onion mixture into an ovenproof dish and top with the herbs.

Place the bream on top of the herbs and season well. Place the remaining butter in pieces on top of the bream.

Cook the dish in the oven for about 15–20 minutes, depending on the thickness of the bream.

Take the fish out of the oven and remove the herbs. Serve with the onions and a salad.

Cinnamon-poached Smoked Haddock with Fried Green Tomatoes
Most people don't associate fish with spices, but fresh cinnamon and naturally smoked haddock go really well together. Try it and see.

SERVES 2

4 green tomatoes (or unripe, firm tomatoes)

1 1/4 cups milk

1/4 cinnamon stick

1 bay leaf

2 pieces smoked haddock, about 5 oz (140 g) each

7 tbsp butter

salt and pepper, to taste

1 tbsp chopped fresh parsley

juice of 1/2 lemon

Cut the tomatoes into thick slices: roughly about four slices per tomato.

Place the milk, cinnamon, and bay leaf into a pan with the fish and cover with a lid. Bring to a boil and simmer slowly for about 2–3 minutes, depending on the thickness of the fish. Turn the heat off, remove the lid, and let stand while you cook the tomatoes.

Melt half the butter in a sauté pan, add the tomatoes, and season with salt and pepper. Sauté quickly until golden brown, then remove the slices from the pan and divide between two plates.

Return the pan to the heat and add the remaining butter, the chopped parsley, lemon juice, and seasoning.

Remove the fish carefully from the milk in the pan, using a slotted spatula. (Discard the milk.) Place the fish on top of the tomatoes, pour over the remaining juices from the sauté pan, and serve.

Many people don't think poached eggs can be prepared in advance, but they can: simply poach the egg, then place it into ice-cold water to cool down. When cold, put it in the refrigerator. When you want the eggs, blanch them in boiling water for 30 seconds and place them on your haddock. This is particularly useful when serving breakfast for a lot of people.

Smoked Haddock with Poached Egg and Horseradish Mash

SERVES 4

3³/4 cups whole milk

juice of 1 lemon

6 black peppercorns

a few fresh parsley stalks

salt and pepper, to taste

4 pieces natural smoked haddock, about 7 oz (200 g) each

4 large free-range eggs

5¹/2 oz (150 g) fresh young spinach leaves, washed

HORSERADISH MASH

2 lb (900 g) Yukon gold or russet potatoes, peeled and chopped

7 tbsp unsalted butter

scant 1 cup whole milk, warmed

2 tbsp creamed horseradish

For the mash, cook the potatoes in boiling salted water until tender, about 15 minutes. Once cooked, drain well and, while hot but not wet, place back in the pan and return to the heat. Mash with the butter and the warm milk. Once you get the texture you want, beat in the horseradish and some salt and pepper to taste and keep warm.

Put the milk, lemon juice, peppercorns, parsley stalks, and a little salt into a medium-size flat pan, and bring to a simmer. At the same time, place a pan of salted water on to boil for the eggs.

Add the haddock pieces to the simmering milk, and cook gently for about 6–8 minutes. While this is cooking, crack the eggs into the stirred, rapidly boiling water, and poach for 2–3 minutes. In another medium pan, quickly wilt the spinach in only the water clinging to the leaves. Season.

Place the spinach, then the mash, on the plates. Drain the haddock and place on the mash. Spoon a little of the flavored milk over this and top with a soft poached egg.

I like this dish how my grandad used to have it: with potatoes straight from the garden and loads of butter! Funny, but it was the only dish my grandad would cook, not just for himself but for anybody who came to visit. From the age of five I can remember eating this, waiting for what was coming next—two hours of cricket, with me being batsman and him bowling against the wall of my grandmother's kitchen.

Grandad's Poached Haddock with Mustard

SERVES 2

1 fillet undyed smoked haddock

2 bay leaves

a few black peppercorns

1/2 onion, roughly chopped

2 cups milk

3¹/₂ tbsp butter

1 tbsp all-purpose flour

2 tbsp Dijon mustard

2 tbsp chopped fresh flat-leaf parsley

salt and pepper, to taste

Cut the haddock in half and place in a shallow pan. Add the bay leaves, black peppercorns, and onion and cover with the milk.

Bring the milk to a boil and gently simmer for about 4–5 minutes to cook the fish.

Carefully remove the fish from the milk, preserving the milk, and keep the fish warm. Remove the bay leaves from the milk.

Melt the butter in a pan and then add the flour and stir over the heat for 15–20 seconds to make the base of a roux. Slowly add the warm milk, a little at a time, stirring all the time until you end up with a nice smooth sauce. You may not need all the milk. Add the mustard and parsley to taste and check the seasoning.

Place the haddock on the plate and spoon over the sauce.

Sea Bass with Onions

I go fishing with my friends Steve and Jo, and a fisherman, Rick, from Poole harbor about once a month. First, we go out and catch sand eels (they're small sardinelike fish), then we use these and live mackerel to catch the bass while drifting over ledges just off the Isle of Wight Needles. Not only is it a great day of beer, sandwiches and chocolate bars, but also the catch is the best fish I have ever eaten. Simply cooked, fresh fish is one of the true pleasures of life, but catching your own makes the experience a little more special.

SERVES 4

3 large white onions, sliced

2 cloves garlic, crushed

olive oil

a dash of white wine vinegar

3 tbsp honey

salt and pepper, to taste

4 small sea bass, about 18 oz (500 g) each, scaled and gutted

1 sprig fresh thyme

2 bay leaves

1 sprig fresh rosemary

Preheat the oven to 400°F/200°C.

Fry the onions and garlic in a little oil in a hot pan. Add the white wine vinegar and honey, and cook until golden brown. Season and let cool.

Place the fish on a baking sheet, and score the skin on top two or three times with a knife. Stuff the cavity with the onion mixture and herbs.

Season with salt and pepper, drizzle with olive oil, and roast in the oven for about 15 minutes.

Remove from the oven, and serve whole with the juices from the sheet poured over the top, and a salad.

Sea Bass with Mango Chutney and Red Pepper Essence

This is another great bass recipe I make with the catch we get from our fishing trips. Bass was always deemed an expensive fish in the past, but due to farming, the price has come down. However, this fish remains the king of the sea, and will always make me look forward to another day out on the boat fishing.

SERVES 4

4 sea bass fillets, about 4 1/2 oz (125 g) each, bones removed, skin left on

olive oil

butter

1 cup bean sprouts

juice of 1 lime

2 tbsp sesame oil

a small bunch of fresh cilantro, chopped

1/2 cup smooth mango chutney

RED PEPPER SAUCE
6 red bell peppers, stalks and seeds removed, chopped

1/3 cup cold water

Make the red pepper sauce by placing the red bell peppers and water in a liquidizer and processing for 2 minutes. Put into a clean dish towel placed over a bowl, and squeeze out the liquid. Put this into a pan and reduce over the heat by three-quarters, until it resembles honey in texture. Let cool.

Pan-fry the sea bass, skin-side down, in a little olive oil and butter. When the skin is crisp and brown, turn the fish over and turn off the heat.

Dress the bean sprouts in the lime juice and sesame oil, and scatter the cilantro over them.

Warm the mango chutney and spoon into the center of each serving plate. Top with the bean sprouts and fish, drizzle the pepper sauce around the edge, and serve.

Halibut is a large, sometimes huge, flatfish that is expensive because chefs love to place it on their menus. It's important that you don't overcook it, or it will become dry. The flavors of the sauce may appear strong, but halibut is a meaty fish like salmon and monkfish, and can take it. Use mussel meat if you want, because it saves a load of hassle, but I think a few mussels left in their shells look good.

Seared Halibut with Mussels and Onion Sauce

SERVES 4

1 tbsp olive oil

2 tbsp butter

salt and pepper, to taste

**4 halibut fillets, about
6 oz (175 g) each**

MUSSEL AND ONION SAUCE

**3 lb 5 oz (1.5 kg) fresh mussels,
beards removed, or 3 oz (85 g)
mussel meat**

2 tsp chopped fresh thyme

1 bay leaf

1 cup Muscat wine

2 tbsp butter

2 onions, finely sliced

1 small leek, finely diced

1/2 fennel bulb, sliced

**3 1/2 cups sliced cremini
mushrooms, sliced**

a pinch of curry powder

2 tbsp Pernod

1/3 cup heavy cream

2/3 cup chopped flat-leaf parsley

a pinch of saffron

Discard any mussels that do not close when tapped on the edge of the sink—they are probably dead. Heat a large saucepan until very hot. Add the mussels, thyme, bay leaf, and one-third of the wine. Cover and heat for a minute or two, then shake the pan well.

Continue to cook for a minute or two, then remove the lid. When the mussels have all opened, drain over a bowl to save the cooking liquid. Discard any mussels that are still closed, and the bay leaf. Remove some or all of the mussels from their shells, and discard the shells.

In the same saucepan, melt a little of the butter and caramelize the onions. Cook gently until the onions are soft and brown in color, about 10 minutes. Add the leek, fennel, mushrooms, curry powder, and Pernod. Cover the pan and gently sweat the vegetables for about 7 minutes, or until softened but not colored. Add the remaining wine and bring to a boil. Cook, uncovered, until the cooking liquid has almost completely evaporated. Add the reserved mussel liquor, and cook, uncovered, for 5 minutes to reduce again.

In a nonstick pan, heat the olive oil and butter for the fish. Season the halibut and place in the hot pan. Cook for 3–4 minutes before turning over to get some nice color on the flesh.

Meanwhile, add the cream and parsley to the sauce and bring back to a boil. Sprinkle in the saffron, heat for 1–2 minutes, and season to taste. Mix the mussels in and season.

Divide the sauce between four warm plates, and serve with the halibut on the top and a few mussels in their shells to decorate.

Hot Tea-smoked Trout with New Potatoes and Rocket

I first learned this dish while doing a television show, and I have loved it ever since. It tastes as good now as it did then. I've used trout here, but you can use salmon, chicken, or duck (the meat needs to be cooked for a few more minutes than the fish). My dog Fudge loves it, but it makes his breath smell like he's been smoking ten a day....

SERVES 2

2 fresh trout, about 10–12 oz (280–350 g) each, gutted and heads removed

olive oil

salt and pepper, to taste

SMOKING MIXTURE

1/4 cup raw brown sugar

1/4 cup long-grain rice

10 tea bags (any kind, but not herbal), torn open and bags discarded

TO SERVE

1 lb (450 g) new potatoes

4 oz (115 g) arugula

2–3 tbsp balsamic vinegar

2 tbsp chopped fresh flat-leaf parsley

1/2 cup freshly grated Parmesan cheese

To make the smoking mixture, put the sugar, rice, and tea leaves into a bowl and mix together. Line a deep roasting pan with foil and pour the tea mixture into the bottom. Cover with another layer of foil, then place on the stove to heat up.

Once it is smoking a little, add the trout on top of the foil. Drizzle with a little olive oil, making sure the fish sits in the foil. Season with salt and pepper before covering with a tight-fitting lid or another piece of foil, and let smoke on the stovetop over a medium heat for 15–20 minutes.

While the trout is smoking, wash and boil the new potatoes in plenty of salted boiling water for 12–15 minutes, depending on size, until cooked.

For the salad, place the arugula in a bowl with the balsamic vinegar, 6 tablespoons of olive oil and a pinch each of salt and black pepper, and toss.

To serve, drain the hot new potatoes and place them in a bowl with the parsley. Finish the salad with the Parmesan and place on the plate, with the hot smoked trout on the side, and the potatoes served separately.

Mackerel with Gooseberry Cream Sauce

Mackerel is such an underrated fish, but it must be eaten as fresh as possible. Just simply broiled, it has a wonderful oily taste, and goes very well with chutneys and sour fruits, such as gooseberry. Don't turn the fish over while cooking; it will cook through from only one side, because it is so thin when filleted.

SERVES 4

4 large fresh mackerel, filleted

salt and pepper, to taste

olive oil

3½ oz (100 g) mixed salad greens, dressed with balsamic vinegar and extra-virgin olive oil

GOOSEBERRY CREAM SAUCE

8 oz (225 g) gooseberries

2 tbsp butter

²/₃ cup heavy cream

granulated sugar (optional)

To make the sauce, trim the gooseberries. Melt the butter in a pan, add the gooseberries, cover them, and let simmer gently until they are cooked, usually about 30 minutes. Mash them down and mix in the cream and some seasoning to soften their sharpness. Add a little sugar if the gooseberries were very young and green, but the sauce should not be sweet like an apple sauce.

Preheat the broiler.

Season the mackerel to taste and brush with olive oil on both sides. Place on an baking sheet, skin-side up, and broil for about 5 minutes to cook through.

Place the salad greens on the serving plates with two fillets of mackerel each and a spoonful of the gooseberry cream sauce.

This is a twist on fish pie. The cheese and the mustard are slipped in between a layer of puff pastry. Use salmon, cod, haddock, or monkfish—and a handful of shrimp like my grandmother does, if you like.

Fish Pie with Cheese and Mustard Pastry

SERVES 4

1 shallot, chopped

1 tbsp olive oil

1/3 cup fish stock

scant 1 cup heavy cream

salt and pepper, to taste

1 1/2 lb (675 g) fish, cut into chunks

2 1/4 cups sliced mushrooms

3 tbsp chopped fresh chives

10 1/2 oz (300 g) prepared puff pastry

2 tbsp whole-grain mustard

4 slices Emmental cheese

1 free-range egg, beaten

Preheat the oven to 400°F/200°C.

Sauté the shallot in a medium pan in the olive oil. After a few minutes add the fish stock and cream and bring to a boil. Season with salt and pepper and set aside.

Place the fish, mushrooms, and chives in an ovenproof dish. Season and cover with the shallot sauce.

Roll out the pastry until it is twice the size of your dish. Spread half of the pastry with the mustard and cheese. Fold the other half over the top to sandwich the mustard and cheese. Top the pie dish with the pastry.

Crimp the edges of the pastry and then brush it with the beaten egg. Bake for 25–30 minutes.

Once cooked, remove from the oven and serve. A good accompaniment is green beans sprinkled with some freshly cracked black pepper.

This dish is as famous as a bucket of chicken. Give me this, some Tartare Sauce (see page 240), and a wedge of lemon, and I'm a happy man.

Goujons of Sole with Lemon

SERVES 4

450 g (1 lb) sole or lemon sole fillets, skinned

2¼ cups fine fresh bread crumbs

½ tsp cayenne pepper

sunflower oil, for deep-frying

⅓ cup all-purpose flour

3 medium free-range eggs, beaten

salt and pepper, to taste

2 lemons, cut into wedges

Cut each sole or lemon sole fillet into strips, on the diagonal, about ½ inch (1 cm) thick. Mix the bread crumbs with the cayenne pepper and set aside. Heat the oil in the fryer to 375°F/190°C/.

Coat the fish in the flour, then dip first in the beaten egg and then in the bread crumbs. Do a few pieces at a time, making sure all the fish is coated in each of the three dips.

Place a few of the nuggets in the fryer at a time and cook for about 1 minute, until crisp and golden brown. Repeat until all the nuggets are cooked. Once cooked, put onto some paper towels to soak up the excess oil.

Pile the nuggets in a dish or on plates, season, and serve with the lemon wedges. They're great with a mixed green salad.

Jugged Fresh Kippers with Cider Butter and Lime

When I was eight, my family had a vacation home near Whitby in North Yorkshire. Whenever we visited, I would spend the day watching the fishing boats go in and out of the harbor, and would invariably park myself next to the open window of a fish smokery. My mom would object vociferously as we traveled back in the car: I smelled like an old kipper.

SERVES 2

2 fresh kippers

7 tbsp butter, softened

3 tbsp chopped fresh parsley

1/4 apple, grated

1/4 cup hard cider

juice and finely grated zest of 1 lime

Place the kippers in a tall pitcher with the tails sticking out of the top, and carefully pour boiling water into the pitcher, up to the top.

Place the softened butter in a bowl and mix first with the chopped parsley, then more slowly with the grated apple and cider. Set aside.

After the kippers have been in the water for about 2–3 minutes, drain off the water and place the kippers first on paper towels to dry and then on plates.

Put half the butter onto each kipper along with the juice and zest of the lime. Eat as is, or with some sliced bread.

Kipper Paste

In England, Manx kippers are the most widely known, but Whitby kippers are my favorite—not because I'm a Yorkshire man, but because I think they are the best (although hard to find if you're not local). They have a strong, smoky flavor.

SERVES 4

2 pairs undyed kippers

plenty of slightly salted butter

3 tbsp heavy cream

salt and pepper, to taste

a pinch of cayenne pepper

juice of 1 lemon

4 slices toasted whole-wheat bread, to serve

Place the kippers in a large pitcher or pan and immerse in boiling water. Let stand for a few minutes before draining off the hot water and removing the skin and bones from the fish.

Weigh the flesh and blend, while still warm, with an equal amount of butter. Add the cream, then season with salt, pepper, cayenne, and lemon juice.

Serve spread on whole-wheat toast. This mixture will keep in the refrigerator for up to a week in an airtight container.

Whole Poached Salmon

My mother used to do this for dinner parties at home in the 1980s, served with lemon and sliced cucumber. With buttered potatoes, a green salad, and a glass of white wine, it's fantastic.

SERVES 8–10

1 whole salmon, about
5¹/₂–6 lb (2.5–2.7 kg)

2 bay leaves

1 onion, chopped

4 tbsp white wine vinegar

1 lemon, quartered

salt and pepper, to taste

TO SERVE

4–5 lemons, cut into wedges

mayonnaise

Place the salmon in a deep saucepan or, if you're like me, in a large roasting pan. (I never think it's worth spending $100 on something you use only a few times, and is awkward to store.)

Pour in enough cold water to cover the fish (it must be covered). Add the bay leaves, onion, vinegar, lemon quarters, a good pinch of salt, and a little coarsely ground black pepper.

Cover with a lid, and bring to a boil on top of the stove. It is easier and quicker to put two burners on underneath the fish. Once it is boiling, turn off the heat and let the fish stand in the water until cool.

Carefully remove the salmon and place on a board. Scrape off the skin, and place on a large, flat serving dish. Serve with the lemon wedges and a bowl of mayonnaise.

Deep-fried Salmon Belly in Beer Batter

Many good fish suppliers sell salmon belly flaps for next to nothing, or even give them away. They are the parts of the salmon that are normally cleaned off and discarded after filleting, and are full of flavor. Keep the skin on; this helps to hold everything together during cooking.

SERVES 2

vegetable oil, for deep-frying

1 lb (450 g) salmon belly,
cut into strips

BATTER

1²/₃ cups self-raising flour

2 tbsp chopped fresh mint

salt and pepper, to taste

2¹/₂ tbsp sesame seeds

1¹/₂ cups ale or lager

Heat the oil in a deep pan to a high heat, or use a deep-fat fryer.

Place the flour in a bowl. Add the mint, salt and pepper, and sesame seeds and slowly mix in the beer. Don't worry about lumps; just make it into a thick consistency.

Mix the salmon strips into the batter. Place them, once coated, into the hot fat one by one to stop them from sticking to each other (keep shaking the basket to stop them from sticking to the bottom). Cook them in two batches to speed up the cooking time.

Once they are golden brown, remove the salmon strips and place on paper towels to drain off any excess oil.

Pile them up in a bowl or on a plate to serve.

Baked Salmon and Dill Hash Brown with Pan-fried Tomatoes

To make it well, this dish needs a lot of fresh dill and you must make sure you cook the potato thoroughly before combining it with the salmon. I've served the dish here with pan-fried tomatoes, but a Caesar Salad (*see* page 64) makes it a good complete summer dish. The egg is used to bind the mixture during cooking.

SERVES 2

1 shallot, chopped

1 clove garlic, chopped

olive oil

1 large baking potato

8 oz (225 g) salmon fillet
(skin on but no bones)

1 free-range egg, beaten

2 tbsp fresh bread crumbs

1/2 cup chopped fresh dill

salt and pepper, to taste

3 plum tomatoes

Preheat the oven to 400°F/200°C. Place the shallot and garlic in a sauté pan with 4 tablespoons of oil and gently start to cook.

Peel the potato and cut it into 1/2 inch (1 cm) dice, add to the pan, and cook until the pieces are golden brown. Remove from the heat.

Cut the salmon into 1/2 inch (1 cm) dice and place in a bowl with the egg, bread crumbs, and chopped dill, then pour on the potato, shallot, and garlic. Mix well and season with plenty of salt and pepper.

Divide the mixture between two 3 inch (7.5 cm) stainless-steel rings placed on a baking sheet, pressing it in well. Place the sheet in the oven and cook for 10 minutes.

Meanwhile, cut each tomato into five slices and season with salt and pepper. Quickly seal in a hot pan with 1 tablespoon of olive oil to color both sides. This should only take a minute or two.

Arrange the tomatoes on two plates, overlapping them into a circle pattern in the center. Remove the salmon from the oven and place each ring in the middle of the tomatoes. Remove the metal rings. Drizzle with olive oil to finish the dish.

Wild Salmon with Samphire

Wild salmon is at its best in the summer, when samphire—one of the best accompaniments for it—is available. There are two types of samphire: rock and marsh. Marsh is found on tidal marshes around Britain, and is also found in the United States; rock grows on—yes, you guessed it—rocky cliffs and slopes around the British coast. They used to use marsh samphire as a source of soda when making glass. No glassmaking here, but picked early in the season samphire can be eaten raw, blanched, or pan-fried. I pickle it in vinegar in mid-season, when it is at its cheapest.

SERVES 2

1 lb 2 oz (500 g) samphire

6¹/₂ tbsp butter, softened

2 tbsp olive oil

4 wild salmon fillets, about 6 oz (175 g) each, bones and skin removed

freshly ground black pepper, to taste

To cook the samphire, remove any of the woody roots with a pair of scissors and wash very well. Blanch in plenty of boiling water for 1 minute and then refresh in a bowl of ice-cold water to retain the color.

Meanwhile, melt 2 tablespoons of the butter in the olive oil in a hot nonstick pan and then fry the salmon fillets over a high heat for 5–6 minutes. Do not shake the fillets.

Let the fillets crisp on the underside before turning over, using a spatula. Add another 2 tablespoons of the butter and remove from the heat. The residual heat in the pan will continue to cook the fish.

Drain the samphire really well before reheating in a pan with the remaining butter. Season with only pepper, because the samphire is quite salty.

Place some samphire on the plate, top with the salmon, and spoon over the warm, buttery juices.

Salmon Fish Cakes with Pickled Cucumber and Ginger Relish

Fish cakes are wrongly thought to be made from poor-quality cuts of fish. But actually they should always be made using the best cuts. I've used salmon because it's readily available to us all, but other fish, such as haddock, smoked haddock, tuna, crab, and cod, are all ideal for fish cakes.

SERVES 4

1 lb 2 oz (500 g) floury potatoes, peeled and cut into large chunks

2 tbsp butter

generous 1/4 cup light cream

1 tsp mild or medium curry powder

2 tbsp chopped fresh parsley

1 large green chile, seeded and finely chopped

1 shallot, finely chopped

salt and pepper, to taste

1 lb 2 oz (500 g) cooked salmon, bones and skin removed

4–5 tbsp all-purpose flour, seasoned

2 medium free-range eggs

generous 1 cup dried bread crumbs

sunflower oil, for frying

CUCUMBER AND GINGER RELISH

1 cucumber

1/2-inch (1-cm) piece fresh ginger

2 cloves garlic

juice of 2 lemons

3 tbsp peanut oil

1 tbsp sesame oil

Boil the potatoes in a saucepan of lightly salted water for about 15 minutes, or until tender. Drain well, then return to the pan. Mash with a fork or potato masher until smooth, beating in the butter, cream, curry powder, parsley, chile, shallot, and plenty of salt and pepper. Let cool completely.

Meanwhile, check the salmon for any remaining bones, then flake. Mix the fish with the potato and shape into eight round patties.

To coat the salmon cakes in bread crumbs requires a methodical approach. Complete each of the three stages for all the cakes before moving on to the next stage. So, first coat each cake in seasoned flour, shake well, and place on a plate. Beat the eggs in a wide shallow bowl, then dip each cake into the egg to coat evenly. Place the bread crumbs in another wide bowl and coat each cake in the crumbs, pressing the crumbs on to coat the surface evenly. Shake off any excess and place on a plate. Chill in the refrigerator for about 30 minutes to "set" the crumbs.

Meanwhile, make the relish. Peel the cucumber, cut it in half lengthwise, and scoop out all the seeds. Slice very thinly lengthwise into ribbons. Put in a bowl. Peel and grate the ginger and garlic and add to the cucumber. Mix together the lemon juice and oils and pour over the cucumber. Season with salt and pepper. Let marinate while you cook the first cakes.

Heat the sunflower oil to a depth of 1/2 inch (1 cm) in a wide, shallow skillet until you feel a good heat rising. Slide in the cakes using a spatula. Cook for about 3 minutes, until crisp and golden on the underside, then turn and cook the other side.

Remove and place on paper towels. Serve the cakes with the relish.

An odd dish, I know, but all the characteristically British flavors work really well when eaten together. You can serve it all cold, but I like the vegetables cold and the salmon hot from the pan.

Salmon with Beetroot, Cauliflower and Horseradish Cream

SERVES 4

1 large cauliflower

juice of 1 lemon

4tbsp horseradish cream

2/3 cup heavy cream, semi-whipped

salt and pepper, to taste

4 salmon fillets, about 4–6 oz (115–175 g) each, skin on

olive oil

BEETS

8 medium beets, cooked

4 shallots, chopped

1 clove garlic, chopped

generous 1/4 cup extra-virgin olive oil

1/4 cup chopped mixed fresh chives, parsley, and dill

2 tbsp balsamic vinegar

To prepare the beets, peel them, cut them into segments, and place these in a bowl.

Sweat the shallots and garlic in a pan in a little of the oil, but don't let them color. Let cool. Mix with the herbs, balsamic, and remaining oil, pour over the beets, and set aside.

Divide the cauliflower into small florets and cook these in boiling water for about 5 minutes. When just cooked, plunge into iced water, drain, and set aside.

Make the horseradish cream by combining the lemon juice and horseradish, then adding the semi-whipped cream and some seasoning. Fold in the cauliflower and place in a serving bowl.

Season the salmon, then cook it in a hot pan in a little oil, for 3–4 minutes on both sides.

Serve the cold beets and cauliflower in separate containers on a plate, with the hot salmon on top of either one.

Char-grilled Smoked Salmon with Rocket and Parmesan

Smoked salmon is superb. Here I've taken an unusual approach and charbroiled it in a grill pan, which gives it great flavor. This dish could also be served as a light main course for two people.

SERVES 4

2 oz (55 g) piece fresh Parmesan

olive oil

2 tbsp balsamic vinegar

salt and pepper, to taste

7 oz (200 g) arugula leaves

8 oz (225 g) sliced smoked salmon

Using a vegetable peeler, shave the cheese into thin strips and set to one side.

Mix 4 tablespoons of the olive oil and the vinegar together with some seasoning. Mix into the arugula leaves quickly and carefully and place on the plates.

Heat a ridged grill pan to high. Remove the salmon from the package, and fold each slice into three to make one thicker slice. Season with black pepper and drizzle on one side with a little olive oil. When the pan is very hot, place the salmon on it, oiled-side down, and leave for about 15 seconds. Turn it 90 degrees, cook for another 15 seconds, then remove. Do not turn it over; cook only on one side.

Sprinkle the arugula with the Parmesan shavings and place the salmon, charred-side up, on top. Serve immediately.

Smoked Salmon Mousse with Cucumber

This dish is what I used to eat as a kid, followed by a steak with onion rings, peas, and carrots, and a baked potato. That in turn would be followed by—but only if I sat still while my sister tormented me – jello and ice cream with sprinkles on the top.

SERVES 4

7 oz (200 g) smoked salmon

7 oz (200 g) cooked salmon, skin and bone removed

2/3 cup heavy cream

1/3 cream cheese

juice of 1 lemon

1/2 tsp horseradish cream

salt and pepper, to taste

TO SERVE
1/2 cucumber, finely sliced

Place the two types of salmon in a blender and blend to a paste. Remove the paste from the machine and place in a bowl. Partly whip the cream in a separate bowl.

Fold the cream cheese into the salmon mixture. Carefully fold in the lemon juice and horseradish, and finally the cream. Do not overmix, or it will split. Season and transfer to a clean bowl or individual ramekins.

Serve with the sliced cucumber, as well as some mixed salad greens and thickly sliced whole-wheat bread with butter.

Gravadlax may be Scandinavian, but it frequently appears on our supermarket shelves and in our restaurants now. It should never be confused with smoked salmon because it is made in a very different way. You don't need a smoker as you do for smoked salmon—all you need is time. Trust me, this stuff is worth the wait.

Gravadlax with Mustard and Dill Sauce

SERVES 6

1/2 cup coarse rock salt

scant 1/2 cup superfine sugar

1 tbsp white peppercorns, crushed

2 large bunches fresh dill

2 thick salmon fillets, about 2 lb (900 g) each, skin on, scaled, and bones removed

arugula leaves, to garnish

MUSTARD AND DILL SAUCE

2 tbsp Dijon mustard

1 tbsp superfine sugar

1 free-range egg yolk

2/3 cup peanut oil

1 tbsp white wine vinegar

1/4 cup chopped fresh dill

salt and pepper, to taste

To make the salmon curing mix, place the salt, sugar, and white pepper into a medium-size bowl. Finely chop most of the dill, add to the salt mixture, and stir to combine.

Choose a large, shallow, rectangular dish that will hold the salmon fillets, and line it with plastic wrap. Sprinkle one-quarter of the curing mixture over the bottom and top with one of the salmon fillets, skin-side down. Sprinkle over half of the remaining curing mix, and top with the other half of the salmon, skin-side up. Sprinkle the remaining curing mixture on top of the fillet and wrap in the plastic wrap.

Weigh the fish down with some cans or weights on top to remove any excess liquid or moisture. Place in the refrigerator, turning the salmon over every 6 hours where possible, for 3–4 days.

Before serving the gravadlax, rinse the cure off the fish to remove the salt and pat dry with paper towels. Sprinkle the remaining finely chopped dill over one side of the salmon, then sandwich the two fillets together again. Wrap tightly in plastic wrap and chill for 6 hours.

To make the mustard and dill sauce, whisk the mustard and sugar together with the egg yolk in a large bowl. Gradually whisk in the oil, making sure the oil is well emulsified. Add the vinegar, the fresh dill, and some salt and pepper, and mix well.

To serve, cut the gravadlax thinly (gravadlax is traditionally served thicker than smoked salmon). Place three or four good slices on a plate along with a spoonful of the sauce, and garnish with arugula leaves. Serve with rye bread.

shellfish

Garlic Prawns

The 1970s and 1980s saw a huge rise in the popularity of garlic—from garlic shrimp and garlic bread to bread-crumb-coated garlic mushrooms. Living in Hampshire, I'm lucky enough to be close to the Isle of Wight, where a lot of British garlic is grown successfully, thanks to the high density of light reflecting off the sea around the island.

SERVES 4

20 cooked jumbo shrimp, tails left on

4 tbsp olive oil

4 cloves garlic, crushed

2 tbsp dry white wine

salt and pepper, to taste

2 tbsp chopped fresh flat-leaf parsley

1 lemon, cut into quarters

1 loaf crusty bread, warmed

Firstly, prepare the shrimp by cutting each one through the length of the back. Pull out the dark vein and discard it. It's a bit fiddly, I know, but you will thank me for this when you eat them—the gritty part you get in your mouth if this is not removed is the remainder of the shrimp's last supper.

Heat a large pan on the stove. Add the olive oil and, when it's hot, add the garlic. Sauté for a few seconds, then add the shrimp and white wine. Sauté well for about 45 seconds to 1 minute. Season with salt and pepper and add the parsley.

Serve immediately with wedges of lemon and some chunks of crusty bread so you can dunk it in the juices while eating. Oops: Don't forget a bowl of warm water on the table for your fingers, because it can get a bit messy.

Oysters

Guinness beer was introduced to the world in 1759 by Arthur Guinness in Dublin. But now, like so many beers, it is brewed all over the world, from Jamaica and Ghana to Canada and Australia. But real lovers of Guinness, like me, will know that the best glass is always going to be served in Dublin—a glass poured with time and care. And the best accompaniment is an oyster.

SERVES 4

12 fresh oysters

1 lemon, quartered

a pinch of cayenne pepper

TO SERVE

whole-wheat bread and butter

4 glasses Guinness

Wash and open the oysters.

Loosen the bottom of the oysters with a knife and arrange on crushed ice. Decorate with the lemon wedges and season with cayenne.

Serve with the bread and butter on the side and a glass of Guinness.

Tiger Prawns Steamed with Beer

I first tasted this dish a few years ago in the United States, and I thought it was fantastic but lacked flavor. I decided this was probably due to the type of beer used. So, of course, I decided to use Yorkshire bitter instead of lager, and now it's a great dish that, for me, has got even better.

SERVES 4–6

1½ cups bottled beer (not lager)

1–1½ lb (450–675 g) raw shrimp, shells on

salt and pepper, to taste

olive oil

TO SERVE

2 lemons, cut into wedges

⅓ cup mayonnaise

4–6 sprigs fresh flat-leaf parsley

Heat a wok to a high heat. Place a bamboo steamer base (or an ordinary steamer) in the bottom of the wok and add 1 cup of the beer.

Season the shrimp in a bowl and drizzle with a little olive oil. Place in the steamer basket with a lid on. Reduce the heat to moderate.

Steam for 5–6 minutes, until the shrimp are cooked. Put the shrimp into a serving bowl and serve with wedges of lemon and a bowl of mayonnaise. Garnish with sprigs of flat-leaf parsley.

Potted Shrimps with Melba Toast

The first thing I look for at farmers' markets are potted shrimp. I have to—I don't know why—it's just my fix. I suppose it dates back to the days when my parents took us to Blackpool and I first tasted the shrimp from Morecambe Bay.

SERVES 4

genenrous ½ cup unsalted butter

a good pinch of cayenne pepper

a good pinch of freshly grated nutmeg

10 oz (285 g) peeled cooked shrimp

salt and pepper, to taste

TO SERVE

4 slices thinly-sliced white bread

green salad with a dressing

1 lemon, cut into wedges

Put the butter in a pan to melt with the cayenne and nutmeg. Once it has melted, add the shrimp. Mix over the heat and season. Put the shrimp in little pots or ramekin dishes and press down. Top with butter left in the pan and chill in the refrigerator.

To make the Melba toast, preheat a broiler until it's nice and hot. Broil the bread on both sides until golden brown. With a sharp knife, remove the crusts, then slice in half horizontally. Put back under the broiler, cut-side uppermost, to toast. The edges will curl up to give the traditional Melba toast effect.

Serve the shrimp with a green salad, a lemon wedge, and slices of Melba toast.

What an appetizer starter! Name one appetizer that has been on a menu in both three-star restaurants and cafés. It must be one of our all-time favorites. I remember eating this as a kid: defrosted shrimp, iceberg lettuce, a quarter of tomato, a slice of cucumber, a wedge of lemon and Marie Rose sauce. And, of course, a must with shrimp cocktail is whole-wheat bread and butter. Who said the British can't produce good food? I have brought it up to date slightly, but the taste remains much the same.

Prawn Cocktail

SERVES 6

2 lb (900 g) large shrimp, shells left on

olive oil, for frying

1 lettuce, preferably romaine

¼ cup arugula

1 ripe avocado

cayenne pepper

COCKTAIL SAUCE

⅓ cup mayonnaise

1 tbsp Worcestershire sauce

a dash of Tabasco sauce

2 tbsp Ketchup (*see* page 241)

juice of 1 lime

To prepare the shrimp, heat the oil in a large, solid skillet and shallow-fry them for 4–5, minutes until they turn a vibrant pink. Put them aside to cool. Reserve six in their shells to garnish and peel the rest. Take a small, sharp knife and cut along the back of each peeled shrimp to remove any black thread.

To make the cocktail sauce, mix the mayonnaise with the rest of the ingredients. Stir and taste to check the seasoning. Keep the sauce covered with plastic wrap in the refrigerator until it is needed.

Shred the lettuce and arugula finely and divide among six plates or glasses. Peel and chop the avocado into small dice and scatter this over the lettuce. Top with the shrimp and then the sauce. Sprinkle a dusting of cayenne pepper on top and garnish with one unpeeled shrimp per serving.

Sweet and Sour Prawns

A nod to all the Chinese who have been running restaurants in Britain since the 1950s. This dish will work with chicken, too: cut the breast into thin strips, then roll it in cornstarch, blanch in boiling water for a minute or two, drain, and make as described below. This will not only cook the chicken a little, but also tenderize it at the same time.

SERVES 4

1½ tbsp peanut oil

1 tbsp coarsely chopped garlic

2 tsp chopped fresh ginger

4 scallions, cut into 1-inch (2.5-cm) pieces diagonally

1 lb (450 g) shrimp, shelled and deveined

½ each medium red and green bell pepper, cut into 1-inch (2.5-cm) squares

8 oz (225 g) canned water chestnuts, drained and sliced

SAUCE

⅔ cup chicken stock

2 tbsp rice wine or dry sherry

3 tbsp light soy sauce

2 tsp dark soy sauce

1 tbsp tomato paste

3 tbsp Chinese white rice vinegar or cider vinegar

1 tbsp superfine sugar

1 tbsp cornstarch, blended with 2 tbsp water

Heat a wok over a high heat, then add the oil. When it is very hot and slightly smoking, add the garlic, ginger, and scallions, and stir-fry for a couple of seconds.

Add the shrimp and stir-fry them for 1 minute. Next add the bell peppers and water chestnuts, and stir-fry for another 30 seconds.

Now add all the sauce ingredients except for the cornstarch mixture, then turn the heat down and simmer for 3 minutes.

Add the cornstarch to thicken the sauce, stir-fry for 2 minutes more, and serve with plain or egg-fried rice.

Crab Cakes
A fabulous taste of the sea and another twist on the traditional British fish cake. Serve these crab cakes piping hot.

SERVES 4

1 lb 2 oz (500 g) floury potatoes, peeled and cut into large chunks

salt and pepper, to taste

2 tbsp butter

2 tbsp heavy cream

1 tsp mild or medium curry powder

2 tbsp chopped fresh cilantro

1 large green chile, seeded and finely chopped

1 tbsp grated red onion

1 lb 2 oz (500 g) flaked crab meat, preferably white meat

2–3 tbsp all-purpose flour, seasoned

2 medium free-range eggs, beaten

3/4 cup dried bread crumbs

corn or sunflower oil, for frying

Boil the potatoes in a saucepan of lightly salted water for about 15 minutes, or until tender. Drain well, and return to the pan. Mash with a fork or potato masher until smooth, beating in the butter, cream, curry powder, cilantro, chile, onion, and plenty of salt and pepper. Let cool completely.

Meanwhile, check the crab meat carefully for any flecks of shell and discard these. Mix the crab meat with the potato mixture, and then shape into eight neat, round patties. If the mixture sticks to your hands, simply dip them in cold water.

Coat the crab cakes with seasoned flour, egg, and bread crumbs as described on page 191, then chill in the refrigerator for about 30 minutes to "set" the crumbs.

Heat the oil to a depth of 1/2 inch (1 cm) in a wide, shallow skillet until you feel a good heat rising. Carefully slide in the crab cakes using a spatula. Cook for about 3 minutes, until crisp and golden brown on the underside, then carefully turn and cook the other side. Remove and place on paper towels. (If you have a medium-size skillet, you may find it best to fry the crab cakes in two batches).

If you're not serving the crab cakes immediately, place them uncovered in a warm oven so that the coating stays crisp.

Potted Crab

Potted shrimp is familiar to most of us, which come in small buttered containers and served with lemon and whole-wheat bread and butter (a must with all potted fish for me). Crab makes a nice change, because it's difficult to find the small brown shrimp in this country.

FILLS 12 RAMEKINS

14 oz (400 g) white crab meat

14 oz (400 g) brown crab meat

1³/₄ cups best unsalted butter

a good pinch of ground mace

a good pinch of freshly grated nutmeg

¹/₃ tsp cayenne pepper

salt and pepper, to taste

lemon juice

Preheat the oven to 300°F/150°C. Put the crab meats into separate bowls. Have ready 12 ramekins.

Clarify 1 cup of the butter by melting it gently, then pouring it carefully into another pan, leaving behind the milky, curdlike solids (which you should discard). Add the mace, nutmeg, and cayenne to the clear butter, then pour the spiced butter into the bowl with the white crab meat. Amalgamate well, and season with salt, pepper, and a squeeze of lemon juice to taste.

Fill each ramekin with a layer of the buttered white crab meat, followed by a layer of brown meat. Finish with a layer of the white meat. You will have just enough room at the top of the ramekin for a final layer of clarified butter (which you will add after the poaching). Place the ramekins in a roasting pan, pour boiling water to come halfway up the sides, and place in the oven for 25 minutes.

Remove the ramekins from the oven and let cool. Clarify the rest of the butter as above, and pour the clear liquid over the ramekins, like a sealing wax. Place in the refrigerator to set.

The ramekins should be removed from the refrigerator before serving. Then slip a slim knife blade all the way around the girth of each ramekin right to the bottom, turn the potted crab out on to the palm of your hand, and put each one, butter-side up, on individual plates.

Serve with warm toasted whole-wheat bread and dressed salad greens.

Thyme-steamed Mussels

Here is a dish that is a little like *moules marinières*, but with fresh thyme. Hot sourdough (or rye) bread is great to dunk in the juices afterward. Mussels should be bought as fresh as possible. A mussel that is dead or even slightly bad can cause unpleasant side effects. Check them before cooking and discard any whose shells refuse to close when tapped briskly, because these are probably dead. Once they are cooked, throw away any that have not opened because they might also be bad. Also, avoid frozen mussels.

SERVES 2

2 lb (900 g) fresh mussels

2 tbsp butter

1/2 red onion, roughly chopped

3 cloves garlic, roughly chopped

generous 1 cup white wine

4 sprigs fresh thyme

generous 1 cup heavy cream

salt and pepper, to taste

3/4 cup roughly chopped fresh flat-leaf parsley

TO SERVE

1 medium sourdough loaf

butter

Wash the mussels in a colander to remove any dirt or grime. Pick through the mussels and remove the stringy parts from the edges; this is what the mussel uses to hold onto rocks or its mates before being taken from the sea. Discard any that do not close when tapped briskly.

Wrap the bread in foil (to prevent it from drying out) and place it in a low oven—about 300°F/150°C—to warm up slowly while you cook the mussels.

Place the butter in a large pan and sauté the onion and garlic for 1 minute before adding the wine. Bring to a boil and add the fresh thyme and mussels. Place the lid on the pan and cook for 3–4 minutes, until the mussels start to open.

Add the cream, salt, pepper, and parsley, stirring the ingredients with a spoon. Heat through, making sure all the mussels are open (discard any that are not).

Divide the mussels between two bowls and pour the sauce left in the pan over them. Remove the bread from the oven and break into large chunks. I like to eat all the mussels first, and dunk the bread (with loads of butter on it) in at the end.

vegetarian

Love it or loathe it, the British cauliflower is a great vegetable. Chefs love to cook with it, but other people are still divided, probably due to the school lunches we used to have—that dreaded gray stuff that was kept warm for hours in steaming trays with lids on. Overcooked cauliflower still scares me to this day.

Cauliflower Cheese

SERVES 4

1 large cauliflower, divided into florets, or use individual baby cauliflowers

salt and pepper, to taste

butter

CHEESE SAUCE

1 clove

1 bay leaf

1 small onion

2 1/2 cups milk

2 tbsp butter

3 tbsp all-purpose flour

freshly grated nutmeg

2/3 cup light cream

1 tsp English mustard

2 cups grated, sharp cheddar cheese

To make the sauce, first stud the clove through the bay leaf into the peeled onion, and place in a saucepan with the milk. Warm the milk slowly to let the flavors impregnate the milk.

Melt the butter in a saucepan. Once melted, add the flour and cook on a low heat for a few minutes, stirring from time to time. Add the simmering milk, a ladle at a time, and stir to a smooth sauce. Bring to a simmer and cook for about 8–10 minutes.

Remove the onion and season the sauce with salt, pepper, and nutmeg. Add the cream, which will loosen the sauce slightly. Add the mustard and 1 3/4 cups of the grated cheddar. Once completely melted into the sauce, taste again for seasoning and strength. Do not boil. Strain through a strainer.

Cook the cauliflower florets in a pan of salted water until just tender, for a few minutes. Drain. (The cauliflower can be cooked ahead of time and refreshed in ice water. To reheat, either microwave or plunge back into boiling water. If using baby cauliflower, you can keep it whole, as in the photograph.) Warm a pat of butter in a skillet and add the florets. Roll these, without coloring, in the butter and season with salt and pepper.

To finish, preheat the oven to 400°F/200°C or preheat the broiler. Spoon a little cheese sauce into an ovenproof dish, arrange the cauliflower on top, and coat with more of the sauce. Sprinkle the last of the grated cheddar on top and place in the oven or under the broiler to melt and color for 10–15 minutes.

Baked Cheese in a Box
Pubs are a great showcase for British food, and that's where I got the idea for this. The Red Lion Pub in Stourbridge, Kent, serves fantastic food and great British beers. I had this baked cheese there with a loaf of bread to dunk into it, and it was well worth the 200-mile round trip!

SERVES 4

1 Bonchester or English Camembert cheese in a box

salt and pepper, to taste

extra-virgin olive oil

1/2 tsp chopped fresh thyme

TO SERVE

fresh crusty bread

Preheat the oven to 375°F/190°C.

Remove the cheese from the box and, if the box is held together only with glue, staple it together because the glue will melt in the oven.

Take a sharp knife and cut the top off the cheese—just the skin. Then place the cheese back in the box, cut-side up.

Season, drizzle with olive oil, and sprinkle with fresh thyme.

Put in the oven for 10–15 minutes, until cooked through and brown on top.

Remove from the oven and serve with warm, crusty bread. It's a little like a dip—kind of a fondue thing.

Stilton Fondue with Pears
This is a Swiss concept, using very British ingredients. If you don't have a fondue set you can improvise with an oven-to-table dish on a rack over nightlights.

SERVES 4

5 1/2 oz (150 g) Stilton cheese, diced

3 oz (85 g) mascarpone cheese

generous 1/4 cup heavy cream

a drizzle of vodka

salt and pepper, to taste

3 pears, cored and sliced

1/2 walnut bread loaf, in chunks

Place the Stilton, mascarpone, and heavy cream in a pan and warm over a low heat until the cheeses have melted.

Add the vodka, remove from the heat, and season.

Place the pears and bread in separate dishes. Serve the fondue warm in the middle of the table. Dip the pear slices and bread chunks into the fondue, and enjoy!

I know it doesn't have vegetables in it, but humor me! This recipe provides the ideal centerpiece for vegetarians.

Double-baked Cheese Soufflés

SERVES 6

3 tbsp unsalted butter, plus extra, for greasing

2³/₄ cups ground almonds

1¹/₄ cups all-purpose flour

1¹/₄ cups hot milk

1¹/₃ cups grated Emmental cheese

5 medium free-range egg yolks

salt and pepper, to taste

generous 2 cups free-range egg whites

3 tbsp lemon juice

SAUCE

5¹/₂ cups heavy cream

generous 1 cup Kirsch

1¹/₄ cups grated Emmental cheese

Preheat the oven to 350°F/180°C. Butter six small soufflé molds, then dust with ground almonds. Put the moulds in a roasting pan.

To make the béchamel base of the soufflés, melt the butter in a pan, add the flour, and stir until smooth. Add the hot milk gradually, stirring, until smooth. While it is still hot, stir in the grated cheese until melted. Let cool. Stir in the egg yolks and season.

Whisk the egg whites with the lemon juice until firm. Add one-quarter of this to the cheese béchamel and fold in. When smooth, slowly fold in the rest. Fill the molds with this. Pour enough boiling water into the roasting pan to come halfway up the molds, then put the pan in the oven for 10 minutes. Let the soufflés cool. (You can freeze them at this stage.) Reduce the oven temperature to 325°F/160°C.

Remove the soufflés from the molds, and place in an ovenproof dish. For the sauce, mix the cream and Kirsch, pour over the soufflés, and top with the grated Emmental. Bake in the cooler oven for 8 minutes. Serve the soufflés hot, with their sauce.

Eggplants are not really English, but I'm growing them in my greenhouse and they taste wonderful. Simply pan-fry slices of eggplant, top with mozzarella cheese and Parmesan, place under the broiler, and serve with a tomato sauce. This is a real classic Italian dish that we Brits have learned to love.

Grilled Aubergine with Tomato Sauce

SERVES 4

all-purpose white flour

4 medium free-range eggs, beaten with a pinch of salt

2 eggplants, cut into 3/8 inch (8 mm) circles

olive oil

salt and pepper, to taste

10 1/2 oz (300 g) buffalo mozzarella cheese, sliced

generous 3/4 cup freshly grated Parmesan cheese

TOMATO AND BASIL SAUCE
extra-virgin olive oil

1 medium onion, finely chopped

2 cloves garlic, finely chopped

2 1/4 lb (1 kg) tomatoes, diced

1/4 tsp dried oregano

8 fresh basil leaves, torn

To make the sauce, heat 4 tablespoons of olive oil in a pan and fry the onion and garlic for 4–5 minutes. Add the tomatoes and oregano, bring to a boil, then reduce the heat and cook for 10–15 minutes. Halfway through the cooking, add the basil leaves. Season and blend to a smooth sauce, then set aside.

Preheat two skillets on the stove top, and preheat the broiler.

Put the flour and beaten eggs in separate shallow bowls. Dip the eggplant slices first in flour and then in beaten egg, and fry in shallow olive oil until golden on both sides. Put each slice on absorbent paper towels.

Place the drained eggplant slices on a broiler pan and season. Top with the sliced mozzarella and grated Parmesan.

Broiler until the cheeses have melted and started to brown, then serve immediately with the heated tomato and basil sauce.

Quick Onion Bhajias

This recipe isn't really mine, because it comes from one of my boys in the bistro kitchen. I promised him I'd put it in the book. I hope you like these as much as I do. I know bhajias are not really British, but we've kind of adopted them. To make a good dip for them, mix some ground cumin, lime juice, and chopped mint into some thick plain yogurt.

MAKES 8–10

2 onions, thinly sliced

1/2 cup self-raising flour

1 tsp medium curry powder

1/2 tsp ground cumin

2 tsp turmeric powder

1/2 tsp salt

2/3 cup plain yogurt

vegetable oil, for deep-frying

Place the onions, flour, spices, and salt in a bowl and then stir in the plain yogurt.

Divide the mixture into small balls in the palm of your hands.

Heat the oil to 350°F/180°C, then deep-fry the bhajias for 1–2 minutes, to color and cook. Drain on paper towels and cool for a while.

Serve as required, with either a spiced yogurt dip (*see* recipe introduction) or some mango chutney.

Garlic Mushrooms

There was a time when to eat anything with garlic in it was considered "daring". Now we just enjoy it, and it goes fantastically with mushrooms. Try different types of mushrooms: buttons would be good, too, as would some of the exotic cultivated varieties, such as oyster mushrooms.

SERVES 4

1 lb 5 oz (600 g) cremini mushrooms

2 tbsp extra-virgin olive oil

4 cloves garlic, finely diced or crushed

2 1/2 tbsp butter

juice of 1/2 lemon

salt and pepper, to taste

2 tbsp chopped fresh flat-leaf parsley

Clean the mushrooms. Heat the oil in a large skillet and add the mushrooms. Fry for about 2–3 minutes over a high heat, stirring all the time.

Add the garlic and butter and cook for another 2–3 minutes.

Finish by quickly stirring in the lemon juice and salt and pepper to taste and the chopped parsley.

Serve in a bowl with some lovely warm, crusty bread.

I love a fried meal, and this is simply a more elegant way of serving the British classic, ever-popular "bubble and squeak", made from mashed potatoes and cabbage.

Bubble and Squeak Cakes

MAKES 4

1 lb 2 oz (500 g) floury potatoes, peeled and chopped

1¼ cups shredded green cabbage

olive or sunflower oil, for frying

1 shallot, chopped

2 cloves garlic, crushed

3 tbsp chopped mixed fresh herbs, such as parsley, dill, or cilantro

salt and pepper, to taste

seasoned flour, for coating

Boil the potatoes in lightly salted water for about 15 minutes, until just tender, then drain well and mash in the pan. Let stand.

Blanch the cabbage in a little boiling water for 2 minutes, then drain, rinse under cold running water, and pat dry with paper towels.

Heat 1 tbsp of oil in a skillet, add the shallot and garlic, and sauté for 3 minutes, until softened.

Add the shallot and garlic to the mashed potato with the cabbage, chopped herbs, and seasoning. Set aside to cool.

Shape the mixture into four cakes. Toss in seasoned flour to coat, shaking off any excess. Heat oil to a depth of ½ inch (1 cm) in a large skillet. Lower the cakes into the hot oil, using a spatula, and cook for about 3 minutes on each side, turning them carefully. Remove and drain on paper towels.

The pizza may not be traditionally British, but it's up there in our favorite things to eat, so it had to be in the book. Add whatever extra toppings you like but, if you use this recipe as a base, you won't go wrong. You can make the pizzas larger if you like and, of course, they can be any shape you fancy.

Pizza Margherita

MAKES 4 X 10 INCH
(25 CM) PIZZAS

olive oil

3 cloves garlic, finely chopped

2 1/4 lb (1 kg) vine-ripened tomatoes, skinned, seeded, and roughly chopped

salt and pepper, to taste

1 tbsp chopped fresh oregano

18 oz (500 g) buffalo mozzarella cheese, thinly sliced

a large handful of basil leaves, torn into pieces

PIZZA BASE

4 cups white bread flour, plus extra for dusting

4 tsp easy-blend yeast

2 tsp salt

2 cups lukewarm water

4 tsp olive oil

4 tbsp polenta or semolina

For the base, sift the flour, yeast, and salt into a bowl, and make a well in the center. Add the warm water and olive oil, and mix together to a soft dough. Pour the dough out onto a lightly floured surface and knead for 5 minutes, or until smooth and elastic. Return it to the bowl, cover with plastic wrap and let stand in a warm place for approximately 1 hour, or until doubled in size.

Meanwhile, for the topping, heat 6 tablespoons of the oil and cook the garlic in a large, shallow pan. As soon as the garlic starts to sizzle, add the tomatoes and some salt and pepper, and simmer vigorously for 7–10 minutes, until reduced to a thickish sauce. Season again if necessary.

Put a large baking sheet into the oven and heat the oven to its highest setting. Punch down the air out of the dough and knead it briefly once more on a lightly floured surface. Divide into four pieces, and keep the spare ones covered with plastic wrap while you shape the first pizza.

Sprinkle a spare baking sheet with some of the polenta or semolina. Roll the dough out into a disk approximately 10 inches (25 cm) in diameter, lift it onto the baking sheet, and reshape it with your fingers into a circle. Spread one-quarter of the tomato sauce to within about 1 inch (2.5 cm) of the edge. Sprinkle with some of the oregano, then cover with one-quarter of the mozzarella cheese slices.

Drizzle with a little olive oil, then open the oven door and quickly slide the pizza off the sheet onto the hot baking sheet on the top shelf. Bake for 10 minutes, or until the cheese has melted and the crust is crisp and golden. Repeat the assembling and cooking process with the remaining pieces of dough, cooking individually.

To serve, scatter with the basil leaves and serve hot.

vegetables

Roast Potatoes

Everyone has a different recipe for roast potatoes; this is mine. It was my grandmother's first, then my mother's, and it's still the best. Use lard or dripping for the cooking fat (or vegetable oil if you don't have either), but best of all use some goose fat.

SERVES 6

10 medium floury potatoes

salt

1/4 cup fat (*see* above)

Preheat the oven to 400°F/200°C. Peel the potatoes and cut each one in half (into three if large). Place in a saucepan, cover with cold water, and add a good pinch of salt. Bring to a boil and simmer for a maximum of 3–4 minutes. Put into a colander and let drain well.

Heat the lard or dripping in a roasting pan on the stove, and fry the potatoes until they start to brown. Turn them occasionally. Sprinkle generously with salt, then roast for about 25 minutes.

Remove from the oven and turn the potatoes in the pan to prevent them from sticking. Roast for another 25 minutes and remove. Serve immediately. (I also love roast potatoes cold—which is why I always make bucketloads of them! I eat them with cold meat and a good pat of butter.)

Roast Parsnips

I love these, at Christmas or any other time of the year.

SERVES 6

2 lb (900 g) parsnips, peeled and quartered

2 tbsp olive oil

leaves from 2 fresh thyme sprigs

salt and pepper, to taste

3 tbsp unsalted butter

4–6 tbsp honey

Preheat the oven to 400°F/200°C. If the parsnips are large and have woody centers, cut these out before cooking. The parsnips can be boiled in salted water for 2 minutes before roasting.

Preheat a roasting pan on the stove top and add the oil. Fry the parsnips until golden on all sides, allowing burned tinges on the edges. Add the thyme and then roast, turning every 10 minutes, for 20–30 minutes.

Remove from the oven and season. Add the butter and honey. Return to the oven for 5–10 minutes. Place in a serving dish and spoon over the juices.

Mashed Potatoes
How fantastic does good mashed potato taste? It goes with anything: it can top fish pies or it can simply be served with sausages and onion gravy. I could eat this just with cold roast lamb—that's my favorite.

SERVES 4

2 lb (900 g) large Yukon gold potatoes, peeled and quartered

1/2 cup unsalted butter

1/2 cup light cream

salt and pepper, to taste

freshly grated nutmeg

Boil the potatoes in salted water until cooked, about 20–25 minutes, depending on size.

Drain off all the water, replace the lid, and shake the pan vigorously, which will start to break up the boiled potatoes. Add the butter and cream, a little at a time, while mashing the potatoes.

Season with salt, pepper, and some nutmeg, according to taste. The potatoes will now be light, fluffy, creamy, and ready to eat.

Dauphinoise in a Pan
Yes, this dish is French, and purists will complain that traditionally it's cooked in layers raw in the oven, and not with cheese. But I'm all for making life easier, and this recipe takes one-quarter of the time to cook. When working in France at a three-star Michelin restaurant, this is all I ate, and it now features on many of my menus.

SERVES 6

2 lb (900 g) Yukon gold potatoes

2 tbsp unsalted butter

2 cloves garlic, chopped

2 shallots, peeled and chopped

2/3 cup milk

2 1/2 cups heavy cream

salt and pepper, to taste

1/4 cup grated cheddar cheese

3 1/2 oz (100 g) mozzarella cheese, crumbled

Peel and slice the potatoes as thinly as possible (preferably using a mandolin). Melt the butter in a medium heatproof dish or in a large pan, and sauté the garlic and shallot lightly. Add the milk and cream and bring to a simmer. Add the sliced potato, and cook on a gentle simmer for about 8–10 minutes to just cook the potato.

Preheat the broiler to medium-hot.

Season the potatoes well, and either leave in the dish to serve or ladle carefully from the pan into six small heatproof dishes. Top with the cheeses, spreading them evenly. Place under the broiler for a couple of minutes, until brown, then serve.

Parsley and Mozzarella Croquettes
This is party food without the mess, because the cheese will melt inside—and a great side dish, too.

MAKES 24

2 1/4 lb (1 kg) potatoes, peeled

a pinch of freshly grated nutmeg

salt and pepper, to taste

2 tbsp unsalted butter

7 oz (200 g) mozzarella cheese, finely diced

2 medium free-range egg yolks

1/4 cup chopped fresh parsley leaves

all-purpose flour

2 medium free-range eggs, beaten

2 1/2 cups fresh white bread crumbs

vegetable oil, for deep-frying

Place the potatoes in salted water, bring to a boil, and simmer until they are tender.

Drain and return to the pan. Place over a low heat and mash-fry with a potato masher. Season with the nutmeg, salt, and pepper, then beat in the butter and let cool.

Once the mash is cold, add the diced mozzarella, the egg yolks, and the chopped parsley.

Divide the mixture into 24 pieces. Roll these into cylinder shapes on a lightly floured surface.

With the beaten eggs in one bowl and the bread crumbs in another, coat the croquettes first in the egg, then in the crumbs. Repeat to give them a double coating.

Preheat the oil to 375°F/190°C and deep-fry the croquettes until golden brown, about 5–6 minutes. Drain on paper towels and serve immediately.

Salt-baked Baby Potatoes with Taleggio and Bacon
I loved baby baked potatoes at Halloween as a kid. There are many cheeses available now—you can use dolcelatte torta or my favorite, Taleggio.

SERVES 6–8

1 2/3 cups sea salt flakes

16–20 baby roasting potatoes

5 oz (140 g) Taleggio cheese, grated

4 streaky bacon strips, rinded, chopped, and blanched in boiling water

Preheat the oven to 450°F/230°C.

Cover a baking sheet with a layer of sea salt flakes. Lay the potatoes on the salt and bake for 30–40 minutes, or until cooked through.

Cut a slit in the top of each potato and stuff with the cheese and bacon.

Place the stuffed potatoes back in the oven or put under a well preheated broiler for a few minutes, until the cheese has melted and the bacon is cooked through and golden.

Serve immediately, while still hot.

Chips and French Fries
Nothing can beat French fries —whether fat or thin—with a little salt and ketchup.

SERVES 4–6

vegetable oil, for deep-frying

4–6 large potatoes, about
3 lb 5 oz (1.5 kg)

salt

Heat the oil in a deep-fat fryer or a deep, heavy pan to 200°F/95°C for blanching.

For good, large steak fries, peel, then trim the potatoes into rectangles. Now cut into 1/2 -inch (1-cm) thick slices, then cut again to give chips 1/2 inch (1 cm) wide. If you want regular French fries, then simply halve the thickness, making them 1/4 x 2 1/2 –3 inches (5 mm x 6–7.5 cm).

The fries now need to be blanched in the preheated fryer. This is very important, because it guarantees the fries will be completely cooked before serving. Frying them at 200°F/95°C will cook them without allowing them to color. The large fries will take up to 10 minutes before becoming tender; the smaller fries will need only 6–8 minutes.

Once cooked, check with a knife. When ready, remove from the oil and drain. The fries can be left to cool on waxed paper and even chilled before finishing in the hot fryer.

To finish, preheat the oil in the fryer to 350°F/180°C. Once hot, place the fries in the fat. These will now take around 2–3 minutes to become golden brown and crispy. Shake off any excess fat and sprinkle with salt before serving.

Jacket Potatoes
Sometimes a little of what hurts you does you good— and a good pat of butter melting into baked potatoes tastes fantastic.

SERVES 4

4 large baking potatoes

olive oil

rock salt or sea salt flakes

5 1/2 tbsp butter

Preheat the oven to 350°F/180°C. Wash and dry the potatoes and prick each one about eight times all over with a fork. Rub with olive oil and sprinkle with rock or sea salt.

Bake the potatoes in the oven for 1 1/2 –2 hours, until cooked. They should be crisp on the outside and soft in the middle.

Cut a cross in the top, then, using your fingers, squeeze in the middle to push the top out. Spoon on a good pat of butter.

Roasted Vegetables with Rosemary and Honey

This is a great way to serve vegetables at a dinner party or Sunday lunch. It's less stressful than five pans of boiling water with overcooked roots inside!

SERVES 6

1 lb (450 g) each of new potatoes, parsnips and carrots

8 oz (225 g) fennel bulbs

8 oz (225 g) red onions

6 cloves garlic

6 lemon slices

6 tbsp olive oil

1/4 cup honey

2 tbsp unsalted butter

1 fresh rosemary sprig, torn into 4 pieces

salt and pepper, to taste

juice of 1 lemon (optional)

Preheat the oven to 425°F/220°C.

Wash the potatoes, parsnips, carrots, and fennel, but don't peel them, then slice into large chunky pieces. Cut the red onions into quarters.

Place all the vegetables into an baking with the garlic and lemon slices, and drizzle with olive oil and honey. Add the butter in pats and sprinkle on the rosemary. Season well. Roast for 30–40 minutes.

Remove from the oven and coat all the vegetables in the glaze in the bottom of the pan. Serve with some lemon juice squeezed over if you like.

Celeriac Rémoulade

This French salad has become popular over here. You can serve celeriac raw, although some people prefer it blanched in boiling water for 1 minute. The sauce is a mustard mayonnaise livened up with my special touches.

SERVES 4

1 lb 2 oz (500 g) celeriac

1 red onion, thinly sliced

generous 1 cup thick mayonnaise

3 tbsp coarse-grain mustard, such as Pommery or Gordons

finely grated zest and juice of 1 lemon

a dash of Worcestershire sauce

salt and pepper, to taste

2 tbsp chopped fresh parsley

Peel the celeriac, then slice it as thinly as possible (use a mandolin if you have one). Stack the slices three or four at a time on top of each other and cut into long, thin julienne or matchsticks.

Place in a bowl and mix with the onion. (If you prefer a milder flavor, first soak the onion in a large bowl of cold water for 1 hour.)

Beat the mayonnaise with the mustard, lemon zest and juice, Worcestershire sauce, and seasoning. Combine with the celeriac and onion. If you find the sauce a little too thick, thin it with 1–2 tbsp milk. Check the seasoning, stir in the parsley, and serve in an attractive bowl.

Roast Squash, Lemon and Mustard Purée

This is a good dish to serve with roast meat, poultry, or game, and makes a nice change from mashed potatoes every time.

SERVES 6–8

2 butternut squashes, about
1 lb 7 oz (650 g) each

2 cloves garlic, crushed

2 lemons, each cut into 4 slices

1 tbsp olive oil

leaves from 1 sprig fresh thyme

6 1/2 tbsp unsalted butter

3 tbsp coarse-grain mustard

5 tbsp heavy cream

salt and pepper, to taste

Preheat the oven to 375°F/190°C.

Cut the squashes in half, scoop out the seeds, then peel and chop the flesh into even-size chunks. Place the squash in a bowl with the garlic, lemons, oil, and thyme.

Melt 4 tablespoons of the butter and add half of this to the bowl. Toss together, then spread out in a roasting pan and roast for about 20 minutes, until the squash feels tender when pierced with a knife.

Scoop the squash into a food processor with the remaining melted butter, the mustard, cream, and seasoning. Blend to a smooth puree. Alternatively, mash the squash and stir in the other ingredients.

Reheat and dot with the remaining butter when ready to serve.

Caramelized Beetroot

A speedy, simple serving idea for cooked beet. You can use cooked beets from a package but be sure to avoid the variety contained in that awful vinegar. But better still, cook and peel your own fresh beets.

SERVES 4

3 tbsp honey

2 tbsp butter

4 whole cooked beets,
cut in half

juice of 1 lemon

salt and pepper, to taste

1 tbsp chopped fresh parsley

Heat a large nonstick skillet until you feel a good heat rising. Spoon in the honey and swirl in the butter.

When you have a golden brown glaze, add the beet halves with the lemon juice and cook for 3–5 minutes, spooning the honey juices constantly over the beets.

Season well and turn into a warmed serving dish. Scatter over the parsley and serve.

Mushy Peas

British fish and "chips", or fries. Can't be without them. Marrow fat peas are plump, mature garden peas. Look for them at specialty suppliers of British products.

SERVES 6

generous 1 cup dried marrowfat peas

1 tsp baking of soda

1 1/2 tbsp butter

salt and pepper, to taste

In a large bowl, soak the peas in three times their volume of water with the baking of soda for at least 4 hours or, if you have the time, overnight.

Drain the peas, rinse under the tap, place on the stove in a large saucepan, and cover with water. Cover and bring to a boil and, once boiled, reduce the heat and simmer the peas for 1 1/2 – 2 hours, stirring from time to time.

The peas should be soft and mushy in texture but not too dry. If they are too wet, continue cooking over the heat with the lid off to dry out a little. Beat in the butter, season, and serve.

Butter Bean and Rosemary Purée

I've used Spanish lima beans but you can use American lima beans, otherwise French haricots are a good alternative. You can make the puree in advance and simply reheat it before serving.

SERVES 4

1 cup dried white beans (*see* above)

1 tbsp olive oil

3 shallots, chopped

3 fat cloves garlic, crushed

3 strips smoked bacon or pancetta, rinded and chopped

leaves from 1 sprig fresh rosemary, chopped

1 sprig fresh thyme

2/3 cup dry white wine

2 cups fresh chicken or vegetable stock

salt and pepper, to taste

2–4 tbsp heavy cream or crème fraîche

Soak the beans in water overnight, then drain and rinse them. Place in a saucepan, cover with cold water, and bring to a boil. Continue to boil for 5 minutes, then drain.

Meanwhile, heat the oil in a skillet, add the shallots, garlic, and bacon or pancetta, and sauté for 5 minutes. Add the blanched beans with the rosemary, thyme, wine, and stock. Bring to a boil, then season with only pepper.

Cover and simmer for about 30 minutes, until the beans are softened. Remove the lid, add salt to season and boil again to evaporate any remaining liquid. Remove the thyme sprig and transfer the bean mixture to a food processor or blender. Add the cream or crème fraîche and blend to a puree.

To make a quicker version of this dish, use 28 ounces (800 g) of canned butter beans in place of the dried beans. Simply rinse and drain the beans, then add them to the sautéed shallots, garlic, and bacon or pancetta with the herbs and wine, but without the stock. Simmer for 15 minutes, then blend with the cream or crème fraîche to make a puree.

Buttered Brussels Sprouts

The old days of putting the Brussels on at the same time as the turkey have, thankfully, long gone. Sprouts cooked properly with a lot of melted butter can be a real joy to eat.

SERVES 4

2¹/4 lb (1 kg) Brussels sprouts

salt and pepper, to taste

butter

Trim off the outer leaves of the Brussels sprouts.

Bring a large saucepan of salted water to a boil. Place the sprouts in the water and bring back to a boil as quickly as possible. Simmer for 3–4 minutes, until just cooked but still with a bit of crunch.

Drain into a colander and place in a bowl with a pat of butter and a good twist of freshly ground black pepper.

Brussels Sprouts with Chestnuts and Bacon

A simple way to make Brussels taste more interesting—although if you use Brussels still on the vine (much more readily available now), the sprouts don't dry out so much and are fresher in flavor. Chestnuts are readily available vacuum-packed in plastic pouches and jars, as well as canned.

SERVES 10–12

3 lb (1.3 kg) Brussels sprouts, or 2 stems Brussels sprouts, trimmed

salt and pepper, to taste

a large pat of unsalted butter

12 smoked streaky bacon strips or dry-cured ham, rinded and cut into thin matchsticks

7 oz (200 g) vacuum-pack cooked, peeled whole chestnuts

Bring a large pan of salted water to a boil, add the sprouts, and cook until just tender, 8–12 minutes, depending on their size. Drain well.

Meanwhile, melt the butter in a large skillet or wok and fry the bacon until crisp. Add the chestnuts and cook for about a minute to heat through.

When warm, tip in the drained Brussels sprouts. Mix well and season with salt and pepper.

sauces

Apple Sauce

The Americans eat apple sauce by itself. I like it best with cold pork and stuffing. Mmm—delicious.

SERVES 4

8 oz (225 g) Granny Smith apples

4 tbsp water

1 tbsp brown sugar

a pinch of freshly grated nutmeg

2 tbsp butter

Peel, core, and thinly slice the apples and put them in a pan with the rest of the ingredients.

Cook over a gentle heat and simmer, stirring all the time, until the apples have reduced to a pulp.

Let cool before chilling in the refrigerator until you're ready to use the sauce.

Spiced Apple Sauce

A change from the normal apple sauce, this goes very well with roast pork and ham, especially the Honey-Glazed Ham on page 110.

SERVES 6

1 lb 2 oz (500 g) Granny Smith apples

2 tbsp butter

2 tbsp water

2 tbsp white wine vinegar

1/4 tsp freshly grated nutmeg

1/4 tsp ground cinnamon

1/4 tsp freshly ground black pepper

2 tbsp dark brown sugar

Peel, core, and cut up the apples.

Put them in a pan with the butter, water, vinegar, and spices. Cover and cook gently until soft enough to beat to a puree.

Add sugar to taste, and more spices if you like.

Real Mint Sauce

This was my grandmother's mint sauce recipe. She never had a sharp knife, so she had to resort to chopping the mint in a grinder—this white plastic thing that you feed the leaves into while turning the handle. It did it in the end, but took about an hour to wash up.

SERVES 4

1 bunch fresh mint

a pinch of salt

1 level tbsp superfine sugar

4 tbsp boiling water

4 tbsp white wine vinegar

Strip the mint leaves off the stalks, sprinkle the leaves with the salt, and chop finely.

Place in a pitcher, add the sugar, and pour over the boiling water. Stir and let cool.

Stir in the vinegar and taste. Add more water or vinegar, and adjust the seasoning to suit your taste.

Horseradish Sauce

The best accompaniment to any roast beef or, indeed, steak.

MAKES SCANT 1 CUP

3 oz (85 g) fresh horseradish, peeled and finely grated

1 tsp Dijon or English mustard

1 tbsp white wine vinegar

1 tsp superfine sugar

3/4 cup heavy cream, whipped

salt and pepper, to taste

Place all the ingredients except the seasoning in a bowl, and whisk together to a soft peak consistency. Season with salt and pepper.

The sauce is best served chilled.

Mum's Gravy
Thanks, mom, for the best gravy recipe I know.

SERVES 4–6

scant 1/2 cup vegetable cooking water

2 white onions, sliced

2 tbsp butter

4 tsp gravy powder

2/3 cup red wine

3/4 tsp mustard powder

1 tsp cornstarch

1 tsp yeast extract

Remove the roasted meat from the roasting pan and pour off any excess fat. Add the vegetable water to the remaining juices in the pan and slowly simmer over a low heat on the stove top.

In a separate pan, fry the onions in the butter to give a lot of color. Dissolve the gravy powder in 1 1/4 cups of hot water. Pour this into with the roasting pan with the red wine and add the onions.

In a small dish, stir the mustard powder and cornstarch into a little water to make a paste. Whisk or stir into the simmering gravy. Add the yeast extract and stir in well. Pour into the sauceboat and serve as required.

Bread Sauce
My grandmother left me an old Be-Ro flour book in her will, which had been passed down from my great-great-grandmother. In it there were alternatives and variations to classic recipes, written in pencil by my great-grandmother: the pages were full of crossings out, and notes. This recipe is based on one in that book.

SERVES 8

8 oz (225 g) stale French bread

3 cups whole milk

1 small onion, studded with 6 cloves

1 bay leaf

a good pat of unsalted butter

a pinch of ground allspice

about 1 cup heavy cream

salt and pepper, to taste

Shave the light-brown crust from the French bread with a bread knife and discard it. Cut the bread center into 2 inch (5 cm) cubes.

In a saucepan, bring the milk, onion, bay, butter, allspice, and 3 tablespoons of the cream to a boil. Reduce the heat, then add the bread. Gently simmer, uncovered, for 5 minutes. Add a little seasoning and then cool. Remove the onion and bay.

The sauce can be refrigerated in a covered container overnight. To serve, warm through gently in a pan, adding enough heavy cream to give a light consistency. Grind over some black pepper and serve.

This is one of the first sauces you learn to make as a chef, and although it's French in origin, us Brits have fallen in love with it. It should never be overheated, otherwise the butter will split. Asparagus is great with this, as are poached eggs. Clarified butter is what you get when it separates from the whey. To do this, place the butter in a small pan and leave it over a very low heat until it has melted. Skim off any scum from the surface, and pour off the clear (clarified) butter into a bowl, leaving behind the milky white solids that will have settled on the bottom.

Hollandaise Sauce

SERVES 4

2 tbsp water

2 free-range egg yolks

1 cup clarified butter, warmed

juice of 1/2 lemon

a good pinch of cayenne pepper

1/2 tsp salt

Put the water and egg yolks into a stainless-steel or glass bowl set over a pan of simmering water, making sure that the bottom of the bowl is not touching the water. Whisk until voluminous and creamy.

Remove the bowl from the pan and gradually whisk in the clarified butter until thick. Then whisk in the lemon juice, cayenne pepper, and salt.

This sauce is best used as soon as it is made, but will hold for up to 2 hours if kept covered in a warm place, such as over a pan of water.

Béarnaise is French as well, not British, but we have taken it to our hearts. It's one of what they call the "mother sauces", the basis for others such as "Choron" and "Maltaise". It's closely related to Hollandaise, based on butter and egg yolks, and has as many uses. It's wonderful with any fish dish and with meat (especially steak) and vegetables. In the best kitchens it's made with clarified butter and by hand—but my version is much easier. The secret of this Béarnaise is to make sure that the butter is bubbling when it is added to the egg yolks for the sauce to thicken.

Béarnaise Sauce

SERVES 4

2 tbsp tarragon vinegar

1/4 cup white wine or water

1 tsp crushed white peppercorns

scant 1 cup unsalted butter

4 free-range egg yolks

2 tbsp chopped fresh tarragon

salt and white pepper, to taste

a squeeze of lemon juice

In a pan, heat the vinegar and wine or water with the peppercorns and bring to a boil. Simmer rapidly until the liquid has reduced by half. Strain out the peppercorns, return the liquid to the pan, and bring back to a boil.

In another pan, gently melt the butter. Add the reduced liquid and bring to a rolling boil.

Place the egg yolks in a food processor and blend. Then, with the motor running slowly, pour the hot vinegar and butter mixture into the food processor in a thin stream through the lid.

Pour the sauce into a bowl and let stand for 3 minutes, stirring occasionally. If the sauce has not thickened enough, pour it back into the pan and stir constantly over the lowest possible heat until it thickens.

Add the chopped tarragon and season with the salt, pepper, and lemon juice. Serve immediately.

Tartare Sauce

Tartare sauce is a classic accompaniment for any fish— broiled, baked, or fried. It's much better if you make it yourself rather than buy it in a jar. In fact, you could make the mayonnaise yourself, too, but perhaps that's a culinary step too far!

SERVES 4

scant 1 cup mayonnaise

1 tbsp each of chopped capers and gherkins

1 tbsp each of chopped fresh parsley, tarragon and dill

juice of 1/2 lemon

salt and pepper, to taste

Combine all the ingredients together and season to taste.

Chill in the refrigerator until ready to use.

Barbecue Sauce

If people knew barbecue sauce was this easy to make, they wouldn't be buying prepared stuff in bottles. Use as a marinade, a basting sauce, *and* a serving sauce.

SERVES 4–6

1 onion, chopped

3 cloves garlic, crushed

2 tbsp olive oil

1 fresh red chile, seeded and finely chopped

1 tsp fennel seeds, crushed

1/4 cup brown sugar

1/4 cup dark soy sauce

11/4 cup ketchup

salt and pepper, to taste

Fry the onion and garlic in the olive oil with the chilli, fennel seeds and sugar.

Add the soy sauce and ketchup (you could use homemade, *see* page 241), and season with salt and pepper. Bring to the boil and simmer for a few minutes to amalgamate the flavours.

Homemade Salad Cream

I know what you're all thinking. Why should I make my own when I can buy it in a bottle? But like the homemade Ketchup below, I wouldn't make that decision until you have tried making it—they are *so* much more delicious. If refrigerated, this sauce will keep for a minimum of 1–2 weeks.

MAKES 1-1/4 CUPS

1 tbsp all-purpose flour

4 tsp superfine sugar

2 tsp mustard powder

a pinch of salt

2 free-range eggs

$1/4$ cup white wine vinegar

$2/3$ cup heavy cream

a squeeze of lemon juice

Mix together the flour, sugar, mustard, and salt in a bowl. Beat in the eggs and white wine vinegar.

Place the bowl over a pan of simmering water—the bottom of the bowl must not touch the water—and stir until warmed and thickened. This will take only 4–5 minutes. Once "cooked", remove the bowl from the heat and let cool.

Now it is time to add the cream. With this you can be as generous as you wish. A minimum of $1/4$ cup will be needed. Finish with a squeeze of lemon juice and the salad cream is ready.

Ketchup

Tomato-based ketchup is a tradition in British cooking. The homemade stuff tastes great. Try making it—you may be surprised.

SERVES 4–6

1 tsp ground allspice

generous 1 cup cider vinegar

8 tbsp raw brown sugar

3 lb 5 oz (1.5 kg) ripe tomatoes, diced

1 bay leaf

1 tsp English mustard

1 clove garlic, chopped

1 tbsp tomato paste

a dash of Worcestershire sauce

a dash of Tabasco sauce (optional)

Put all the ingredients into a large pan and bring to a boil, stirring all the time. Reduce the heat and simmer for about 40 minutes, stirring occasionally to make sure it doesn't stick to the bottom of the pan.

Blend in a food processor and pass through a fine strainer. Pour into a sterilized bottle (*see* page 368 for sterilizing instructions), and keep in the refrigerator.

sweet
pastries
& fritters

Sweet Shortcrust Pastry

Making pastry may seem like hard work, but it's worth it. It's not just that the flavor and texture are better than that of the store-bought stuff—but it makes you feel good, too.

MAKES ABOUT 1 9-INCH (23-CM) PIE SHELL

1/2 cup cold unsalted butter, cubed

generous 3/4 cup all-purpose white flour

a pinch of salt

2 tbsp superfine sugar

2 tbsp ground almonds

1 free-range egg, lightly beaten, plus extra to glaze

Place the butter, flour, salt, sugar, and almonds in a food processor. Blend until you have a fine bread-crumb texture, but do not overwork. Add the egg and 1/2 an eggshell full of cold water and mix well, using the pulse button until the pastry balls; again, do not overwork.

Turn the dough out of the processor and knead very gently, just to bring it together. Flatten the dough slightly (this makes it easier to roll when chilled) and wrap in plastic wrap, then chill in the refrigerator for at least 20 minutes—an hour or two would be better.

Grease a 9-inch (23-cm) diameter, 11/2 -inch (4-cm) deep tart pan. Lightly flour the work surface. Roll the dough out so you end up with a circle about 11/2 inch (4 cm) larger in diameter than the tart pan. Carefully roll the dough onto the rolling pin and then unroll it over the tart pan, being careful not to stretch the dough too much.

Immediately ease the dough into the pan and use your thumb to gently push it into the bottom and corners; do not leave any creases in the outside or air between the dough and the ring. Let about 1/2 inch (1 cm) overhang the top edge of the pan. Then trim off with a sharp knife or roll a rolling pin over the top to remove the excess. Use your thumb to squeeze up the top edge again (the pastry will shrink back a little during cooking), and pinch with your thumb and index finger to make the edge more decorative. Using a piece of well-floured leftover dough, push the bottom of the dough into the corners so it's flush. Chill for 30 minutes. Preheat the oven to 400°F/200°C.

Cut out a round piece of wax paper 11/2 inches (4 cm) larger than the pan and place it inside the dough-lined tart pan. Fill with dried beans and bake for 15 minutes, or until the top edge is slightly brown. Remove the paper and beans, turn the oven down to 325°F/160°C, and cook for another 10 minutes, until the pastry is set but has not colored. Remove from the oven, brush with extra beaten egg (to stop the pastry from getting soggy when you add the filling), and then put it back in the oven for 2 minutes to seal. Cool for a little while before adding the filling.

What can I say? Just look at the photograph and try the recipe. I promise you won't be disappointed.

Apple Pie and Custard

SERVES 4–6

1 1/2 lb (675 g) perpared pie crust

1 lb 9 oz (700 g) Granny Smith apples

1/2 cup superfine sugar, plus extra for sprinkling

finely grated rind and juice of 1/2 lemon

2 tbsp butter, plus extra for greasing

ground cinnamon (optional)

1 free-range egg, beaten

CUSTARD

1 vanilla bean

1 1/4 cups milk

1 1/4 cups heavy cream

6 free-range egg yolks

1/2 cup superfine sugar

Butter an 8 1/2 -inch (22-cm) pie plate and preheat the oven to 375°F/190°C.

Roll out two-thirds of the pie crust on a floured work surface and carefully line the pie plate.

Peel, quarter, and core the apples, then slice them thickly into a bowl to which three-quarters of the sugar and all the lemon juice and rind have been added. Stir gently to mix.

Put the apple slices and sugar into the pie plate. Dot with a little butter and a sprinkling of cinnamon.

Roll out the remaining pie crust and put it on top of the apples. Seal and crimp the edges well and then make a small hole in the top to allow the steam to escape.

Make decorations from any pie crust trimmings (I like to do a few leaves) and seal them with a little water. Brush with the beaten egg, dredge with the remaining sugar, and then bake for 35–40 minutes, until the fruit is tender and the top is golden brown.

For the custard, split open the vanilla bean and scrape the seeds out into a heavy saucepan. Add the vanilla bean, milk, and cream and bring slowly to a boil.

Place the egg yolks and sugar in a bowl and whisk together until they lighten in color.

Pour the milk and cream onto the eggs, whisking well. Return the mixture to the pan. Place the pan over a low heat and cook the custard for about 5 minutes, stirring all the time, until it thickens slightly and coats the back of the spoon. Do not boil or the custard will curdle. Strain through a strainer and serve with the warm apple pie.

This is a great dish! Roughly pureed Granny Smith apples form the base, and are topped with slices of Cortland. Custard is poured on the top. Don't rush cooking the custard, or you'll risk it "souffléing" and so splitting on the surface. If you are unsure, cook the tart a little longer and put it in the refrigerator to firm the custard before you serve it.

Bramley Apple, Custard and Honey Tart

SERVES 4–6

9-inch (23-cm) Sweet Shortcrust Pastry pie shell (*see* page 245)

FILLING

2 large Granny Smith apples

caster sugar, to taste

1 large Cox's apple

1¹/₂ tbsp unsalted butter

4 medium free-range egg yolks

2 medium free-range eggs

2 tbsp honey

scant 3 cups heavy cream

a pinch of saffron strands (optional)

TO SERVE (OPTIONAL)

1 large Cortland or Jonagold apple

confectioners' sugar

a little whipped cream

Preheat the oven to 325°F/160°C.

Peel, core, and roughly slice the Granny Smith apples. Put them in a pan with a little water, and cook over a medium heat for 5–10 minutes, until soft. Add some sugar to taste and beat to a puree.

Peel and core the Cortland apple, and cut it into neat ¹/₄inch (5 mm) slices. Fry gently in the unsalted butter until softened and lightly colored. Place the apple puree in the bottom of the pie shell and overlap the apple slices on top.

In a bowl, beat together the egg yolks, eggs, and honey. Place the cream and saffron (if using) in a small pan and bring to a boil. When boiling, whisk the cream into the egg mix, beating all the time. Pour into the prepared and precooked pie shell, over the apple, and bake for 20 minutes, until the mixture has set and is golden brown.

If you want to garnish with caramelized apple, peel and core the Cortland apple and cut it into slices, 1¹/₄ inches (3 cm) thick. Sprinkle with confectioners' sugar and toast under a hot broiler until caramelized.

Serve the tart warm or at room temperature with a few pieces of caramelized apple and a dollop of cream on each slice.

This is a twist on a prune and almond tart, but it works better because the plums stew down while the tart is cooking. Use dark plums to give the frangipane a rich color. Fluff the butter and sugar for the frangipine together well before adding the eggs and flour, as this will create a much lighter filling—and never put the cooked tart in the refrigerator.

Plum and Almond Tart

SERVES 4–6

butter, for greasing

9-inch (23-cm) Sweet Shortcrust Pastry pie shell (*see* page 245)

all-purpose flour, for dusting

2 lb (900 g) plums, dark if you can get them

confectioners' sugar

FRANGIPANE

1 cup unsalted butter

generous 1 cup superfine sugar

4 free-range eggs, beaten

4 tbsp brandy

1 1/4 cups ground almonds

4 tbsp all-purpose flour

TO SERVE

generous 1/3 cup heavy cream

cassis to taste (optional) or 4 tbsp homemade custard (*see* page 246)

a few blackberries (optional)

Preheat the oven to 400°F/200°C.

Grease and line a 13 1/2-inch (34-cm) round, fluted or rectangular tart pan. Roll out the pastry on a lightly floured surface, press it into the tin, trim the edges, and prick the bottom lightly with a fork. Cover and chill.

Meanwhile, make the frangipane. Using an electric mixer, beat together the butter and sugar until pale and creamy. Gradually beat in the eggs. Stir in the brandy, almonds, and flour. Spread the frangipane evenly over the bottom of the pie shell.

Remove the pits from the plums and cut into quarters. Gently push the plum quarters vertically into the frangipane.

Place the tart on a baking sheet and bake for 10–15 minutes, or until the pastry is beginning to brown. Reduce the oven temperature to 350°F/180°C and continue to bake for 35 minutes.

Remove the tart from the oven and let cool slightly, then remove from the pan and dust lightly with confectioners' sugar.

Serve the tart at room temperature. Cut it into wedges and serve it warm with plain, thick heavy cream, heavy cream flavored with cassis, or custard, and perhaps a few blackberries.

I find this hard to cook, because it appears to be cooked long before it is. If you're unsure, turn the oven a little lower and cook for a while longer or else the nuts will burn.

Pecan Pie

SERVES 4–6

12 oz (350 g) pecans (or walnuts)

2 oz (55 g) dark chocolate, grated

1 tsp vanilla extract

2 pinches salt

1¹/₂ cups good maple syrup

4 large free-range eggs

1¹/₂ cups granulated sugar

¹/₂ cup unsalted butter, melted

9 inch (23 cm) Sweet Shortcrust Pastry pie shell (*see* page 245)

Preheat the oven to 325°F/160°C.

Place the nuts, grated chocolate, vanilla extract, salt, and maple syrup in a bowl. Beat the eggs in a separate bowl, then stir into the nut mixture together with the sugar. Finally add the melted butter and stir well.

Pour into the prepared and precooked pie shell and bake for 55–60 minutes, or until set in the middle. Let cool completely before cutting.

Bakewell Tart

Here is a British classic dessert. The original did not contain almonds, and was more like a custard tart. One tip for this is to mix the ingredients well at the start, as this will make the mixture lighter and give a nice texture.

SERVES 6

generous 1/2 cup superfine sugar

scant 2/3 cup ground almonds

scant 1 cup all-purpose flour, plus extra for dusting

7 tbsp butter, finely diced

1 large free-range egg, plus 1 extra free-range egg yolk

finely grated zest of 1 small lemon

a pinch of salt

FILLING

6 tbsp butter

scant 1/2 cup superfine sugar

2 medium free-range eggs

3 drops almond extract

1 cup fresh white bread crumbs

scant 1 cup ground almonds

8 tbsp raspberry jam

3 tbsp slivered almonds

First, make the dough. Put the sugar, almonds, and flour into a food processor, and turn on to full speed for a few seconds. Add the butter and work again until just blended in. The mixture will resemble fine bread crumbs.

Add the egg and extra yolk, the lemon zest, 2 teaspoons of water, and a tiny pinch of salt. Work again until the dough balls. Wrap in plastic wrap and refrigerate.

Preheat the oven to 375ºF/190ºC.

Roll out the chilled dough on a flour-dusted surface and use to line an 8 inch (20 cm) loose-bottom tart pan. If it breaks it can be repaired by pressing with your fingers. Make the shell as even as possible, and ensure that around the edges it is pushed right up to the top, because it will shrink as it bakes. Be careful to press into the bottom edges to eliminate air between the pan and pastry. Chill.

To make the filling, put the butter and sugar in a food processor, and blend until light and fluffy. With the machine running on full speed, add the eggs and almond extract until combined to a smooth paste, then fold in the bread crumbs and ground almonds.

Put the pastry shell on a baking tray, prick the bottom with a fork, and line with foil. Fill with dried beans and bake for 10 minutes. Remove the foil and beans, and let cool slightly, then spread the bottom with a layer of raspberry jam. Cover this with the almond filling. Scrape the surface smooth and level, and sprinkle with the slivered almonds.

Return the tart to the oven and bake for 25–30 minutes, until risen and lightly browned.

Yorkshire Curd Tart

My aunt's favorite, and a tart that is famous all over the country. Thought to originate from the 13th century, this is otherwise known as cheesecake. You can make small tarts as well: cook these for slightly less time.

SERVES 4–6

9-inch (23-cm) Sweet Shortcrust Pastry pie shell (*see* page 245)

FILLING

2 1/4 cups whipping cream

8 free-range egg yolks

1/3 cup superfine sugar

1 tsp ground allspice

Preheat the oven to 250°F/120°C.

To make the filling, put the cream into a saucepan over a medium heat and bring to the boil. Mix the egg yolks with the caster sugar and half the allspice in a bowl. Pour the cream on to the egg mixture, being careful not to let the yolks curdle, then pass through a sieve. Pour into the prepared and precooked pie shell.

Sprinkle the curd tart with the remaining allspice and bake in the oven for 23–45 minutes, until the custard is set. Remove from the oven and allow to cool.

Serve at room temperature.

Syrup and bread in pastry...whoever invented this? But whoever you are, what a combination! I feel, though, that you must eat this warm and never place it in the refrigerator. Serve with heavy cream, ice cream, whipped cream, or fruit. It's up to you.

Treacle Tart

SERVES 6–8

butter, for greasing

18 oz (500 g) prepared pie crust

all-purpose flour, for rolling

FILLING

1³/₄ cups dark corn syrup

2¹/₄ cups fresh bread crumbs

2 free-range eggs, lightly beaten

finely grated zest and juice of 1 lemon

Preheat the oven to 350°F/180°C, and butter a 14 inch (35 cm) ovenproof tart pan.

Roll out the dough on a floured surface until very thin and, using the tart pan as a template, cut around the pan, allowing enough to go up the sides of the pan. Place the disk of dough in the bottom of the pan and up over the sides. Prick the bottom with a fork, line with foil, and fill with dried beans. Bake for 10–12 minutes, until lightly golden. Remove from the oven, and lower the oven temperature to 275°F/140°C. Remove the foil and beans.

In a bowl, mix together the corn syrup, bread crumbs, eggs, and lemon juice and zest. Once combined, spoon into the pie shell and bake at the reduced temperature for 50–60 minutes.

Trim off the edges of the pastry, and cut the tart into portions. Let the tart cool slightly before serving. It is best eaten warm, with a spoonful of whipped cream.

Chocolate and Raspberry Tarts with Fennel

This is on my restaurant menu. It might seem peculiar to put fennel with chocolate, but it's a combination I love. You can use fennel, aniseed or Pernod.

SERVES 4

butter, for greasing

1/2 recipe Sweet Shortcrust Pastry pie shell (*see* page 245)

all-purpose flour, for dusting

FILLING

12 oz (350 g) bittersweet dark chocolate, broken into pieces

4 medium free-range eggs

generous 1/4 cup superfine sugar

6 tbsp heavy cream

7 oz (200 g) raspberries

GARNISH

cocoa powder

vanilla ice cream

4 fresh mint sprigs

fennel oil (*see* below)

Preheat the oven to 375°F/190°C, and grease eight 3 inch (7.5 cm) plain-edged tart pans.

Roll out the dough on a lightly floured surface and use to line the pans (*see* page 245). Prick the bottoms with a fork, line with foil, and fill with dried beans. Bake for about 15–20 minutes. Let cool and then keep in the pans. Remove the foil and beans.

For the filling, melt the chocolate carefully in a bowl over simmering water. In another bowl, whisk the eggs and sugar, then fold in the cream and melted chocolate.

Spoon this mixture into the baked pastry shells and sprinkle with the raspberries. Bake for 10 more minutes, until just lightly cooked.

Serve warm with a dusting of cocoa powder, a scoop of vanilla ice cream, a sprig of fresh mint, and some fennel oil drizzled around the edge.

Fennel Oil

I used to make this with a stock syrup and blended fennel through it, but it works better with olive oil.

MAKES 1 1/4 CUPS

salt

1 1/4 oz (30 g) fresh flat-leaf parsley leaves

1 large fennel bulb, finely chopped

1 1/4 cups good olive oil

Bring a pot of salted water to a boil. Place the parsley leaves in a strainer and dip them into the water for 10–15 seconds, keeping the water at a strong boil. Remove the strainer and plunge the blanched parsley into an ice-water bath to chill. Drain the cold parsley and squeeze as dry as possible.

Place all the parsley and chopped fennel in a food processor with enough of the oil just to cover. Turn the food processor to medium speed and blend for a minute. Turn the speed to high and continue to blend for 2 minutes.

Pass the finished oil through a fine strainer or a clean dish towel. Store the oil in the refrigerator or freeze. Use as required.

Chocolate and Marron Glacé Tart

Marrons glacés and chestnuts preserved in a sweet syrup, are a must at Christmas. Even if you haven't stuffed chestnuts inside your turkey, try the sugared ones in this quick and simple dessert. This is one of those desserts that gets a little better after a day in the refrigerator.

SERVES 8

generous ¼ cup dark rum

2 oz (55 g) superfine sugar

7 oz (200 g) marrons glacés, chopped

14 oz (400 g) good-quality chocolate cake

13 oz (375 g) good dark chocolate, broken into pieces

2½ cups heavy cream

good cocoa powder

scant ½ cup heavy cream, semi-whipped

Heat the rum and 2fl oz (50 ml) of water in a pan with the sugar. When hot, remove the pan from the heat. Allow to cool, then add the chopped marrons glacés.

Slice the chocolate cake and use it to line the base of a 10 inch (25 cm) flan tin. Scatter an even layer of the rum and marron glacés mixture over the top, using up all the mixture.

Melt the chocolate in a bowl over a pan of hot water. Allow to cool slightly before adding the cream. The mixture should go smooth and glossy. Spoon this over the surface of the marrons and cake.

Place the tart in the fridge to set for a few hours or overnight before serving.

Dust with cocoa powder, then serve sliced with a drizzle of cream or a spoonful of the semi-whipped cream on the side.

Bitter Chocolate Tart

You need the best chocolate for pastries, but don't listen to chefs who tell you to use over 70 percent cocoa solids. The maximum you need is 70 percent, otherwise you can't eat the stuff. Serve this tart warm and never refrigerate it once cooked. To make it even more special, make a chocolate pastry shell: substitute 1/4 cup of the flour with cocoa powder.

SERVES 6–8

7 oz (200 g) bittersweet dark chocolate, 70 percent cocoa solids (no more)

3 1/2 oz (100g) milk chocolate

2 large free-range eggs, plus 2 large free-range egg yolks, at room temperature

1/3 cup superfine sugar

scant 3/4 cup unsalted butter, melted

9-inch (23-cm) plain or chocolate Sweet Shortcrust Pastry pie shell (*see* page 245)

confectioners' sugar

COFFEE BEAN SYRUP

2 tbsp liquid glucose

10 fresh coffee beans, crushed

1 cup superfine sugar

juice of 1/2 lemon

Preheat the oven to 425°F/220°C.

Break the two chocolates into pieces, and melt together in a heatproof bowl over a pan of gently simmering water.

Place the eggs, egg yolks, and sugar in a bowl and using an electric mixer, whisk at high speed until very thick. Carefully stir in the melted chocolate, being careful not to knock too much air out of the eggs. Fold in the melted butter, again very carefully.

Place the prepared and prebaked pie shell on a baking sheet, pour the chocolate mixture into the pie shell, and bake for 7–8 minutes, or until just set—do not let the edges soufflé up. Remove from the oven and let cool on a wire rack.

Meanwhile, make the coffee bean syrup. Place 1 cup of cold water, the glucose, coffee beans, and sugar in a pan and bring to a boil. Remove from the heat, cover, and let cool. Finally, add lemon juice to taste to the cooled syrup, then strain to remove the coffee beans.

Eat the tart at room temperature, cut into wedges, dusted heavily with confectioners' sugar, accompanied by the coffee syrup.

Quick Chocolate Tart

As you can see by the number of chocolate tarts I've included in this book, it's one of my favorite things to eat! This one is quick to prepare, but looks and tastes no less special because of that.

SERVES 6–8

PASTRY

generous 1 cup unsalted butter, softened, plus extra for greasing

1/3 cup confectioners' sugar

1 medium free-range egg

3 1/2 cups all-purpose flour, sifted

CHOCOLATE FILLING

1 1/2 cups heavy cream

2/3 cup whole milk

14 oz (400 g) dark chocolate (70 percent cocoa solids), broken into pieces

3 medium free-range eggs, beaten

Preheat the oven to 350°F/180°C. Place a baking sheet on the middle shelf in the oven.

Cream the butter and sugar in a food processor, or in a bowl with a wooden spoon, until pale and fluffy, then add the egg. Turn the food processor to its lowest setting and add the flour. Mix until the dough comes together. Wrap in plastic wrap and chill for at least 30 minutes.

Grease an 8-inch (20-cm) tart pan or loose-bottom tart pan. Roll out the pastry into a circle 1/8 inch (3 mm) thick and about 2 inches (5 cm) bigger than the tart pan. Line the tart pan with the dough, pressing it down gently and leaving a 1 inch (2.5 cm) overhang.

Prick the bottom with a fork, line with foil, and fill with dried beans. Bake for 20 minutes, or until starting to brown. Remove and trim the overhanging pastry level with the top of the ring, using a sharp, heavy knife. Remove the foil and beans.

Turn the oven down to 250°F/120°C. To make the filling, in a saucepan heat the cream and milk until trembling, just under boiling point. Take off the heat. Add the chocolate to the cream and milk and stir until fully blended, then add the beaten eggs and mix again.

Pour the chocolate mixture into the pie shell and bake for about 1 hour. The tart is done when it is still a bit wobbly in the middle. Let set for at least 45 minutes before serving.

I know you're going to look at this mincemeat recipe with horror because of the raw meat I've used in it. But this is the traditional way of making mincemeat. Most prepared mincemeat doesn't have meat in it, but I thought it would be interesting to explore. You can easily omit the steak if you want to. The recipe makes far more than you need for the pies, so perhaps use some in the Real Christmas Bread on page 365.

Traditional Mince Pies

MAKES 24

9-inch (23-cm) Sweet Shortcrust Pastry pie shell (*see* page 245)

butter and flour, for greasing and dusting

milk and confectioners' sugar, for finishing

TRADITIONAL MINCEMEAT

1 1/3 cups seedless raisins

2 cups currants

6 oz (175 g) ground sirloin steak

1 3/4 cups shredded beef suet

generous 1 cup dark brown sugar

3-4 tbsp each candied citron, lemon and orange peel

1/4 small nutmeg, grated

finely grated zest and juice of 1/2 lemon

12 oz (350 g) peeled and cored apples, finely chopped

generous 1/4 cup brandy

Make the mincemeat at least two weeks in advance of making the mince pies. Mix all the ingredients together in the order given, pouring in the brandy when everything else is well mixed together. Press closely into sterilized jars to exclude the air (*see* page 368 for sterilizing instructions). Cover and let stand for at least two weeks. You'll need about 1 pound (450 g) for the mince pies.

Grease two 12-hole muffin pans. Have ready a 3 inch (7.5 cm) pastry cutter and a 2 1/2 inch (6 cm) pastry cutter, either plain or fluted. Preheat the oven to 400°F/200°C.

Roll out just over half of the pastry on a lightly floured board to about 1/8 inch (3 mm) thick. Cut out 24 larger circles, gathering up the scraps and re-rolling if necessary. Cut the remaining pastry into 24 circles, using the smaller cutter.

Line the muffin pans with the larger circles, and then fill, not all the way to the top, with the mincemeat. Dampen the edges of the pastry with water, and press on the smaller circles. Crimp to seal, and make a couple of holes in the top with scissors. Brush with milk.

Bake near the top of the oven for 25–30 minutes, until golden brown. Cool on a wire rack, and dust the tops with confectioners' sugar.

Chocolate Profiteroles

Chocolate eclairs and cream puffs were my downfall, causing me to get to nearly 280 pounds while I was working as a pastry chef in a hotel. I used to eat about 20 of them before 11 in the morning. What a pig I was!

MAKES ABOUT 40

CHOUX PASTRY

scant 1 cup cold water

4 tsp superfine sugar

6 tbsp unsalted butter

generous 3/4 cup all-purpose flour

a pinch of salt

4 medium free-range eggs, beaten

vegetable oil, for greasing

CREAM FILLING

2 1/2 cups heavy cream

CHOCOLATE SAUCE

6 oz (175 g) good-quality dark chocolate, broken into pieces

5 tbsp water

1 tbsp unsalted butter

Preheat the oven to 400°F/200°C. To make the choux pastry, place the water, sugar, and butter in a large saucepan. Place over a low heat to melt the butter. Increase the heat and add the flour and salt all at once. Remove from the heat and quickly beat the mixture vigorously with a wooden spoon until a smooth paste is formed, stirring continuously to dry out the paste. Once the paste curls away from the side of the pan, transfer the mixture to a large bowl and let cool for 10–15 minutes.

Beat in the eggs, a little at a time, until the paste is smooth and glossy. Continue adding the eggs until you have a soft dropping consistency. It may not be necessary to add all the eggs. The mixture will be shiny and smooth, and will fall from a spoon if it is given a sharp jerk.

Lightly oil a large baking sheet. Dip a teaspoon into some warm water and spoon out 1 teaspoon of the profiterole pastry. Rub the top of the mixture with a wet finger and spoon onto the baking sheet. This ensures a crisper topping. Cover the whole of the sheet with dollops of pastry, working as swiftly as you can. Place the sheet in the oven and, before closing the door, throw a little water into the bottom of the oven. Shut the door quickly. This will make more steam in the oven and make the choux pastry rise better. (Top pastry chef tip there!)

Bake for 25–30 minutes, until golden brown. Remove from the oven and prick the bottom of each puff. Place onto the baking sheet with the hole facing upwards and return to the oven for 5 minutes. The warm air from the oven helps to dry the middle of the puffs.

To prepare the filling, lightly whip the cream until soft peaks form. Do not overwhip. When the puffs are cold, use a piping bag with a plain nozzle to pipe the cream into the holes of the puffs.

To make the sauce, melt the chocolate with the water and butter in a bowl over a pan of boiling water. Stir without boiling until smooth and shiny. Arrange the puffs on a dish and pour over the hot sauce. Eat hot or cold.

Baby Coffee Eclairs
This is the kind of party food that always impresses: delicious éclairs packed with thick pastry cream.

MAKES ABOUT
40–50 ECLAIRS

butter, for greasing

1 quantity choux pastry (*see* opposite)

1 free-range egg, beaten

COFFEE PASTRY CREAM

1¼ cups whole milk

2 tbsp freshly ground coffee

4 large free-range egg yolks

⅓ cup unrefined superfine sugar

scant ½ cup all-purpose white flour, sifted

1¼ cups heavy cream, lightly whipped

ICING

5 tsp instant coffee

3 tbsp boiling water

about 2 cups confectioners' sugar

Preheat the oven to 425°F/220°C. Lightly grease two baking sheets. Spoon the choux pastry into a large piping bag fitted with a ⅝ inch (1.5 cm) nozzle. Pipe the pastry on the baking sheets into 1¾-inch (4-cm) long éclairs. Brush with beaten egg and refine the shape at the same time. Bake for 15–20 minutes, or until well risen and golden.

Once the éclairs are fully formed and golden, turn the oven down to 325°F/160°C and cook the éclairs for another 5–10 minutes to dry them out until they are very crisp. The crisper they are, the easier they are to pipe and ice. Remove from the oven and cool completely—don't store them in an airtight container because this makes the pastry soggy.

Meanwhile, make the coffee pastry cream: bring the milk and ground coffee to a boil in a pan, stirring all the time. Remove from the heat and let stand for 10 minutes.

Meanwhile, whisk the egg yolks and sugar together. Add the flour and mix well. Strain the milk and coffee mixture through a fine strainer onto the egg-and-sugar mixture and stir well. Return to the pan and bring to a boil slowly, stirring all the time in a figure-eight so it doesn't catch. Once boiling, remove from the heat and pour into a clean bowl. Cover with plastic wrap and let cool.

Whisk the cooled coffee pastry cream to loosen and break it down, then add the whipped cream and whisk together. Spoon into a piping bag fitted with a ¼ inch (5 mm) nozzle. Using a little knife, make small incisions in the bottom of each éclair large enough to fit the nozzle. Pipe the coffee cream into the éclairs one by one, until they feel heavy and full.

For the icing, mix together the instant coffee and boiling water, then gradually add enough confectioners' icing sugar to make an icing of coating consistency. Dip the éclairs into the icing one at a time and smooth off with your finger. Let set for 15 minutes and then serve piled high.

Choux Pastry
Don't be put off making choux pastry by rumors of it being difficult. It's not that hard—honest—and well worth it!

1/2 cup unsalted butter, cubed

a pinch of sugar

a pinch of salt

1 cup all-purpose white flour, sifted

3–4 free-range eggs, beaten

Bring the butter and 1 1/4 cups of cold water to a boil in a pan. Add the sugar and salt, and then immediately add the flour and beat well until the mixture comes away from the pan. Let cool completely (more egg is absorbed when the mixture is cold).

Gradually add 3 of the beaten eggs to the cooled dough, a little at a time (it's best to do this in a food processor) and then beat small amounts of the last egg into the mixture until you get the right consistency. The reason for only adding 3 eggs at the start is that the mixture needs to be tight; if you add too much egg, the end product will not rise correctly and, of course, you can always add the extra egg but you can't take it out. The finished paste should just fall off the paddle on the machine. It's best to use choux dough straight away, but it will keep for a couple of days in the refrigerator.

Puff Pastry Hearts
This is such a simple idea, using prepared puff pastry. Don't refrigerate the pastry once cooked because it will become too hard. Glazing it in this way with confectioners' sugar requires a very hot oven.

MAKES 15–20 HEARTS

10 1/2 oz (300 g) prepared puff pastry

all-purpose flour, for dusting

1/2 cup superfine sugar

1 tbsp ground cinnamon

2/3 cup heavy cream

1/4 cup raspberry or strawberry jam

If necessary, roll out the pastry on a floured work surface until it is about 1/4 inch (5 mm) thick. You should have a rectangle of about 12 x 8 inches (30 x 20) cm.

Mix the superfine sugar and cinnamon together in a bowl. Brush the pastry with some water, then sprinkle some of the spiced sugar liberally over the top. Fold each long side over to meet in the middle.

Brush the top with water again, then sprinkle again with some of the spiced sugar, then repeat the above, folding the long sides over to meet in the middle. Brush with water and sprinkle with the sugar again, and fold over. You should have eight layers. Place in the refrigerator to chill.

Meanwhile, preheat the oven to 400°F/200°C. Using a sharp knife, cut the pastry into strips about 1/4 inch (5 mm) wide and place on a baking sheet with the cut-side up. Bake for 10–15 minutes to open to a heart shape and give a golden brown color. Remove the hearts from the oven and let cool completely.

While cooling, whip up the heavy cream until stiff, and place in a piping bag with a plain or starred nozzle. Take one of the pastries and add a spoon of the jam in the middle. Pipe the heavy cream on top. Add another piece of pastry on top—at a slant so you can see the filling inside—and serve.

Jam or Marmalade Roly Poly
This dessert was often served at school. But this recipe is good enough to serve at a dinner party, and everyone will love it. Let's face it, what could be better?

SERVES 4–6

1²/₃ cups self-raising flour

1 tsp baking powder

a pinch of salt

finely grated zest of 1 lemon or orange

³/₄ cup shredded vegetarian or beef suet

1/₃–²/₃ cup milk, plus extra for brushing

1/₂ cup orange marmalade or raspberry jam

Sift together the flour, baking powder, and salt into a bowl. Add the lemon or orange zest, and suet, and rub the mixture gently with your fingertips until it resembles bread crumbs. Add the milk a little at a time, and squeeze with your hands until a soft texture is formed. Wrap in plastic wrap and let rest in the refrigerator for 20–30 minutes.

Roll the dough into a rectangle approximately 14 x 10inches (35 x 25 cm). Spread the marmalade or jam on the dough, leaving a border of 1/2 inch (1 cm) clear. Brush the border with extra milk or water.

Roll the dough from the shorter edge and pinch at either end to retain all of the marmalade or jam. Wrap the roly poly loosely in wax paper, followed by loose foil, and tie with string at either end.

Steam the dessert in a steamer for 2 hours, filling up with hot water, if necessary, during cooking. Once cooked, unwrap, slice, and serve (it's great with custard or ice cream).

Apple Fritters
Whichever way you do fritters, they are always a winner.

SERVES 6

6 large firm eating apples

superfine sugar, to taste

a good dash of brandy

vegetable oil, for deep-frying

vanilla ice cream, to serve

BATTER

generous ³/₄ cup all-purpose flour

1 free-range egg plus 1 free-range egg yolk

1 tbsp oil or clarified butter

up to 1¹/₄ cups milk

a pinch of saffron strands (optional)

Peel, core, and slice the apples thickly. Put them into a dish, sprinkle with sugar, and pour on the brandy. Let stand to one side for an hour or so, turning occasionally in the liquid.

Meanwhile, for the batter, mix the flour, egg, egg yolk and oil or clarified butter. Beat in about half the milk. Pour 3 tablespoons of almost boiling water over the saffron, if using, and let steep for a little while. When the water is a good crocus yellow, strain it into the batter. Add more milk if the batter is too thick.

Drain the apple slices well and coat them with the batter. Heat the vegetable oil in a deep-fryer to 350ºF/180ºC. Dip the coated apple slices into the batter, and fry them in hot oil until golden brown. Drain on paper towels and serve sprinkled with sugar, with a scoop of vanilla ice cream.

fruit puds

This can also be made as individual trifles. Use four medium ramekins, and just make the trifles in miniature, cutting the Swiss roll slices smaller, if necessary.

White Chocolate and Raspberry Trifle

SERVES 4

6 oz (175 g) white chocolate

2 medium free-range egg yolks

2 tbsp superfine sugar

1¹/₄ cups milk

2³/₄ cups heavy cream

8 slices Swiss roll (bought or homemade), 1¹/₂ inches (4 cm) thick

2 tbsp Kirsch

1 lb 5 oz (600 g) raspberries

4 fresh mint sprigs

Put a 2 oz (55 g) piece of white chocolate in the refrigerator—this will make it easier to grate later. Break the remainder into small pieces.

Cream the egg yolks and superfine sugar together in a large bowl. Whisk for about 2–3 minutes, until the mixture is pale, thick, and creamy and leaves a trail.

Pour the milk and 1 ¹/₂ cups of the cream into a small, heavy saucepan and bring to a boil. Pour this onto the egg mixture, whisking all the time, then pour it back into the pan and place over a moderate heat. Stir the mixture with a wooden spoon until it starts to thicken and coats the back of the spoon. Add the broken-up pieces of chocolate and stir in until completely incorporated. Remove the pan from the heat and let cool slightly. Cover the custard with plastic wrap to stop a skin from forming.

Place half the Swiss roll slices in a large glass bowl and sprinkle with half the Kirsch. Scatter over one-third of the raspberries, then repeat. Pour the white chocolate custard over the top and let set in the refrigerator.

To serve, whip the remaining heavy cream. Top the custard with the whipped cream, scatter over the remaining raspberries, grate over the chilled white chocolate, and place the mint sprigs on top.

Sherry Trifle with Raspberries

Trifles are ancient—they go back to medieval times. Some contained gelatin and some used syllabub as a topping instead of cream. You can also use ladyfingers or macaroons instead of the sponge cake.

SERVES 6

1/4 cup raspberry jam

8 oz (225 g) plain sponge cake, sliced

2/3 cup sherry

7 oz (200 g) fresh raspberries

Custard made with 2 1/2 cups milk (double the quantity on page 246)

finely grated zest of 2 oranges

1 3/4 cups heavy cream

2 tbsp slivered almonds, toasted

Spread the jam over the slices of sponge cake and place in the bottom of a large glass dish, or divide evenly among six glasses or glass dishes.

Pour the sherry over the cake and sprinkle the fresh raspberries evenly over the top.

When you have made the custard, pass it through a strainer, add the orange zest, and let cool. Pour over the sponge and fruit.

Whip the heavy cream and either pipe it over the top of the trifle or, if you are like my mother, whose piping bag is collecting dust at the back of a drawer in the kitchen, spread it on and spike it with a fork.

Cover and refrigerate overnight, and sprinkle with the toasted slivered almonds just before serving.

Raspberry Pavlova

Named after a ballerina, this is a national dish in both New Zealand and Australia, but we love it here as our own. I have made the pavlova in a slightly different way, in what is called boiled or Italian meringue; I think this is the best way to make a pavlova. My top tip with a pavlova is to fill it full of seasonal fruit.

SERVES 4

generous 1/3 cup superfine sugar

5 free-range egg whites

TO SERVE

3 1/2 oz (100 g) white chocolate, melted

generous 1 cup heavy cream, whipped

12 oz (350 g) fresh raspberries

confectioners' sugar, for dusting

4 mint sprigs, to garnish

Preheat the oven to 250°F/120°C, and cover a large baking sheet with nonstick parchment paper. In a pan, boil a scant 1/2 cup of water and the sugar to the soft ball stage (239°F/115°C). Remove from the heat.

Whisk up the egg whites in a food mixer bowl, and pour in the liquid sugar while still beating. Keep on beating until the mixture is cool. Spoon the mixture onto the baking sheet, and spread it out into four circles. Using a spoon, mold the centers into a pavlova shape, with an indentation. Place the baking sheet in the oven and cook for 3–4 hours, or overnight.

Remove from the oven, cool, then arrange on a plate. Spread the melted white chocolate across the top of each meringue (this will stop the cream from softening it). Let it set.

Fill the indentation with heavy cream, top with raspberries, a little dusting of confectioners' sugar, and a sprig of mint and serve.

Eton Mess

A dessert that is said to originate at Eton College in England, and which is a mixture of fruit, cream, and crushed meringue. My variation contains a little balsamic vinegar to boost the flavor of the fruit. It's an economical dish, particularly if you get the meringues from discount shelves at a supermarket—where they come already crushed—and strawberries that are marked down in price because they are nearly past their best.

SERVES 4

1 lb 2 oz (500g) strawberries

1 3/4 cups heavy cream

3 meringue nests, 3 inches (7.5 cm), crushed into small chunks

1 tbsp balsamic vinegar

Grand Marnier (optional)

Hull the strawberries (remove the green tops) and puree half in a blender. Chop the other half into small dice.

Whip the heavy cream until stiff, and fold in the strawberry purée and crushed meringue. Mix the chopped strawberries in the vinegar and fold them in as well. Stir in a tablespoon or so of Grand Marnier to add a little orangey spice, if you like.

Divide between cold wine glasses and serve, or keep in the refrigerator until needed (but for no longer than a couple of hours).

Strawberry and Vanilla Soft Iced Terrine

This is based on a *semifreddo*. You can use most soft berries that are in season, and nougat or meringue added to the mixture is also really nice. A simple, great-tasting dessert that you can make, keep in the freezer and take a slice of whenever you fancy.

SERVES 4–6

4 free-range eggs, separated

4 tbsp superfine sugar

1 vanilla bean, split

14 oz (400 g) mascarpone cheese

7 oz (200 g) strawberries, diced

olive oil

STRAWBERRY SAUCE

10 1/2 oz (300 g) strawberries, diced

1/4 cup water

2 tbsp confectioners' sugar

STRAWBERRY COMPOTE

4 oz (115 g) strawberries, diced

1/4 cup strawberry sauce (*see* above)

4 fresh mint leaves, finely chopped

TO GARNISH

2 tbsp superfine sugar

1 tsp ground cinnamon

4 small doughnuts (the mini supermarket ones are fine)

4 sprigs fresh mint

Put the egg yolks in one bowl, and the whites in another. Add the sugar to the egg yolks, along with the seeds from the vanilla bean, and whisk until very light and frothy. Add the mascarpone and keep mixing.

Whip up the egg whites to stiff peaks, then fold them into the mascarpone mixture carefully, along with the strawberries.

Grease an 8 x 4 x 2 inch (20 x 10 x 5 cm) loaf pan with olive oil, then line with plastic wrap. Pour the mixture into the mold, and freeze until set, overnight if possible.

For the strawberry sauce, blend all the ingredients together, then pass them through a strainer. For the strawberry compote, mix all the ingredients together.

Mix the superfine sugar and cinnamon together in a bowl, and add the doughnuts one at a time to coat them.

Tip the iced terrine from the pan and slice. Place a slice on each plate, with a doughnut alongside. Put a little strawberry compote in the doughnut hole, garnish with a sprig of fresh mint and pour around some of the remaining strawberry sauce.

Summer Fruit Pudding

This is another classic British dessert, but most people are put off making it as they think it needs to be kept in the refrigerator for two weeks. This alternative recipe is a tribute to my mother. It can be eaten immediately.

SERVES 4–6

8 oz (225 g) each of strawberries (hulled), blackberries, and red currants

14 oz (400 g) mixed frozen fruit, defrosted

approx. ²/₃ cup superfine sugar

vegetable oil, for greasing

15 slices white bread

Quarter half of the fresh strawberries and add to three-quarters of the frozen fruit. Add 1/4 cup of the superfine sugar. Place the rest of the frozen fruit in the blender and puree for the sauce. Add more sugar to taste.

Line four to six small molds with a little oil and then with plastic wrap. Remove the crusts from the bread. Cut a bread circle for the base, slices for the sides, and a circle for the top, dipping the bread in the fruit puree sauce on one side before placing it, puree-side out, in the mold.

Fill the center with the strawberry mixture, blackberries, and red currants, and press well. Top with bread. Remove each pudding from the mold and place on a plate. Remove the plastic wrap. Spoon over the fruit puree sauce and garnish with the remaining strawberries.

Spun Sugar

Sugar work was probably my trademark on the British television program *Ready Steady Cook*. It looks really impressive.

SERVES 4–6

1 cup superfine sugar

In a very clean pan, heat the sugar until it turns a deep brown and becomes a caramel. Cool slightly.

Using a clean small metal spoon and a knife-sharpening steel, dip the spoon into the caramel and lift it out again. Move backward and forward over the steel until a cotton-candylike texture is achieved.

Place the spun sugar on top of the dessert you want to decorate in a tall pile.

Gooseberry Fool

In my yard these are one of the first fruits of the spring, but the British seem to be the only people to embrace this fantastic fruit. Other than with mackerel, I feel the gooseberry should just be used for puddings alone. It is good in a pie and in a fool, a traditional British dessert of fruit and cream.

SERVES 6–8

4 tbsp butter

1 lb 2 oz (500g) young green gooseberries, topped and tailed

superfine sugar, to taste

1¼ cups heavy cream, or half-and-half

juice and finely grated zest of 1 orange

Melt the butter in a large pan, add the gooseberries, cover, and let cook gently for about 5 minutes. When the fruit looks yellow and softened, remove the pan from the heat and crush the fruit with a wooden spoon, then a fork. Do not try to produce too smooth a puree by straining or liquidizing the gooseberries; they should be more of a mash. Sweeten with sugar to taste. Let cool.

Whip the cream until you have half-whipped but soft peaks, and fold in the cooled fruit, orange juice, and most of the zest. Taste and add more sugar if necessary, but do not make the fool too sweet.

Serve lightly chilled, sprinkled with the remaining orange zest, and accompanied by almond cookies or shortbread.

Rhubarb Fool with Toasted Oatmeal

Yorkshire is fabulous for a lot of foodie things, but in the area of Bradford, Leeds, and Wakefield the most famous ingredient is rhubarb. These three cities form the area of the "Rhubarb Triangle", which is where the best rhubarb in England, and indeed the world, comes from.

SERVES 4

1 lb 2 oz (500 g) forced rhubarb

4 tbsp superfine sugar

3 free-range egg whites

generous 1 cup heavy cream

juice and finely grated zest of 2 oranges

TO SERVE

⅔ cup toasted cracked oats

4 strawberries, hulled

4 sprigs fresh mint

Preheat the oven to 400°F/200°C. First, wash and cut the stems of rhubarb into 2-inch (5-cm) pieces. Place in an ovenproof dish and sprinkle with the sugar and 4 tablespoons of water. Bake for about 20 minutes, until soft. Remove from the oven and let cool.

Meanwhile, whip up the egg whites and cream—separately—to soft peaks. Fold the rhubarb into the cream, together with the orange juice and zest, then fold in the whipped egg whites.

Spoon the mixture into four glasses and chill. Serve each one topped with the toasted oats, a strawberry, and a sprig of mint.

Baked Bananas with Toffee Sauce

Bananas and rosemary are like pineapple and black pepper, pears and saffron, and apples and tarragon: a weird combination, but one that is literally made in heaven.

SERVES 4

4 large bananas

4 sprigs fresh rosemary

TOFFEE SAUCE

6 tbsp butter

2^1/$_2$ cups heavy cream

scant ^{1}/$_2$ cup dark brown sugar

2 tbsp dark corn syrup

2 tbsp blackstrap molasses

TO SERVE

1 pint (475 ml) vanilla ice cream

Preheat the oven to 400°F/200°C.

Do not peel the bananas. Using a sharp knife, make a slit in the top of each banana and insert a sprig of rosemary. Place the bananas on a baking sheet and bake in the oven for about 10 minutes, until they are brown in color and soft inside.

While the bananas are cooking, put the butter, cream, sugar, corn syrup, and molasses into a pan, bring to a boil, and keep warm.

Remove the bananas from the oven and cut lengthwise, skin and all. Place on plates, pour the sauce over, and spoon the vanilla ice cream on the side!

Poached Pears with Cinnamon and Goat's Milk Sauce

The more you cook the sauce in this recipe, the better it is (it should be a dark caramel color). Cook it in a large pan because when you add the baking powder it will boil all over the place.

SERVES 4

1 vanilla bean, split in half lengthwise

1 cup superfine sugar

4 Comice pears

juice and finely grated zest of 1 lemon

1¹/2 cups good vanilla ice cream

SAUCE

2¹/2 cups goat's milk

1 cup superfine sugar

¹/4 cup dark corn syrup

1 cinnamon stick

1 tsp baking powder

Start the sauce by putting the milk, sugar, and corn syrup in a pan. Bring to the boil. Crumble the cinnamon stick into the milk and add the baking powder. Take the pan off the heat and stir well because the mix will rise quickly. Continue to whisk the mixture until it stops rising.

Place the sauce on the heat again and bring back to a boil, whisking all the time. Turn down the heat and simmer for about 45 minutes, stirring from time to time to prevent the mixture from burning. When the sauce is ready it should be a caramel color. Burned or black is no good. Strain out the cinnamon.

Meanwhile, place the vanilla bean in a pan with the sugar. Peel the pears, leaving the stalks on, and use the peeler to remove the core from the bottom of the pears. Place in the pan with the sugar and vanilla, and cover with hot water. Pour in the lemon juice and zest, and cover. Bring to a boil with the lid on. Turn down the heat and simmer for 20–30 minutes, until the pears are cooked, testing them with a knife.

Remove the pears from the pan and drain for a minute on paper towels. Using a sharp knife, fan the pears by cutting five slits in each of them. Place the pears on serving plates, pour the hot sauce over the top, and serve with vanilla ice cream.

The original *Pêche Melba* was created by the great Savoy chef, Escoffier, for Dame Nellie Melba. I have made a few changes, for a much simpler version.

Peach Melba

SERVES 2

1 small can peach halves

2 tbsp apricot coulis

2 brandy snap baskets

2 scoops vanilla ice cream

4 tbsp raspberry coulis

1/4 cup fresh raspberries

a sprig of mint

2 chocolate curls

Drain the peaches. Pour 1 tablespoon of apricot coulis onto the center of each of two plates and add a brandy snap basket to each, pressing it down to secure it in place. Top with a scoop of ice cream and a peach half.

Pour 2 tablespoons of raspberry coulis around each peach half. Garnish with fresh raspberries, mint, and a chocolate curl.

Here's a recipe borrowed from our American cousins. They will freeze well, but must be layered between sheets of wax paper or else they'll all stick together. Warm them up on a baking sheet in a low oven.

Risen Pancakes with Fresh Fruit and Maple Syrup

SERVES 8

1¼ cups self-raising flour

1 tbsp baking powder

½ cup superfine sugar

2 medium free-range eggs, beaten

scant 1¼ cups milk

unsalted butter

TO SERVE

7 oz (200 g) mixed fresh fruit (strawberries, raspberries, and blueberries)

scant ½ cup maple syrup

To make the pancakes, sift the flour into a bowl with the baking powder and superfine sugar. Add the eggs and milk and whisk together, but be careful not to overmix.

Heat a little butter in a nonstick pan, then add 2 tablespoons of batter for each pancake. Once golden brown, turn over and cook on the other side, about 2 minutes in all. Repeat, using a little more butter, until you have used all the batter.

Serve the pancakes with the fresh fruit on top. Drizzle with maple syrup.

While filming, I visited the famous "Rhubarb Triangle", which is located between Leeds, Wakefield, and Bradford. It is well worth a visit, as you can see rhubarb growing in forcing sheds. The plants grow in complete darkness for about six to eight weeks, and you can actually hear the rhubarb growing; it sounds like two rubber boots rubbing together. Harvesting is the best part: it is done, by candlelight, by hand to give the stalks their unique color and flavor. Sadly, forced rhubarb production has declined, because it is so labor-intensive and expensive. But if you see it growing and taste it, you will be a rhubarb convert for life.

Rhubarb and Ginger Crumble

SERVES 6

10 stalks young forced rhubarb

4 tbsp water

generous 1/2 cup superfine sugar

3 tbsp preserved ginger in syrup, chopped

CRUMBLE

7 tbsp butter, softened

1/2 cup raw brown sugar

11/4–11/2 cups all-purpose flour

Preheat the oven to 350°F/180°C.

Cut the rhubarb into 2-inch (5-cm) slices and place on a baking sheet. Sprinkle with the water and superfine sugar and roast for 10 minutes.

Once the rhubarb is cooked, remove it from the oven and sprinkle the ginger over it. Mix together and place in an ovenproof dish about 1 1/4 –1 1/2 inches (3–4 cm) deep.

In a separate bowl, rub the butter and flour together until the mixture resembles bread crumbs. Then mix in the raw brown sugar to make the crumble.

Sprinkle the crumble over the rhubarb and bake for 10 minutes. Remove and let cool slightly before serving with ice cream or heavy cream.

Apple Charlotte

This is a classic that never fails to impress. It has to be made with Granny Smith apples. If you don't want to use apples, try rhubarb or a mix of apples and rhubarb. You can make it in one large dish (when it would take 30–40 minutes to cook) or four small ones, as here. Chuck custard, heavy cream, or ice cream on it and dive in.

SERVES 4

2¼ lb (1 kg) Granny Smith apples

juice of 1 lemon

¾ cup unsalted butter

generous ¾ cup superfine sugar

4 tbsp smooth apricot jam

10 thin slices white bread, crusts removed

Preheat the oven to 350°F/180°C.

Peel, core, and slice the apples, place them in a bowl, and pour over the lemon juice.

In a large pan, melt 2 tablespoons of the butter, then add the sugar, apples, and any lemon juice. Put the lid on and cook over a gentle heat for about 10 minutes, stirring occasionally.

Remove the lid and cook for another 5–10 minutes, until you have a smooth sauce. Add the apricot jam and let cool.

Meanwhile, melt the remaining butter. Cut the slices of bread in half, and then cut each half into four slices to get small fingers. Dip each piece of bread into the melted butter and use to line four small dariole molds about 2½ inches (6 cm) wide. Reserve some slices, dipped in butter, for lids.

Once the molds are lined, spoon in the apple sauce and top with the remaining bread slices. Bake for 15 minutes, or until golden on top.

Remove from the oven and let cool slightly. Carefully turn out and serve immediately.

Warm Blackberries with Cheat's Brown Bread Ice Cream

When in season, blackberries are one of my favorite foods. I like them best with nothing much done to them—as here. Whole-wheat bread ice cream is traditional (well, since Victorian times), but this is the quick, "cheat's" way to make it.

SERVES 4

1 lb 2 oz (500 g) fresh blackberries

1 1/2 tbsp superfine sugar

sprigs of fresh mint

ICE CREAM

2 slices whole-wheat bread

2/3 cup vanilla ice cream

Preheat the oven to 400°F/200°C. Place the sliced bread in a blender and reduce to crumbs, then place on a baking sheet and bake for 10 minutes. Let cool and rub together in your hands to break up the larger pieces.

Heat a small pan on the stove, then add the blackberries and sugar. Sauté for about 1 minute, until the berries are warm but not too mashed. Spoon the berries into the serving bowls, top with a scoop of vanilla ice cream, then sprinkle the bread crumbs over the ice cream. Serve with a sprig of mint on top of the ice cream.

Spiced Oranges

This sweet and spicy orange accompaniment is simple to prepare and has the versatility to complement a wide range of sweet (and not sweet) dishes.

SERVES 4–6

8 oranges

scant 1/2 cup water

scant 1/2 cup superfine sugar

1 cinnamon stick

3 large pinches ground allspice

Remove the zest from four of the oranges using a swivel vegetable peeler and place in a large saucepan with the water, the sugar, and spices. Bring to a boil, then reduce the heat and simmer for 15 minutes.

Meanwhile, cut away the pith from all eight fruit. Cut between the membranes to remove the orange segments, working over a bowl to catch the juice. Add the juice to the pan. Place the orange segments in a heatproof bowl.

Strain the contents of the pan over the orange segments and let cool. When cool, transfer to the refrigerator to chill.

steamed & sponge puds

Syrup Sponge with Custard
English purists will say, "Steamed pudding in a microwave? You've got to be joking!" But try this recipe. It takes only a few minutes to cook, a few to prepare, and a few to eat.

SERVES 4

generous 1 cup all-purpose flour

1 tsp baking powder

generous 1/2 cup butter, melted

scant 1 cup superfine sugar

2 free-range eggs

finely grated zest and juice of 2 small lemons

milk

vegetable oil, for greasing

TO SERVE

4 tbsp dark corn syrup or jam

Custard (see page 246)

Sift together the flour and baking powder.

Put the butter, sugar, eggs, and flour- and- baking- powder mix into a food processor and mix.

Add the lemon juice and zest and continue to mix, adding enough milk to make a dropping consistency.

Spoon the mixture into a greased 1 quart (1 liter) ovenproof dish (suitable for the microwave). Cover and microwave on full power for 4 minutes, or until the sponge begins to shrink from the side and is springy to the touch.

Let stand for 2–3 minutes before turning out and serving with corn syrup or jam, and custard.

Spotted Dick and Custard
This should always be made with lemon and currants. The currants give it its British name, "Spotted Dick".

SERVES 4

butter, for greasing

2 1/2 cups all-purpose flour

2 tbsp baking powder

3/4 cup shredded suet

generous 1/3 cup superfine sugar

3/4 cup currants

5 tbsp milk

5 tbsp light cream

2 tbsp butter, melted

juice and finely grated zest of 2 lemons

TO SERVE

Custard (see page 246)

Butter a 1 quart (1 liter) ovenproof dish.

Place all the dry ingredients in a bowl. Separately, mix together the milk and cream. Add the melted butter to the dry ingredients and then stir in the lemon juice and zest. While stirring, slowly add enough of the milk- and- cream mixture to create a dropping consistency.

Pour the mixture into the prepared ovenproof dish, cover, and place in a colander over a pan of boiling water for about 1 hour, until cooked.

Turn the dessert out of the dish and serve it, cut into wedges, with hot custard.

Sticky Toffee Pudding with Toffee Sauce

This is the king of all puddings, and my recipe is well over a hundred years old. It's not for dieters, but forget about diets and just enjoy yourself. It can be made either in one 5 inch (13 cm) ovenproof dish or, better still, two to three small 3 inch (7.5 cm) metal dishes.

SERVES 2–3

6 tbsp butter, softened

2 tbsp all-purpose flour

scant 1 cup raw brown demerara sugar

generous 1 cup pitted dried dates

1¼ cups water

1 tbsp dark corn syrup

2 tbsp blackstrap molasses

2 free-range eggs

½ tsp vanilla extract

scant 1½ cups self-raising flour

1 tsp baking soda

TO SERVE

Toffee Sauce (*see* page 280)

vanilla ice cream

Preheat the oven to 400°F/200°C. Take 2 tablespoons of the soft butter and butter the mold(s) very well. Scatter the all-purpose flour over the buttered inside to coat it thoroughly. Discard any excess flour.

Using a food mixer with a bowl and a whisk attachment, blend the remaining butter and the raw brown sugar.

While mixing, bring the dates and water to a boil in a small pan.

Add the corn syrup, molasses, eggs, and vanilla extract to the butter mixture and carry on mixing. Then slowly add the self-raising flour on a slow setting. Once mixed together, turn off the mixer.

Puree the water and date mixture in a blender, add the baking soda, and quickly stir this, while hot, into the egg-and-butter mix.

Once combined, pour into the mold(s) and bake in the oven for 20–25 minutes, until the top is just firm to the touch.

Remove the pudding(s) from the mold(s) and place on a plate with a lot of toffee sauce on top. Vanilla ice cream is a must when eating this dish.

Sussex Pond Pudding

One of the best desserts ever, but be warned that it takes a while to make. This is not a dish ever likely to appear at a Weight Watchers' convention dinner—the amount of butter and sugar is scary! But you'll forget all about that when you pour heavy cream over it and have a spoon in your hand....

SERVES 4–6

1²/₃ cups self-raising flour

1/2 cup shredded beef suet

1/4 cup milk

scant 1 cup slightly salted butter, diced

1 cup soft light brown or superfine sugar

2 large lemons

Mix the flour and suet together in a bowl. Combine the milk with 1/4 cup of water in a pitcher. Mix enough of the wet ingredients into the dry ingredients to make a dough that is soft, but not too soft to roll. Roll this dough out into a large circle, then cut out a quarter of the circle to be used later as the lid of the pudding.

Butter a 1 1/2 quart (1.5 liter) ovenproof bowl. Drop the three-quarter circle of pastry into it and press the cut sides together to make a perfect joint.

Put 1/2 cup each of the butter and sugar into the pastry-lined dish. Prick the lemons all over so the juices can escape, then put them on to the butter and sugar. Fill the rest of the cavity with the remaining butter and sugar, adding more if you want to.

Lay the reserved pastry on top of the filling and press the edges together so the pudding is sealed in. Put a piece of foil right over the dish with a pleat in the middle. Tie it in place with string and make a string handle over the top so the pudding can be lifted out easily.

Put a large pan of water on to boil and lower the pudding in, sitting it on a trivet (or upturned saucer). The water must be boiling, and it should come halfway, or a little further, up the sides of the basin. Cover and let boil for 3–4 hours. If the water gets low, replenish it with boiling water.

To serve, remove the bowl from the pan and take off the foil lid. Put a deep dish over the bowl and quickly turn the whole thing upside down. It is a good idea to ease the pudding from the sides of the bowl with a knife first. Put on the table and serve immediately, making sure everyone gets a piece of lemon.

Make Christmas pudding at least a month in advance—ideally in August or September. Let it sit in the refrigerator or a cupboard like my grandmother used to, with an old fly net over the top to stop flies nibbling. I like to make this recipe in two 2 quart (1.5 liter) bowls rather than one large one, because I find this makes a better-tasting pudding.

Christmas Pudding

SERVES 10

2 cups golden raisins

2 cups currants

generous 3/4 cup dried figs

1 1/4 cups mixed candied peel, chopped

generous 1/2 cup chopped dried apricots

1/3 cup candied cherries, halved

2/3 cup brandy

4 oz (115 g) preserved stem ginger in syrup, chopped, plus 3 tbsp of the syrup

2 Granny Smith apples, peeled, cored and grated

juice and finely grated zest of 2 oranges

6 medium free-range eggs, beaten

1 1/4 cups shredded suet

1 3/4 cups dark brown sugar

4 1/2 cups fresh white bread crumbs

scant 1 1/2 cups self-raising flour

1 tsp ground allspice

unsalted butter, for greasing

In a large bowl, soak the golden raisins, currants, figs, peel, apricots, and cherries in the brandy, covered, overnight if possible—or for at least a few hours.

In a larger bowl, mix the ginger and syrup, apple, orange juice and zest, eggs, suet, sugar, bread crumbs, and flour. Using a wooden spoon or your hands, stir in the soaked fruit and allspice and mix well.

Butter the bowls, and divide the mixture between them. Cover with circles of wax paper with a folded pleat down the center to let the pudding expand. Tie in place with some string and make a string handle over the top so each pudding can be lifted out easily. Steam as described on page 295 for 3 hours.

Let the puddings cool before removing the paper. Cover them with plastic wrap over the top of pudding and bowl, and store in a cool, dry place if you aren't using them immediately. You can soak them with more booze in the run-up to Christmas, if you like.

To reheat, steam the puddings for 2 hours before turning out and flaming with hot brandy.

Quick Christmas Pudding with Baked Ice Cream

This is a great way of saving time on Christmas Day. The ice cream packages are better made in advance (at least the day before) and placed in the freezer. Look for Christmas puddings from a specialty supplier of British products.

SERVES 4

8 prepared filo pastry sheets

1 medium free-range egg, beaten

4 scoops bought or homemade vanilla ice cream

confectioners' sugar

4 x 115g small bought Christmas puddings

scant 1 cup brandy sauce (*see* opposite)

4 fresh mint sprigs

Preheat the oven to 425°F/220°C.

Unroll the filo and cut into 4 inch (10 cm) squares. Layer three of the squares at slight alternate angles and brush with some beaten egg.

Place a scoop of the ice cream in the center of each filo square, and bring up the sides of the pastry to stick together. Brush with beaten egg.

If cooking immediately, dust with confectioners' sugar, place on a baking sheet, and bake for about 3–4 minutes. Alternatively, place in the freezer until ready to use (much better).

Meanwhile, cook the puddings according to the package instructions and warm the brandy sauce through on the stove.

Spoon the warm sauce into the center of the plates, and place a Christmas pudding in the middle. Remove the ice cream package from the oven and place on top of the pudding.

To finish, simply dust the top with confectioners' sugar and garnish with a sprig of mint. Serve immediately.

Brandy Sauce

This is one of the few recipes I use granulated sugar in. As you can probably imagine, it was used in my grandmother's recipe (although she had to grate sugar from a large lump or chop sugar cubes). I remember her bringing this sauce back home to the farmhouse, and me fighting with my sister to remove the wax paper from the top.

SERVES 4–6

1 cup heavy cream

2³/₄ cups whole milk

¹/₄ cup cornstarch, mixed with 4 tbsp cold water

4 tbsp unrefined granulated sugar

4 tbsp unsalted butter, cubed

brandy, to taste

Bring the cream and milk to a boil together, and then stir in the cornstarch mixture. Bring back to a boil, stirring, to thicken.

Remove from the heat and stir in the sugar and butter, until dissolved. Finally, stir in brandy to taste.

Cover to stop a skin from forming, and keep warm.

cream, eggs & vanilla

Hot Chocolate Fondants

Hands up all those who love a dark and delicious hot chocolate soufflé? Almost everyone, I bet. Well, this recipe is sure to please. This is a dessert in which a rich sauce oozes from a cakelike fondant. You can cook the mixture as soon as you've finished making it, but it also freezes wonderfully and can be baked once it has thawed.

SERVES 8

8 oz (225 g) dark chocolate with at least 60 percent cocoa solids

4 tbsp heavy cream

7 tbsp unsalted butter

1/3 cup ground almonds

2 large free-range eggs, separated

1/4 cup cornstarch

scant 1/2 cup superfine sugar

Finely grate 1 1/2 oz (40 g) of the chocolate and set aside. Gently melt one-third of the remaining chocolate with the cream in a small saucepan, stirring well to mix. Remove and let cool.

Line a small plate with plastic wrap and pour on the mixture. Place in the freezer for about 8 hours until set hard, then stamp out eight small circles using a 1 1/4 inch (3 cm) round cutter. Set aside.

Melt half the butter and brush liberally all over the inside of eight small ramekins. Dust well with the grated chocolate, shaking out any excess. Set aside on a baking sheet.

Melt the remaining chocolate (including any shaken-out excess) and butter in a small heatproof bowl over a pan of barely simmering water, or in a microwave-proof bowl in the microwave on high for 2–3 minutes, stirring once. Do not overheat or the chocolate will "seize", or turn solid. Scrape this mixture into a bigger bowl, then beat in the ground almonds, egg yolks, and cornstarch.

Whisk the egg whites in a separate bowl until they form stiff but not dry peaks. Gradually beat in the superfine sugar. You may like to use a handheld electric mixer for this.

Fold this meringue mixture into the melted chocolate mixture. Spoon half the combined mixture into the bottom of the ramekins to fill them halfway, place a chocolate disk on top, then fill each ramekin with the remaining mixture. Smooth the tops of the fondants and chill in the refrigerator while you heat the oven to 350°F/180°C.

Bake the fondants in the oven for 10–15 minutes, until risen and slightly wobbly, then remove and eat as soon as possible.

Baked Chocolate Mousse

This mousse-cake contains no flour and needs to be baked and eaten fresh. As it starts to cool it will collapse, but don't worry—it still eats well, as long as you don't put it in the refrigerator.

SERVES 6–8

10 1/2 oz (300g) dark bittersweet dark chocolate, broken into pieces

generous 1/2 cup unsalted butter, diced

6 free-range eggs, separated

1/3 cup superfine sugar

heavy cream, to serve

Line the bottom and sides of a 8 inch (20 cm) loose-bottomed cake pan with wax paper, and preheat the oven to 350°F/180°C.

Melt the chocolate and butter in a metal bowl over a pan of simmering water (the bowl must not touch the water). Whisk the egg yolks with 2 tablespoons of the sugar. Stir in the melted chocolate and mix well.

Beat the egg whites with the remaining sugar until very stiff. Quickly stir one-third of the whites into the chocolate mix, then gently fold in the remainder and pour the mix into the prepared cake pan. Place on the middle shelf of the oven and bake for 20 minutes.

Remove from the oven and let cool slightly, before serving with the heavy cream poured over.

Cranachan

I bet that no more than a few weeks after this book's out some Scot will come up to me to say this recipe is all wrong. It's great, but then how could it not be? Cream, whiskey and raspberries—it's one of the few cold desserts I know that will warm your cockles on a winter's day.

SERVES 8

1 cup oats

3 tbsp whiskey

600ml (1 pint) heavy cream

scant 1/2 cup superfine sugar

1 lb (450 g) raspberries

Put the oatmeal on a baking sheet and toast briefly under the broiler, being careful not to burn it. Remove and, while still warm, sprinkle over the whiskey and let stand for 10 minutes.

While the oatmeal is absorbing the whiskey, whip the heavy cream, adding the sugar as it starts to hold, and continue to whisk until it forms soft peaks. Be careful not to take it too far, or the cream will split.

Fold the oatmeal into the cream and spoon the mixture into some large wine glasses.

Divide the raspberries between the glasses, sitting them on top of the cream. Chill for 30 minutes to firm up before serving.

Angel Delight, blancmange, strawberry and orange jello and chocolate mousse—all great foods British kids love to eat. I remember the blancmange my grandmother used to make. It was bright pink and was made in old gelatin molds. I'm not giving you the recipe for that, as the best is out of a package. Another great treat, of course, was chocolate mousse. This, I suppose, is the grown-up version.

Chocolate Mousse

SERVES 6

7 oz (200 g) dark chocolate (70 percent cocoa solids), broken into pieces

1/2 cup warm water

3 large free-range eggs, separated

3 tbsp golden superfine sugar

TO SERVE

a little whipped cream

Place the broken-up chocolate and warm water in a large, heatproof bowl and sit it over a pan of barely simmering water, making sure the bowl doesn't touch the water.

Keep the heat at its lowest setting and let the chocolate melt slowly— it should take about 6 minutes.

Remove it from the heat and stir thoroughly until the chocolate is smooth and glossy. Let the mixture cool before adding the egg yolks. Mix them in thoroughly with a wooden spoon.

In a clean bowl, whisk the egg whites to the soft-peak stage. Whisk in the sugar gradually, then continue whisking until the whites are glossy. Using a metal spoon, fold the egg whites into the chocolate mixture. Be careful to avoid knocking the air out of the egg whites.

Divide the mousse between six ramekins or glasses and chill for at least 2 hours. Serve with a dollop of whipped cream on top.

Bananas and Custard Soufflé

Bananas and custard was the best dessert ever when I was growing up, but when you reach a certain age you never seem to eat it again, apart from when you're ill. I've played around here with a real British classic. It's a great dish to serve at a dinner party, or just for a cosy dinner for two.

SERVES 2

3¹/2 tbsp butter

3 tbsp superfine sugar

4 free-range egg whites

finely grated zest of 2 oranges

8 tbsp fresh custard
(*see* page 246)

3 medium bananas

TO SERVE
¹/2 cup vanilla ice cream
(optional)

Preheat the oven to 350°F/180°C.

Rub two ramekin dishes with half the butter and sprinkle with 1 tablespoon of the sugar. Whisk the egg whites and, when they are stiff, beat in another tablespoon of the sugar.

Mix the orange zest into the custard and then gently fold in the whisked egg whites. Spoon the mixture into the prepared ramekins and place on an baking sheet. Bake for 15–20 minutes.

While the soufflés are cooking, peel the bananas and cut in half lengthwise.

Heat up a wide, nonstick pan and add the remaining butter. When it's nut-brown, add the remaining sugar and the halved bananas. Fry them on both sides, being careful not to break them, to give them a nice golden color.

To serve, place the warm bananas on the plate, serve the soufflé on the side, and, if you dare, a dollop of vanilla ice cream on the side, too!

Baked Cheesecake

Americans have mastered the art of making cheesecakes, but they started in Britain and were taken across the Atlantic. This is a great recipe, light in texture and delicious served with caramelized bananas.

SERVES 6

a little butter, for greasing

10 inch (25 cm) prepared sponge flan shell

1 cup superfine sugar

finely grated zest of 3 lemons

4 tbsp cornstarch

3 tbsp golden raisins, soaked in a little bourbon

1 lb 14 oz (850 g) soft cream cheese

3 medium free-range eggs

1 vanilla bean

¼ cup Jack Daniels or bourbon, to taste (optional)

generous 1¼ cups heavy cream

TO SERVE

10 small bananas

2 tbsp butter

2 tbsp superfine sugar

caramel sauce or maple syrup

Preheat the oven to 350°F/180°C.

Butter a 10 inch (25 cm) loose-bottom cake pan. Cut the sponge horizontally into two disks. Use one to line the buttered cake pan (I'd suggest using the other to line a trifle).

In a bowl, mix together the sugar, lemon zest, cornstarch, and raisins using a wooden spoon, then beat in the cream cheese. Add the eggs, one by one, beating constantly until all of them are well incorporated.

Slice open the vanilla pod, remove the seeds with a sharp knife, and place them in the cream cheese mixture. Add the Jack Daniels or bourbon, if using, and mix everything together well. Add the cream and beat well until the mixture is smooth. Pour gently over the sponge base in the cake pan.

Sit the pan in a baking sheet filled with ⅛ inch (2–3 mm) of warm water to help create steam during cooking. Bake for 50 minutes, until the top is golden. Remove from the oven and let cool and set completely before removing from the pan.

Just before serving, peel the bananas and fry in the butter and sugar until brown and slightly caramelized.

Serve the cheesecake cut into wedges, with the bananas and a drizzle of caramel sauce or maple syrup.

How can I describe this dish? Well, it's like a custard tart and lemon meringue pie rolled into one. I remember my aunt used to make it, along with stuff like pink blancmange, jam tarts—oh, and Dripping Cake (*see page 342*). They all tasted good then, and they taste even better now, because they bring back so many memories.

Queen of Puddings

SERVES 6–8

generous 1 cup milk

generous 1 cup double cream

1 vanilla bean, split

1/2 cup superfine sugar

6 medium free-range egg yolks

2 1/2 cups fresh bread crumbs

finely grated zest of 2 lemons

generous 1/2 cup raspberry jam

MERINGUE

4 medium free-range egg whites

generous 1/2 cup superfine sugar

1 tbsp confectioners' sugar

To make the custard, pour the milk and cream into a pan and add the split vanilla pod. Bring to a boil over a medium heat.

In a bowl, whisk the sugar into the egg yolks until it is well dissolved and the mixture is light and creamy. Slowly pour in the hot milk and cream, whisking all the time. Remove the vanilla pod.

Mix in the bread crumbs and lemon zest, then pour into an ovenproof glass or ceramic baking dish of about 8 x 10 x 2 inch (20 x 25 x 5 cm). Let stand for 10–15 minutes.

Meanwhile, preheat the oven to 300°F/150°C, and have a roasting pan ready, filled halfway with boiling water (a bain-marie).

Place the baking dish in the bain-marie in the center of the oven and bake for 25–30 minutes, until the custard is still slightly wobbly in the center. Remove and let cool.

Turn up the oven temperature to 375°F/190°C.

For the meringue, whisk the egg whites until stiff, then whisk in the superfine sugar—apart from 1 tablespoon.

Melt the jam in a pan and spread it over the custard. Cover the pudding with the meringue mix, sprinkle with the remaining superfine sugar and the confectioners' sugar, and bake for 10–15 minutes, until the top is crisp and lightly browned. Serve immediately.

School lunch always seemed to include a milk-based dessert, such as rice pudding, tapioca, or sago, which will probably have put you off them for life. But rice pudding is great, its reputation tarnished only by a lack of thought and care put into making it over the years. Try this one, and you'll be a convert.

Baked Rice Pudding

SERVES 4

2 tbsp butter, plus extra for greasing

1/2 cup short-grain pudding rice

2 cups milk

2 cups heavy cream

1 vanilla bean, split (optional)

generous 1/3 cup superfine sugar

a little freshly grated nutmeg

Preheat the oven to 350°F/180°C.

Lightly butter an ovenproof dish about 1–1 1/2 quarts (1–1.8 liters) in capacity.

Wash the rice under cold water and drain.

Bring the milk and cream to a boil with the vanilla bean (if using) and add the rice and sugar. Stir well.

Pour into the oven dish and grate a little nutmeg over the top. Dot with pats of butter.

Bake for about 15 minutes, then lower the temperature to 300°F/150°C, and bake for another 1 1/4 hours. It should be golden brown on top and creamy underneath.

Classic Lemon Posset

Simple is always the best, and this is incredibly simple! For something extra special, serve with some crushed cookies and a dollop of lemon curd. Homemade lemon curd is best, but you can use a prepared one from a gourmet market or supermarket.

SERVES 6

2 1/2 cups heavy cream

3/4 cup superfine sugar

juice of 2 large lemons and finely grated zest of 4 large lemons

Put the heavy cream in a large pan and add the sugar. Bring this slowly to a boil, boil for 3 minutes, then let cool.

Add the lemon juice and half the lemon zest and whisk well until thickened. Pour into six large serving glasses and refrigerate for 3 hours.

Sprinkle with the remaining lemon zest before serving.

Lemon Syllabub

Not a real syllabub made with egg yolks and sugar, this was invented when I was filming *Housecall* for the television. I think it is a fantastic recipe, quick to make, and really tasty to eat.

SERVES 4–6

1/2 cup superfine sugar

juice and finely grated zest of 2 lemons

2–3 tbsp brandy

2 1/2 cups heavy cream

Whisk together the sugar, lemon juice, lemon zest, and brandy.

In another bowl, whisk the cream until thick, then slowly whisk in the lemon mixture. Pour into wine glasses and refrigerate overnight.

Serve with ratafia cookies or brandy snaps.

Lemon Verbena Crème Brûlée

I grow lemon verbena in my yard—it is so nice, even the dog likes it. You have to get some of this herb for your yard at home, beacuse its smell and flavor are different to any other herb. I use it mainly for desserts, because the flavor lends itself well to being steeped in a liquid, as in this crème brûlée.

SERVES 4–6 DEPENDING ON SIZE OF RAMEKINS

generous 1 cup milk

5 sprigs fresh lemon verbena, chopped

10 free-range egg yolks

1¼ cups superfine sugar

3 cups heavy cream

¼ cup raw brown sugar

Preheat the oven to 250°F/120°C. Heat the milk in a pan with the lemon verbena until just boiling, then remove from the heat to cool and let the flavors blend.

Place the egg yolks in a bowl, add the superfine sugar, and whisk together until combined. Add the milk and cream, and whisk well. Pass through a strainer to remove any egg shell and the lemon verbena.

Ladle the cream mixture into small ramekins, and place on a baking sheet. Bake in the oven for 1½–2 hours, until set. Remove and let cool. Either refrigerate or use immediately.

When ready to eat, sprinkle the raw brown sugar over the top and caramelize with either a blow torch or by putting under a hot broiler.

ices

Blood Orange Ice Cream

The custard base here can be used for other ice creams: add a little vanilla extract for vanilla or some other fruit flavorings. You can also add some brandy to this custard for a brandy sauce for Christmas pud.

SERVES 6

1 lb 2 oz (500 g) blood oranges, preferably unwaxed

1³/₄ cups superfine sugar

6 medium free-range egg yolks

1 cup heavy cream

2 cups whole milk

Finely grate the orange zest into a bowl, then quarter the fruits. Put the quarters into the bowl as well, and pour over 1¹/₄ cups of the superfine sugar. Refrigerate, covered, for a day or so.

Squeeze the juice from the mixture—start by using your hands, then press through a nylon strainer. Measure the juice and discard the pulp.

Make the custard for the ice cream by whisking the egg yolks and remaining sugar together until thick and pale. This should take 10 minutes in a food mixer.

Bring the cream and milk to the boil in a heavy pan, then whisk this into the eggs. Return the pan to the heat and cook gently, stirring constantly, until the custard begins to thicken. Do not let the mixture boil or it will scramble. (If you prefer, you can cook the custard in a bowl set over a pan of simmering water.) Check whether it is thick enough by coating the back of a wooden spoon with it; if, when you slide your finger through it, it leaves a trail, it is ready. Remove from the heat and cool.

Whisk the juice with 1¹/₂ times its volume of cooled custard, then churn in an ice-cream maker. Alternatively, pour the mixture into freezerproof containers and freeze halfway, then whisk again to remove the ice crystals. Return to the freezer.

Arctic Roll

I spoke to a load of chefs one day, while cooking, about food for this book. When asked what dessert they used to eat as kids, this was the one that brought back the best memories. The hardest thing was trying to replicate that frozen dessert your mother used to buy from the stores, and the best way that I have found of doing this is to use a piece of drain pipe. Yes, a piece of drain pipe! I'll say no more; just read on try.

SERVES 4–6

2 1/2 cups vanilla ice cream

about 5 1/2 oz (150 g) fresh raspberries

3–4 tbsp raspberry jam

2 tbsp chopped fresh mint

confectioners' sugar

SPONGE

butter, for greasing

3 free-range eggs

1/3 cup superfine sugar, plus extra for sprinkling

1/2 cup all-purpose flour, plus extra for dusting

Preheat the oven to 375°F/190°C. Start the sponge by lining a 12 x 8 inch (30 x 20 cm) shallow Swiss roll pan with butter and wax paper. Whisk together the eggs and superfine sugar until they reach ribbon stage, then sift in the flour and gently fold it in. Once the mixture is well blended, pour it into the pan and push it to the edges, leveling with a spatula. Bake in the preheated oven for 8–10 minutes, until golden brown. Once cooked, you should be able to test it with your finger by pressing lightly on the top; if it springs back, then it's cooked.

Remove from the oven and put onto a clean dish towel sprinkled with superfine sugar. Remove the wax paper from underneath the sponge, cover with a dampened dish towel and let cool.

For the ice cream, you need a piece of clean drain pipe, 12 inches (30 cm) long and 4 1/2 –6 inches (12–15 cm) in diameter. Place the ice cream in a bowl and fork in the raspberries, leaving a 1/2 cup for garnish. Fill the drain pipe with ice cream. Press down well, then put in the freezer.

Spread the sponge evenly all over with jam, then sprinkle over the mint. Use a hot cloth to remove the ice cream from the drain pipe, by wrapping the cloth around the outside and then pushing the ice cream out from one end. Place the ice cream on the sponge and roll the sponge around it by pulling the dish cloth toward you.

Once the sponge covers all the ice cream, trim off any excess sponge and put the roll on a plate, seam-side down, with a dusting of confectioners' sugar, the remaining raspberries, and a sprig of mint.

To serve, cut into slices. I bet you never thought you'd be able to make this one at home!

I made this while playing with my new ice-cream machine, and it works, but be careful with the sugar in the recipe. Standard recipes for ice cream say 1 cup of sugar per litre 4 cups of liquid, but sugar will act as a de-icer, and the ice cream won't freeze properly if there is too much. The same applies to alcohol, so remember to reduce the quantity if making a high-sugar or alcoholic ice cream. This ice cream is great served with seasonal fresh berries or with a toasted croissant and some hot chocolate sauce.

Orange Marmalade Ice Cream

SERVES 4–6

1 vanilla bean

generous 1 cup milk

3 cups heavy cream

generous 3/4 cup superfine sugar

10 free-range egg yolks

6 tbsp orange marmalade

Taking a sharp knife, cut the vanilla bean in half lengthwise, and scrape out and retain the seeds.

Place the milk, cream, vanilla seeds and pod, and superfine sugar in a pan, and bring to a boil.

In a separate bowl, whisk the egg yolks. When the cream mixture has boiled, pour the mixture slowly onto the eggs, whisking all the time. Pour into a clean pan and mix quickly over a gentle heat until the mixture has thickened. Pass through a strainer.

Place the mixture into an ice-cream machine and churn until the ice cream is nearly set. Add the marmalade and continue to churn. Once set, transfer the ice cream from the machine into a container, and place in the freezer.

This is a simple way of using leftover Christmas pudding. Please invest in a decent ice-cream maker that blends while the ice cream is freezing. Make sure Santa Claus comes down the chimney with one! Serve the ice cream with a large glass of brandy and some brandy snaps. Get the Christmas pudding from a supplier of British products.

Christmas Pudding Ice Cream

SERVES 4–6

3 oz (85 g) leftover Christmas pudding, chopped into small pieces

2 tbsp brandy

3/4 cup superfine sugar

1 cinnamon stick

1/2 tsp ground allspice

1 cup custard base for ice cream (*see* page 314)

2/3 cup heavy cream

Soak the Christmas pudding in the brandy.

To make the stock syrup, heat 2/3 cup of water and the sugar together in a heavy pan until the sugar has melted, then simmer to reduce to 3/4 cup. Transfer to a small pan and add the cinnamon stick and allspice. Remove from the heat and let cool and steep for 15 minutes.

Mix the custard with the cream. Strain the stock syrup to remove the cinnamon and add to the cream mixture. Mix in the Christmas pudding and brandy.

Churn in an ice-cream maker until thick and frozen, then transfer to a freezerproof container. Store in the freezer for up to a couple of weeks.

I know what you're thinking, squash in an ice cream? Sounds weird, but trust me: I won't let you down. It really is a delight!

Ginger and Butternut Squash Ice Cream

SERVES 4–6

2 cups heavy cream

2 tbsp peeled and chopped fresh ginger

4 medium free-range egg yolks

1/2 cup superfine sugar

2/3 cup cooked, cooled, and pureed butternut squash

a dash of lemon juice

Bring the cream and ginger to a boil together. Cover, remove from the heat, and let steep for 30 minutes.

Return the cream to a boil. Whisk together the egg yolks and sugar in a pitcher and pour in some of the hot cream mixture. Mix quickly, then pour into the cream mixture left in the pan. Continue cooking over a gentle heat for 3–4 minutes, or until the mixture coats the back of the spoon. Cool over ice, stirring occasionally, until cold.

Mix the cooked and cooled squash puree into the cooled custard, add lemon juice to taste, and strain through a fine strainer. Freeze in an ice-cream machine or in a freezerproof container. Keep frozen until ready to use.

Apricot Yoghurt Ice Cream

This is such a great idea. It's so quick and easy, and works with most pureed fruit. Strawberries work best after apricots, I think, because the orange juice complements their taste.

SERVES 20

1 lb 7 oz (650 g) apricot puree

3 cups confectioners' sugar

2 vanilla beans

1 tbsp Amaretto

1/4 cup liquid glucose

1/3 cup orange juice

1 1/4 cups whole yoghurt

generous 1 cup crème fraîche or sour cream

Slowly stir the apricot puree into the confectioners' sugar to form a paste.

Using a sharp knife, split the vanilla beans lengthwise and scrape the seeds out into the apricot purée. Mix in the remaining ingredients, and whisk them until smooth.

Churn in an ice-cream machine until it is just set, then place in a container in the freezer. Let defrost a little before serving.

Vanilla Ice Cream

Here's a real vanilla ice cream recipe if you want to try making it yourself.

SERVES 4–6

generous 2 cups milk

generous 2 cups heavy cream

2 vanilla beans, split

generous 1 cup superfine sugar

10 free-range egg yolks

Place the milk and cream in a saucepan and add the seeds from the vanilla beans. Slowly bring to a simmer. Meanwhile, whisk the sugar and egg yolks together in a large bowl.

Pour the hot milk and cream mixture onto the eggs, whisking all the time. Return the pan to a very low heat and keep stirring until the mixture coats the back of a wooden spoon. (A quick chef's tip: keep stirring until most of the bubbles disappear, do not boil. The bubbles disappearing is a sign that the mixture is starting to thicken.)

Freeze in an ice-cream machine or a metal container. If you use the latter, freeze for about 1 hour, then take out of the freezer and beat with a whisk to break up the ice crystals and re-freeze for at least 3 hours.

Cheat's Raspberry and Cassis Ripple Ice Cream
When serving this, hide the ice-cream cartons to make it look like you did it all yourself. It tastes fantastic!

SERVES 8

2 quarts (2 liters) vanilla ice cream, partly thawed in the refrigerator until just soft

CASSIS SAUCE

10 1/2 oz (300g) frozen raspberries

2 tbsp superfine sugar

juice and finely grated zest of 1/2 lemon

3 tbsp cassis

To make the cassis sauce, blend the raspberries, sugar, lemon juice and zest, and cassis. Pass it through a strainer to remove the raspberry seeds.

Drizzle the sauce over the ice cream and quickly marble it through, using a folding motion with a spoon.

Place the ice cream in a freezerproof container and freeze it for 3–4 hours before serving.

Instant Banana Ice Cream
This may be instant, but it is one of the most delicious ice creams around.

SERVES 4

4 bananas

1/4 tsp vanilla extract

3–4 tbsp superfine sugar, to taste

2/3 cup buttermilk

Peel the bananas, cut them into chunks, and place in a single layer on a freezerproof dish or tray, as you would if freezing raspberries, then freeze so that you have separate pieces.

Put the frozen banana chunks into the food processor. Add the vanilla extract, sugar, and half the buttermilk.

Turn on the processor and let it run for a few moments. Then, while it is still running, pour in the remaining buttermilk in a thin, steady stream. Let the machine run until the mixture is smooth and creamy. Serve at once.

cakes

I remember my aunt making this cake at Christmas. She used to eat it with a glass of Madeira, and dunk it in the glass. Then she'd down the remains, crumbs and all, with a smile on her face—whether because of the wine or the cake, I don't know, but possibly as a result of both....

Madeira Cake

MAKES A 7 INCH
(18 CM) CAKE

**3/4 cup butter, plus extra
for greasing**

generous 3/4 cup superfine sugar

3 large free-range eggs

13/4 cups self-raising flour

about 3 tbsp milk

finely grated zest of 1 lemon

**several thin pieces of candied
citron or lemon peel, to decorate**

Preheat the oven to 350°F/180°C. Grease a 9 x 5 x 3 inch (23 x 13 x 8 cm) loaf pan, line the bottom and sides with wax paper and grease the paper.

Cream the butter and sugar together in a bowl until pale and fluffy. Beat in the eggs, one at a time, beating the mixture well between each one and adding a tablespoon of the flour with the last egg to prevent the mixture from curdling.

Sift the flour and gently fold in with enough milk to create a mixture that falls reluctantly from the spoon. Fold in the lemon zest. Spoon the mixture into the prepared pan and lightly level the top. Bake on the middle shelf of the oven for 30 minutes.

Place the candied peel on top of the cake and bake for another 30 minutes, or until a warm skewer inserted into the center comes out clean. Let the cake cool in the pan for 10 minutes, then turn it out on to a wire rack and let cool completely.

This is obviously German, but it has always been very popular here. My version is the same as the classic, but with the addition of chocolate shards around the edge. I love it, but I only use canned cherries. Who wouldn't love it? Chocolate sponge, heavy cream, and cherries all piled up, with even more chocolate....

Black Forest Gâteau

SERVES 4

SPONGE

butter, for greasing

6 free-range eggs

3/4 cup superfine sugar

scant 1 cup self-raising flour

1/4 cup cocoa powder

FILLING AND TOPPING

2 lb 13 oz (1.27 kg) canned black cherries

2 tbsp cornstarch

a good dash of Kirsch

3 cups heavy cream, whipped

1/2 cup toasted slivered almonds

CHOCOLATE SHARDS

10 1/2 oz (300 g) dark chocolate, broken into pieces

Preheat the oven to 350°F/180°C. Grease and line a deep 12 inch (30 cm) round cake pan.

For the sponge, break the eggs into a mixing bowl, add the sugar, and whisk well until it reaches the ribbon stage, or is very light and fluffy. Carefully fold in the sifted flour and cocoa powder. Pour the mix into the prepared pan and bake for about 40–45 minutes, until cooked.

Turn out on to a wire rack and let cool.

For the filling, drain the cherries, reserving the juice. Put the juice into a pan and bring to a boil. Meanwhile, mix the cornstarch with a little water to make a paste. When the cherry juice is boiling, mix the cornstarch paste into it. Strain through a strainer over the cherries, also pouring through the Kirsch. Let stand to one side to cool.

Cut the sponge into three layers horizontally using a sharp knife. Sandwich the three layers together using the whipped cream, half of the cherries, and all of the almonds.

Melt the chocolate, spread onto a tray lined with plastic wrap, and place in the refrigerator to set. When the chocolate is set, break it into large shards and stick them randomly around the edge of the cake.

Pile the remaining cherries on top of the cake and serve.

Carrot and Orange Cake

Carrot cake is good eaten with slightly whipped cream. The version made in the United States is heavier and darker than this. The cake is at its best served simply.

SERVES 8

butter, for greasing

5 medium carrots, trimmed, scraped, and sliced

juice of 2 oranges

1/2 cup corn oil

4 free-range eggs, separated

13/4 cups superfine sugar

21/2 cups "00" pasta flour, or all-purpose flour

11/2 tsp baking powder

TO SERVE

scant 1 cup heavy cream

2–3 tsp Cointreau

Preheat the oven to 350°F/180°C and butter a cake pan of 12 inches (30 cm) in diameter.

Put the carrots in a pan, cover with water, and add the orange juice. Bring to a boil and cook until tender. Drain and cool, then discard the liquid. Put the carrots in a food processor with the corn oil and the egg yolks, and blend to a puree. Transfer to a bowl.

Beat the egg whites until stiff, and set aside.

In another bowl, mix the sugar, flour, and baking powder together, then fold into the carrot puree, until well combined. Now gently fold in the egg whites. Pour the mixture into the prepared pan and bake for 30–35 minutes.

When the cake is cooked, take it out of the oven and let cool on a wire rack.

Whip the heavy cream and stir in the Cointreau. Cut a slice of cake and serve with a dollop of the cream.

Carrot and Cinnamon Cake

Carrots were used in cakes as a cheap substitute for expensive imported dried fruit for hundreds of years. Serve with a dollop of crème fraîche or sour cream.

SERVES 8

11/4 cups sunflower oil, plus extra for greasing

generous 1 cup brown sugar

4 medium free-range eggs

generous 1/2 cup dark corn syrup

21/2 cups self-raising flour

2 tbsp ground cinnamon

1 tsp baking soda

21/2 cups grated carrot

Preheat the oven to 350°F/180°C. Grease two 8 x 4 x 2 inch (20 x 10 x 5 cm) loaf pans with sunflower oil.

Put the oil, sugar, eggs, and corn syrup into a food processor and then add the flour, cinnamon, baking soda, and grated carrots.

Blend everything together, pour into the loaf pan and bake in the preheated oven for 40–50 minutes. Once cooked, let rest for 10–15 minutes before turning out of the pans.

Whoever is quickest gets a slice. Dive in!

Parkin

In Yorkshire, we would eat this on Bonfire Night, a British holiday in November, and it is a cake that gets better after three to four days in a pan. It's dark and rich and, cut into squares and placed in a sealed container, becomes moister and eats even better.

SERVES 4

1²/₃ cups self-raising flour

generous ¹/₂ cup superfine sugar

2 tsp ground ginger

1 tsp baking soda

4 tbsp butter

¹/₃ cup dark corn syrup

1 free-range egg

scant 1 cup milk

Preheat the oven to 300°F/150°C. Line an 8 inch (20 cm) cake pan with wax paper.

Sieve the flour, sugar, ginger, and baking soda into a bowl. In a small pan, gently heat the butter and syrup until melted. Beat the egg into the milk.

Gradually pour the butter and syrup into the flour mixture and stir well. Pour in the egg and milk mixture and combine until smooth.

Pour into the lined pan and bake for 1 hour.

Banana Cake

The great thing I find about this recipe is that the bananas help keep the cake nice and moist. A lot of banana cake recipes contain nuts, such as almonds or walnuts, but I think it's nicer plain.

MAKES 1 CAKE

4 large ripe bananas

generous ¹/₂ cup butter, softened, plus extra for greasing

1³/₄ cups self-raising flour

1 cup superfine sugar

3 medium free-range eggs

3 tbsp dark corn syrup

Preheat the oven to 350°F/180°C. Butter a large loaf pan.

Peel the bananas and put them into a food processor. Blend for 10 seconds to break them up.

Add all the other ingredients and blend again for 10 seconds. Scrape down the sides and blend again for a few seconds to mix everything in.

Spoon the mixture into the buttered loaf pan and spread evenly. Bake for 1¹/₄–1¹/₂ hours, until well risen and firm to the touch. At this point, insert a small knife to test the cake; if it is pulled out clean and the tip is not wet, then the cake is ready.

Remove from the oven and let rest for 10 minutes before turning out of the pan and placing on a wire rack to cool a little. Serve the cake warm.

My grandmother used to swear by this sponge recipe and my aunt by the other one (see page 332), so you choose—they're both great.

Victoria Sponge

MAKES AN 8 INCH (20 CM) SPONGE

scant 1 cup unsalted butter, softened, plus extra for greasing

scant 1 1/2 cups self-raising flour, sifted, plus extra for dusting

1 cup superfine sugar

1 tsp vanilla extract

4 free-range eggs

TO SERVE

heavy cream, whipped

raspberry jam

confectioners' sugar, for dusting

Preheat the oven to 375°F/190°C. Lightly grease and flour two 8 inch (20 cm) cake pans, at least 1 1/2 inches (4 cm) deep. Line the bottoms with parchment paper.

Beat the butter and superfine sugar together until well creamed. Add the vanilla extract. Gently mix the eggs together in a small bowl, then add, little by little, to the butter mixture. Once all the eggs have been combined, fold in the sifted flour and divide the mixture between the pans.

Bake for 20–25 minutes, until well risen and golden brown on top. Once cooked, turn out and let cool on a wire rack.

Spread one of the sponges with whipped heavy cream and raspberry jam. Top with the second sponge and sprinkle with a dusting of confectioners' sugar.

Auntie's Sponge

Granny's sponge is the classic creamed sponge, while this one is a whisked sponge. It won't last as long as the other, but it's just as delicious.

MAKES AN 8 INCH (20 CM) SPONGE

3 1/2 tbsp butter, melted, plus extra for greasing

1 1/4 all-purpose flour, sifted, plus extra for dusting

6 medium free-range eggs

generous 3/4 cup superfine sugar

TO SERVE

heavy cream, whipped

raspberry jam

confectioners' sugar, for dusting

Preheat the oven to 400°F/200°C. Grease and flour a deep 8 inch (20 cm) cake pan.

Place the eggs and sugar in a bowl and whisk to the ribbon stage. This will take a few minutes, so be patient.

Once the mixture has doubled in volume, fold in the flour. Carefully, but quickly, fold in the butter at the same time.

Pour into the pan and bake for 30 minutes. Test with a skewer in the center—if it comes out clean, the sponge is ready.

Let cool for 10 minutes before turning out.

Finish by cutting in half horizontally and filling with whipped heavy cream and raspberry jam. Sprinkle with a dusting of confectioners' sugar if you want to—I would!

Chocolate Biscuit Cake

This is any kid's favorite, big or little. Use this recipe as a starting point and experiment with other combinations of cookies, dried fruits, and nuts. Ginger cookies or amaretti work well for a more grown-up version.

SERVES 8

4¹/₂ oz (125 g) dark chocolate, broken into pieces

1 tbsp dark brown syrup

generous ¹/₂ cup butter

1¹/₄ cups roughly crushed graham crackers

¹/₂ cup plump dried apricots, chopped

²/₃ cup raisins

¹/₂ cup candied cherries, halved

6¹/₂ cups shelled hazelnuts, roughly chopped

Line an 8 x 4 x 2 inch (20 x 10 x 5 cm) loaf pan with plastic wrap, leaving enough to fold over the top when the pan is full.

Melt the chocolate, syrup, and butter in a bowl in the microwave, giving it a stir to make sure all the ingredients are well blended.

Add the crushed cookies, dried fruits, and hazelnuts and stir well.

Pour the mixture into the loaf pan and shake to level it off. Fold over the plastic wrap and put it in the refrigerator to set—this will take 1–2 hours.

This mixture will keep for up to two weeks in the refrigerator, if you can resist temptation for that long.

To serve, turn it out onto a plate, carefully peel off the plastic wrap and slice. The cake is very rich, so try thin slices at first.

I don't care what all my chef friends think of me for putting this in a British book. I bet these little cakes won't even be able to set in the refrigerator before they're eaten.

Chocolate Cornflake Cakes

MAKES 12

3¹/₂ tbsp butter

3¹/₂ oz (100 g) dark chocolate, broken into pieces

5 tbsp dark corn syrup

generous 3 cups cornflakes

Place the butter and the chocolate pieces in a pan with the corn syrup and slowly melt over a low heat. When the mixture has melted and amalgamated, stir in the cornflakes.

Place paper cases on a baking sheet and fill each one with a tablespoon of the mixture. Put in the refrigerator to set.

Everybody loves Yule Log for Christmas, which must be something to do with the amount of chocolate that goes into it. For me, it's a bit sickly, but for all you chocolate lovers, it has to go into the book!

Yule Log

SERVES 8

sunflower oil, for greasing

6 oz (175 g) good dark chocolate, broken into pieces

6 medium free-range eggs, separated

generous 3/4 cup superfine sugar

FILLING

3 oz (85 g) good dark chocolate, broken into pieces

scant 1 cup heavy cream, whipped

COATING

3 1/2 oz (100 g) good dark chocolate, chopped

scant 1 cup heavy cream

cocoa powder, for dusting

confectioners' sugar, for dusting

Preheat the oven to 350°F/180°C. Lightly grease a 12 x 8 inch (30 x 20 cm) Swiss roll pan with sunflower oil and line with parchment paper.

Put the chocolate into a small heatproof bowl over a pan of hot water (the bowl must not touch the water) and heat gently, stirring occasionally, to melt. Let cool.

Whisk the egg yolks and sugar together in a large bowl until light and creamy. Place the bowl over a pan of hot water, add the cooled chocolate, and stir to blend evenly.

In a separate bowl, whisk the egg whites until stiff but not dry. Carefully fold into the chocolate mixture.

Turn the chocolate mixture into the prepared pan, tilting the pan so that the mixture spreads evenly into the corners. Bake for 20 minutes, or until firm to the touch.

Remove from the oven. Place a clean, dry dish towel on the cake, and on top of this layer another dish towel that has been soaked in cold water and well wrung out.

For the filling, melt the chocolate as above. Cool.

Remove the dish towels from the sponge and turn it out onto a piece of parchment paper. Peel the lining paper from the cake. Spread the melted chocolate over the cake, then spread the whipped cream on top. Roll up the cake from the long edge, using the paper to lift and help roll it forward.

For the coating, melt the chocolate as above. Let it cool slightly before adding the cream. The mixture should turn smooth and glossy. Roughly spread this over the Swiss roll, then dust with cocoa powder and confectioners' sugar. Serve.

There are many recipes for classic Christmas Cake. This is my aunt's old recipe, which worked for her, so it's good enough for me!

Christmas Cake

4¹/₂ cups mixed dried fruit, (about 1¹/₂ lb/675 g)

1 generous cup slivered blanched almonds

1 cup mixed candied peel, chopped

generous ¹/₂ cup candied cherries, well rinsed, then quartered

scant 2¹/₄ cups all-purpose flour

1 tsp ground cinnamon

1 tsp freshly grated nutmeg

finely grated zest and juice of 1 lemon

1 cup lightly salted butter

generous 1 cup soft brown sugar, light or dark

1 tsp vanilla extract

1 tbsp blackstrap molasses

4 medium free-range eggs

¹/₂ tsp baking soda

1 tbsp milk

brandy

Preheat the oven to 275°F/140°C, and line an 8 inch (20 cm) cake pan with a layer of brown paper, then a layer of parchment paper.

Mix the dried fruit, almonds, peel, and cherries in a huge bowl. Turn them well and add the flour, spices, and lemon zest and juice.

Cream the butter and sugar thoroughly, then add the vanilla extract and molasses. Still beating, incorporate the eggs, then stir the mixture into the fruit and flour. Finally, dissolve the baking soda in the milk and stir this into the fruit thoroughly as well. Add brandy to taste by the spoonful, until you have a soft dropping consistency.

Pour the mixture into the prepared pan and hollow out the top slightly. Bake for 3 1/2 hours, then test it with a skewer (if this is just dry, the cake is ready). Remove the cake from the oven, when it is done, and let it cool in its pan.

When cool, remove from the pan and peel off the parchment paper and brown paper. Wrap in plastic wrap, and then put into an airtight container (or in foil). The usual thing is to keep the cake for at least a month before icing it, and to sprinkle it occasionally with more brandy.

To finish off the cake for Christmas, you will need Marzipan and Royal Icing (*see* page 341). Do not buy the marzipan prepared—your own may not look as yellow as it does in the store, but it will taste much better, I promise!

Marzipan

Why buy prepared marzipan for a Christmas cake you've spent ages making when it can so easily be made at home?

COVERS AN 8 INCH (20 CM) CAKE

2 cups confectioners' sugar, plus extra for dusting

5 1/2 cups ground almonds

1 large free-range egg (weighing about 75g / 2 3/4 oz)

3–4 tsp lemon juice

GLAZE
1 tbsp apricot jam

Sift the sugar into a bowl and mix in the almonds. Beat the egg well, then add it and the lemon juice to the dry ingredients. Using a wooden spoon, beat to a firm paste, then knead on a work surface that has been sprinkled with confectioners' sugar. (If you don't find most marzipan too sweet, add another 2 cups confectioners's sugar and use 2 medium eggs instead of 1 large egg.)

Boil the jam and 1 tablespoon of water in a small pan, strain it into a bowl and, while it is hot, brush it over the top and sides of the cake.

Roll out the marzipan to a circle a little larger than the cake. Using the rolling pin to lift up the marzipan, place it on top of the cake and smooth down over the sides.

Pat everything into place with your fingers, closing the cracks, and put the cake back on its rack.

Royal Icing

COVERS AN 8 INCH (20 CM) CAKE

4 small free-range egg whites

4 tsp lemon juice

9 cups confectioners' sugar, sifted

Whisk the egg whites until they are white and foamy but not stiff. Stir in the lemon juice, then the sugar, bit by bit, using a wooden spoon. When everything is combined, continue to beat the mixture until it is a dazzling white. Cover the bowl and let stand for an hour before using.

To ice the cake, have a bowl of hot water handy. Put half the icing on the cake, dip the palette knife into the hot water (it shouldn't be too wet), then use it to spread the icing. Cover the cake, then put on the remaining icing, either roughly to make a snowy effect or with the aid of a forcing bag and nozzles. Let stand for at least two days to set before eating.

Dripping Cake

When I was a young boy, there always seemed to be jars of good country dripping in the kitchen. Beef and lamb fat were both added to the same jar ready to be spread on bread or toast to fill us up. My grandmother, Marjorie, was the ultimate country cook—the type nostalgic movies now feature in comforting soft focus. Except mine was for real. This is her favorite family cake, which always seemed to be on hand whenever we wanted a hunk. It's what cookbooks would call a boiled fruit cake. Nowadays, not many of us have dripping jars, but you can still buy dripping. If it comes with a nourishing layer of meat jelly at the bottom, just scrape it off (save for adding to a stew) and use the clarified fat on top.

MAKES A 6 INCH (15 CM) ROUND CAKE

1½ cups mixed dried fruit (with candied peel included)

scant ½ cup clarified beef dripping

¾ cup brown sugar

1 cup water

1⅔ cups whole-wheat flour

1 tsp baking powder

½ tsp baking soda

a good pinch each of ground cinnamon, nutmeg and allspice

4 medium free-range eggs

Place the fruit, dripping, sugar, and water in a saucepan and bring to a boil, stirring. Remove from the heat and let cool. (My grandmother would do this the night before.)

Heat the oven to 350°F/180°C. Meanwhile, grease and line a deep round 6 inch (15 cm) cake pan.

Sift the flour, baking powder, baking soda, and spices into a large bowl. Mix the fruit mixture into the dry ingredients with the eggs, beating well.

Turn the cake mixture into the prepared cake pan. Level the top and bake in the oven for about 1–1¼ hours, until the top is golden brown and a clean metal skewer comes out clean when inserted into the center of the cake.

Let cool in the pan for about 30 minutes, then turn out onto a wire rack and let stand until cold. Peel off the lining paper and store in an airtight container for up to three days. Slice and top, if you like, with jam and cream.

biscuits

These unusual shortbread cookies are delicate and, once made, need to be handled with care, or otherwise they will fall apart. To prevent this from happening, let them cool right down on the baking sheet before lifting them off.

Jam Shortbreads

MAKES 20–24

generous 3/4 cup confectioners' sugar

1 1/3 cups all-purpose flour, plus extra for dusting

scant 1/2 cup cornstarch

generous 1 cup ground almonds

250g (9oz) unsalted butter, diced, plus extra for greasing

a few drops of almond extract

raspberry or strawberry jam

Sift the confectioners' sugar, flour, and cornstarch together into a bowl. Add the ground almonds then, using your fingers or a food processor, rub or mix the butter in until there are no visible lumps. Pour in the almond extract and mix well.

Turn the mixture out onto a lightly floured surface and knead a few times, just to form a smooth dough.

Butter a baking sheet. Roll the dough out to about 1/4 inch (5 mm) thick. Cut into cookies using a 2 inch (5 cm) cutter. Use a spatula to move them to the greased baking sheet. Make a small indentation in the middle of each. Chill for 30 minutes or so.

Preheat the oven to 350°F/180°C.

Bake the shortbreads until they are a light gold color, about 8–12 minutes. Let cool on the baking sheet.

Fill the indentation in each cookie with jam, and serve.

Shortbread

Who would have thought it? The origins of shortbread appear to be 500–600 years old. It was made as a festive treat, and was not meant to be dunked into your coffee, but how times have changed! The best shortbread is to be found, I think, in Perthshire in Scotland. Not long ago, the Scottish Association of Master Bakers challenged the government, which wanted to change shortbread from being a special confection into a common cookie! What is the world coming to?

MAKES 20 COOKIES

1 cup chilled unsalted butter, plus extra for greasing

1²/₃ cups all-purpose flour, plus extra for dusting

1/₃ cup superfine sugar, plus extra for dusting

a pinch of salt

1 tsp vanilla extract

Butter a baking sheet.

Dice the butter and put it into a mixing bowl to soften. Sift the flour on top with the superfine sugar, salt and vanilla extract. Rub together gently to form into a ball (alternatively, blend all the ingredients in a food processor until they form a ball).

Lightly flour the work surface and then roll out the shortbread mixture until it is about 1/4 inch (5 mm) thick. Using a fork, prick all over the surface.

With a sharp knife, cut the shortbread into fingers about 2 inches 5 cm long and 1/2 inch (1.5 cm) wide. Carefully lift onto the buttered baking sheet and rest in the refrigerator for 30 minutes or so. Dust with a little superfine sugar before baking.

Preheat the oven to 350°F/180°C.

Bake the shortbread for 20 minutes, or until golden brown and firm to the touch. Let stand until completely cooled before removing from the baking sheet.

Grandma's Caramel Banana Shortbread

This is a dish I remember my grandmother making. She also used to make millionaire's shortbread. I never told her which tasted the best, but I had to fight my sister for the burned parts of this one on the baking sheet.

MAKES 8 COOKIES

2 x 14 oz (397g) cans condensed milk (or 2¹/2 cups)

generous 1 cup unsalted butter, at room temperature

³/4 cup superfine sugar

1 cup cornstarch

scant 2¹/4 cups all-purpose flour

4 large bananas, peeled and chopped

CARAMEL SAUCE

scant ¹/2 cup superfine sugar

scant ¹/2 cup water

TO SERVE

vanilla ice cream

fresh mint

Put the unopened cans of condensed milk in a deep saucepan and cover with water. Bring to a boil, then reduce the heat and put on the lid. Let simmer rapidly for 2 hours, filling up with more water if necessary—it's important that the saucepan doesn't boil dry. Cool down completely before you open the cans to find a golden sticky caramel. (Once cooked, a can of caramelized condensed milk will keep in the refrigerator for two weeks.)

Preheat the oven to 400°F/200°C. Cream the butter with the sugar until light and fluffy. Sift together the flours, then combine with the butter and sugar to form a dough. Gently knead until it all comes together in a firm ball.

Line a 8 x 12 inch (20 x 30 cm) baking sheet with nonstick parchment paper. Roll out two-thirds of the dough to fit the sheet and lay it inside, pressing it neatly into the edges. Spread three-quarters of the caramelized condensed milk evenly over the bottom. Add the banana, then crumble the remaining third of the dough over the top.

Bake for 20–25 minutes. The caramel should have bubbled up a little through the dough and the top of the shortbread should be golden. Let it cool in the baking sheet for 5 minutes before cutting it into eight 3 x 4 inch (7.5 x 10 cm) oblongs. Let cool completely in the tin.

To make the caramel sauce, place the sugar in a clean, dry pan. Heat gently until the sugar melts and turns a light caramel color. Carefully pour in the water, stir, then bring to a boil. Let cool.

Remove the squares from the sheet and reheat them gently in the oven before serving with vanilla ice cream, a sprig of fresh mint, and a drizzle of the caramel sauce.

Gingerbread men never used to reach the cookie jar at my grandmother's house when I was there. This recipe is more than 40 years old, and tastes the same every time I make it. But bear in mind, if you have ground spices, such as ginger, in your cupboard, eight times out of ten you will have bought them for a dish some years before. Once the label has changed color and the expiration date says something like 1972, the spices are no good and you should buy fresh.

Gingerbread Biscuits

MAKES ABOUT 20

1²/₃ cups all-purpose flour

¹/₄ tsp salt

2 tsp baking soda

1 heaped tsp ground ginger

¹/₄ tsp ground cinnamon

4 tbsp unsalted butter

generous ¹/₂ cup brown sugar

¹/₃ cup dark corn syrup

1 tbsp evaporated milk

Sift the flour, salt, baking soda, and spices together into a bowl. Heat the butter, sugar, and syrup together until dissolved, then let cool. Once cooled, mix into the dry ingredients with the evaporated milk to make a dough. Chill for 30 minutes.

Preheat the oven to 375°F/190°C and grease two baking sheets. Roll out the cookie dough to about ¹/₄ inch (5 mm) thick and cut into fingers, circles, or even gingerbread men.

Place on the baking sheets, allowing a little space to spread, and bake for 10–15 minutes. Remove from the oven. Let cool slightly on the baking sheets before transferring to a wire rack.

Shortbread Sugar Thins
There are many variations of shortbread, and in this book I have given you several of them. This one is more like a cookie.

MAKES AS MANY
AS YOU LIKE

generous 1 cup butter

1¹/₄ cups superfine sugar, plus extra to sprinkle

1 free-range egg, beaten

1 tbsp heavy cream

scant 2¹/₄ cups all-purpose flour

¹/₂ tsp salt

1 tsp baking powder

a few drops of vanilla extract (or lemon juice or 2 tsp ground ginger)

Cream the butter and sugar together, then add all the remaining ingredients. Mix well. If you like, you can divide the dough into three, and flavor each part differently (with vanilla, lemon juice, and ground ginger).

Form the dough into a long roll or rolls, about 2 inches (5 cm) in diameter, and wrap in foil. Put in the refrigerator until the next day.

Preheat the oven to 375°F/190°C. Shave off the dough into the thinnest possible slices. Put them on a baking sheet, sprinkle them with sugar, and cook them for only 5 minutes. They should remain pale in color.

There is no need to bake the dough all at once; cut off what you need and put the excess back in the refrigerator or the freezer.

Brandy Snaps with Whipped Cream

I used to eat loads of these as a kid. Worst of all, my mother would bring a plate through while all my friends were around watching television and playing Atari and track-and-field on the Commodore 64 (that's an old computer to anyone who hasn't lived!). I used to sit and watch them devour the snaps one by one, thinking how much my fingers hurt from trying to make a competitor do the 110-meter hurdles, and how they could eat them without a care in the world, because when I went to their houses you were lucky if you got a boiled candy....

MAKES 30

generous 1 cup superfine sugar

2 pinches ground ginger

generous 1/2 cup unsalted butter, softened, plus extra for greasing

generous 3/4 cup all-purpose flour

1/3 cup corn syrup

TO SERVE
2 1/2 cups heavy cream, whipped

Slightly cream together the sugar, ginger, and butter. Add the flour and corn syrup, and mix to a firm paste. Roll into a long sausage about 1 1/2 inches (4 cm) in diameter, then wrap tightly in plastic wrap, making sure not to catch the wrap inside the roll. Chill well (overnight is best).

Preheat the oven to 350°F/180°C. Lightly grease a baking sheet.

Remove the plastic wrap from the sausage and cut off 1/4 -inch (5-mm) thick slices. Arrange the slices on the baking sheet, spacing them out well. Bake for about 8–10 minutes, or until well spread out and golden.

Remove from the oven and let cool for a few seconds to firm up slightly. Using a spatula, carefully remove one brandy snap at a time from the baking sheet, then immediately loosely wrap it around the handle of a wooden spoon to shape into a roll. (If the brandy snaps cool too quickly and start to break, a good tip is to put them back in the oven for a minute or so to soften slightly.) Slide the brandy snaps off the spoon handles and let cool. Store in an airtight container for three or four days.

To serve, fill with whipped heavy cream using a piping bag and small nozzle.

Chorley cakes come, not surprisingly, from Chorley, a small town in Lancashire, England. They are made from pastry (usually leftover pastry) and dried fruit. Similar cakes appear elsewhere in the country: Banbury cakes, Eccles cakes, Coventry God cakes, and Hawkshead cakes, all of them in different shapes. You can make these Chorley cakes as individual round cakes, or in a slab as here, which you cut into slices. You can also add alternative dried fruit, perhaps some raisins or citrus peel.

Chorley Cakes

MAKES AS MANY AS YOU LIKE

1 2/3 cups all-purpose flour, plus extra for dusting

1 tsp freshly grated nutmeg

1/2 cup unsalted butter, softened

1/4 cup brown sugar

1/4 cup water

1 cup currants

2 tbsp milk

confectioners' sugar, for dusting

Preheat the oven to 400°F/200°C.

Sift the flour and nutmeg into a large bowl. Add the butter and sugar, and mix with your fingers until the texture is like bread crumbs.

Turn the mixture out onto a lightly floured surface and make a well in the center. Add the water to the well, and gradually work the flour mixture in to form a dough. Then knead in the currants.

Dust the surface lightly with more flour and roll the pastry out to form a slab about 1/2 inch (1 cm) thick. Neaten the edges.

Place on a baking sheet, brush with the milk, and bake in the oven for about 20 minutes.

When cooked, remove from the oven, dust with confectioners' sugar, then cut into slices of whatever size you want.

bakes

Scones

American biscuits are the closest equivalent to these. The British eat them with "clotted" cream and jam. Scottish by origin, they can be made with mashed potato, and they can be griddled or baked in the oven—there are so many variations.

SERVES 4

1 2/3 cups self-raising flour, plus extra for dusting

2 tbsp superfine sugar

a pinch of salt

1 1/2 tbsp butter, diced, plus extra for greasing

2/3 cup milk

GLAZE

1 free-range egg, lightly beaten with a little milk

TO SERVE

clotted cream, whipped cream, or butter

strawberry jam

Preheat the oven to 425°F/220°C. Grease a baking sheet.

Put the flour, superfine sugar, and salt in a food processor and blend briefly to mix. Add the butter and blend again until the mixture forms crumbs. Add the milk in a thin stream while mixing, stopping when the dough forms a ball. It should be moist, but not sticking to the sides.

Turn the mixture out onto a heavily floured surface, and form into a ball, then press gently into a 3/4 -inch (2-cm) thick circle. Cut out the scones using a 5cm (2in) round cutter and put onto the greased baking sheet. Brush the scones with the beaten egg and milk.

Bake for 12–14 minutes. Remove and let cool slightly on a rack. Serve while still warm with clotted cream (found in specialty stores selling British products), whipped cream, or butter and strawberry jam.

Griddle Scones

These are so good eaten warm with some butter or with jam. But if you let them become cold they can be eaten like normal scones with jam and whipped cream.

MAKES 20

1 1/2 cups all-purpose flour

1 1/2 tsp baking powder

1 tbsp superfine sugar

a pinch of salt

1 free-range egg, beaten

2/3 cup whole milk

a pat of butter, for frying

Sift the flour into a bowl with the baking powder, sugar, and salt. Make a well in the middle, put in the egg, then the milk, and whisk to a thick batter, adding a little more milk if the mixture is too dry (you want the consistency of heavy cream). Let stand for 30 minutes at room temperature before using.

Preheat the skillet, add a little butter, and test by cooking one scone first, then cook the rest in batches. A tablespoon of batter will make one scone. As the bottom of the scones cook, after about 2 minutes, bubbles will come to the surface. Turn them onto the other side and cook for another 2 minutes.

Keep the scones warm, wrapped in a cloth in a low oven, until all are done. Eat while still warm, with butter and jam.

You might think doughnuts are difficult, but they are made in much the same way as a simple bread—apart from the deep-frying, of course! They may take a while, but they're worth the wait, trust me.

Doughnuts

MAKES 5–10

1 3/4 cups white bread flour, plus extra for dusting

a pinch of salt

scant 1/4 cup superfine sugar, plus extra for coating

2 tbsp butter, softened

2/3 cup water

1 1/2 tbsp active dry yeast

some good jam (optional)

vegetable or sunflower oil, for deep-frying

Put all the ingredients except the jam, oil, and coating sugar into a large bowl and mix together. Turn out onto a lightly floured surface and knead for 5 minutes. Put the dough back in the bowl, cover with a cloth, and let stand for about 1 hour, until doubled in size.

Divide the dough into 5–10 pieces and shape into balls. If you want, put 1 teaspoon of jam inside each ball. Put on your floured surface, cover lightly with a cloth, and let rise until doubled in size again.

Pour some oil into a large heavy pan and heat to 340°F/170°C, or a medium heat. Carefully lower each of the doughnuts into the oil and fry until brown, then roll them over and fry the other side. (If you have a problem with rolling the doughnuts over, then pierce them slightly with a knife to help you.) The frying should take no more than 5 minutes for both sides.

When they are browned, drain well on paper towels and put them straight into a bowl full of superfine sugar and coat well. Cool on a wire rack, then enjoy with a nice cup of coffee.

Elizabeth Botham, a coffee and cake store in Whitby, was where I first tasted Yorkshire brack. It's a little like a fruit cake, but lighter, and has the taste and texture of British sticky toffee pudding. The store has either tea-steeped or ginger-flavored brack, and it's made fresh on the premises.

Yorkshire Brack

SERVES 6–8

4 cups sultanas

4 cups raisins

2 1/4 cups light brown sugar

scant 1 1/4 cups cold strong breakfast tea

1/2 cup whiskey or bourbon

butter, for greasing

scant 4 cups all-purpose flour

4 tsp baking powder

a large pinch of salt

1 tsp freshly grated nutmeg

1 tsp ground allspice

3 free-range eggs, beaten

finely grated rind of 1 lemon

Soak the raisins and sugar in the tea and whiskey or bourbon in a large bowl for 12 hours or overnight.

The next day, preheat the oven to 300–325°F/150–160°C, and grease a 10 inch (25 cm) round cake pan.

Sift together the flour, baking powder, salt, nutmeg, and allspice, and add to the raisin mixture along with the beaten eggs and lemon rind. Combine well.

Put the batter into the greased pan, and bake for 60–80 minutes, until firm to the touch.

When done, remove from the pan and let it cool on a wire rack. You can leave it simple and serve it with butter, or top it with a little icing.

These taste so good that you shouldn't just make them at Easter. They are great for breakfast with some Blueberry Sauce (see page 26) or fried caramel bananas, or toasted with strawberries and balsamic vinegar with a dollop of clotted or whipped cream. Better still, just serve with some good old homemade jam.

Hot Cross Buns

MAKES 18

BASIC BUN DOUGH

3 1/4 cups all-purpose flour

1 level tsp each of ground cinnamon, nutmeg, and allspice

1/2 tsp ground mace

1/2 tsp salt

2 tbsp active dry yeast

1/4 cup superfine sugar

2/3 cup milk

6 tbsp unsalted butter, plus extra for greasing

1 free-range egg, lightly beaten

1/2 cup raisins

1/2 cup candied peel, chopped

ALMOND PASTE

2 cups confectioners' sugar, plus extra for dusting

5 cups ground almonds

1 large free-range egg

3–4 tsp lemon juice

BUN WASH

a little beaten free-range egg

1/4 superfine caster sugar

5 tbsp water

Put the flour, spices, and salt into a large warmed mixing bowl. Crumble the yeast into another bowl, add 1 heaped teaspoon of the sugar and scant 1 cup of flour from the first bowl. Pour the milk into a measuring pitcher, and make up to a generous 1 1/4 cups with boiling water straight from the kettle. Using a wooden spoon, mix this hot liquid into the yeast mixture. Go slowly to make as smooth a batter as possible. Let it stand in a warm place to rise and froth up—this takes about 20 minutes.

Mix the rest of the sugar with the remaining flour, and rub in the butter. Form a well in the center, and put in the egg and the frothy yeast mixture. Mix to a dough with a wooden spoon. Turn it out onto a floured surface and knead for 10 minutes, adding more flour as required, until the dough is coherent and tacky, but not sticky.

Wash and dry the mixing bowl, then grease with butter. Place the dough in it. Cover with a damp cloth, or put the whole thing inside an oiled plastic bag. Let rise to double its size. This can take 1–3 hours, depending on the room temperature.

Punch down the dough, and knead in the fruit and peel. Roll the dough into a long sausage shape on a floured surface and cut it into 18 disks. Shape into round buns, then place them on baking sheets lined with parchment paper. Leave plenty of room to rise and spread.

To make the almond paste, sift the confectioners' sugar and mix it with the almonds. Beat the egg thoroughly in a bowl, then add the lemon juice and the dry ingredients. Use a wooden spoon to beat everything to a firm paste. Knead it on a board or smooth surface, sprinkled with confectioners' sugar. Roll out the almond paste and cut into thin strips.

To finish, brush the buns with the beaten egg and lay two strips of almond paste on each bun to form a cross. Let the buns rise for about 30 minutes. Preheat the oven to 450°F/230°C. Bake the buns for 10–15 minutes. Meanwhile, boil the sugar and water together until syrupy. Brush over the hot buns when they emerge from the oven.

Crumpets

This is a real Yorkshire thing, although they have them in Lancashire as well. I call them crumpets, but in some areas they are called muffins, though they are different from American muffins. This recipe shouldn't be confused with the Scottish crumpet.

SERVES 4

3¹/₂ cups all-purpose flour
1 tbsp salt
generous 1 tbsp active dry yeast
generous 2¹/₂ cups warm water
butter, for greasing and cooking

Sift the flour and salt together into a bowl.

In a separate bowl, mix the yeast with 5–6 tablespoons of the warm water. Whisk the rest of the water with the flour and salt then stir in the yeast mixture.

Cover and let rest in a warm place to rise. After 15–20 minutes, the batter is ready. If it is a bit too thick, loosen with a little warm water.

Warm a nonstick pan on the stove and lightly butter some metal crumpet rings or scone cutters. (Or use old tuna cans with the tops and bottoms removed—but be careful because the edges will be sharp.) Melt some butter in the pan, too.

Place the rings in the pan and pour a little of the batter into each one, half filling them with the batter.

Cook on a gentle heat until holes appear in the top and the mixture starts to dry slightly around the edge. Turn over, remove the rings, and cook lightly on the other side.

Real Christmas Bread

There are many variations of Christmas breads from country to country. This is my version, and it was invented purely because so often at Christmas we find we've a lot of mincemeat left over. It's very simple to make and uses few ingredients. I use fresh yeast, but if you can't find it, use dried (read the instructions on the packet).

MAKES 1 LOAF

generous 3¹/₂ cups white bread flour, plus extra for dusting

¹/₃ cup mincemeat (bought or homemade, *see* page 260)

finely grated zest and juice of 2 oranges

finely grated zest and juice of 2 lemons

4 tbsp unsalted butter

2 tbsp salt

1 oz (25 g), or 4 tbsp active dry yeast

scant 1¹/₄ cups warm water

Place the flour, mincemeat, citrus zest and juice, butter, salt, and yeast in a bowl and mix together. Gradually mix in the warm water to form a dough.

Place the dough on a lightly floured surface and knead for 4 minutes. Shape into a rough sausage shape, around 6 inches (15 cm) across. Place on a baking sheet lined with parchment paper and let stand to rise for 1 hour, covered with a dish towel.

Preheat the oven to 425°F/220°C.

Slash the top of the loaf with a knife and dust with flour. Bake for 25 minutes, until golden brown and hollow when tapped. Cool on a wire rack.

Grissini and Dips

This is a quick and simple party idea, hardly a recipe, and it's good for an appetizer to a dinner party, too.

MAKES AS MANY
AS YOU LIKE

thin breadsticks or grissini

selection of dips, perhaps including garlic mayonnaise, cream cheese, and tapenade

toasted sesame or poppy seeds or fresh herbs, finely chopped

Dip the ends of the breadsticks or grissini in the garlic mayonnaise, cream cheese, or tapenade. Then dip the dipped end of the stick into the toasted seeds or herbs.

Serve, dipped end up, in tall glasses or in a large pitcher, so people can dive in and help themselves.

Alternatively, you can just wrap the grissini in some Parma ham, which makes a great snack as well.

chutneys, jams & jellies

Plum Chutney

A fruit-based accompaniment, chutneys go well with curried dishes, spread on bread, or served with cheese. I make this one from the plums from my trees in the yard. They are the dark flesh and skin type. If you can't get those, any plums will do.

MAKES 12 OZ (350 G)

1 lb 2 oz (500g) dark red plums

2 shallots, chopped

1 tbsp olive oil

generous 1/3 cup white wine vinegar

3 tbsp water

1 cinnamon stick

1/2 cup raw brown sugar

Cut the plums in half down the crease, twist the halves in opposite directions, and pull apart. Pry out the pits and discard. Roughly chop the flesh.

Place the shallots in a heavy saucepan with the oil and heat until sizzling. Sauté gently for 5 minutes, until softened.

Add the plums, vinegar, water, cinnamon stick, and sugar. Stir until the sugar is dissolved, then simmer for about 15 minutes, stirring occasionally, until softened and slightly thickened.

Meanwhile, heat the oven to 225–250°F/110–120°C. Place a sterilized jam jar in the oven to warm (see below for sterilizing instructions). When the plum chutney is ready, spoon it into the jar. Seal with a lid and let cool completely before labeling. Store in a cool, dark place.

Gooseberry, Raisin and Green Peppercorn Chutney

This chutney is particularly good with broiled fish, such as mackerel or tuna. It also goes well with most cheeses.

MAKES 2 LB (900 G)

1 lb 5 oz (600 g) fresh gooseberries

2 medium onions, chopped

1 clove garlic, crushed

1/2 tsp mustard powder

juice of 1/2 lemon

11/4 cups cider vinegar or white wine vinegar

11/4 cups raisins

a large pinch of salt

11/3 cups brown sugar

3 tbsp green peppercorns

To sterilize the jam jars, place them in a large pan and cover them with cold water. Bring to a boil and simmer for 10–15 minutes. Remove from the water and let stand upside down to dry.

Put the gooseberries, onions, garlic, mustard, and lemon juice in a preserving pan and pour in two-thirds of the vinegar. Bring to a boil, then reduce the heat and simmer for about 45 minutes, stirring occasionally, until thick.

Add the raisins, salt, sugar, and the rest of the vinegar. Stir over a low heat until the sugar has dissolved, then simmer for up to 1 hour, stirring frequently, until thick and syrupy.

Stir in the peppercorns, then remove from the heat. Pour immediately into the hot, sterilized jars, and seal. Label and store in a cool, dark place.

Tomato and Apple Chutney
I love this just with cheese on its own or even with some pan-fried cod or salmon.

MAKES 4 LB (1.8 KG)

1¼ cups malt vinegar

generous 1 cup brown sugar

²/₃ cup golden raisins

1-inch (2.5-cm) piece fresh ginger, peeled and finely chopped

2 red chiles, seeded and chopped

2¼ lb (1 kg) tomatoes, roughly chopped

9 oz (250 g) apples, peeled, cored, and chopped

7 oz (200 g) chunky shallots, roughly chopped

salt and pepper, to taste

Place the vinegar and sugar in a preserving pan and heat on the stove to reduce a little. Add the raisins and cook until the vinegar and sugar start to caramelize. Add all the other ingredients, and bring to a simmer. Cover and cook gently for 20–30 minutes, stirring all the time.

Leave the chutney chunky, and not overcooked, which would make it more like a purée. Spoon into hot, sterilized jars, and label when cool (*see* page 368 for sterilizing instructions). Store in a cool, dark place.

Pear Chutney
I did say I liked chutney!

MAKES 2 LB (900 G)

4 tbsp olive oil

1 tsp finely chopped fresh rosemary leaves

1¼ cups golden raisins

²/₃ cup raisins

½ cup raw brown sugar

½ cup cider vinegar

1 cup crystallized ginger, finely sliced

1¾ lb (800 g) pears, cored and cut into wedges

½ tsp salt

½ tsp freshly grated nutmeg

2 tsp ground allspice

a good pinch of saffron

Heat a preserving pan and add the oil, rosemary, golden raisins, raisins, and sugar. Fry them until the fruit begins to caramelize.

Pour in the vinegar and boil on a high heat for 3 minutes. Add the rest of the ingredients, bring to a boil, then turn down to a simmer and cook until most of the liquid has evaporated. Because of the fruit, this chutney tends to stick to the bottom of the pan, so stir it well and keep an eye on it.

Spoon into hot, sterilized jars, filling them as full as you can, and seal while hot (*see* page 368 for sterilizing instructions). Label and store in the refrigerator when cool. It is important not to cook this too much because the pear wedges need to keep their nice shape.

Courgette and Black Peppercorn Chutney

I love this recipe, which I came across while in Yorkshire filming in a man's vegetable plot. He was an amazing gardener who taught me the ins and outs of the carrot and the humble potato. His wife was an equally amazing cook, and she gave me a jar of this zucchini chutney. I took it home, but didn't try it until some four months later. It was so good I tracked them down again, and she kindly gave me her recipe.

MAKES 2 LB (900 G)

2 small lemons

3 medium courgettes

2 onions, peeled and thinly sliced

scant 1/2 cup dry white wine

3 tsp brown sugar

24 black peppercorns, coarsely crushed

1-inch (2.5-cm) piece of fresh ginger, peeled and finely chopped

a good pinch of salt

Peel the lemons, cutting away all the pith, then slice them thinly and discard the seeds. Cut the zucchini in half lengthwise, then across into 1-inch (2.5-cm) pieces.

Combine all the ingredients in a preserving pan. Cover and cook over a moderate heat for 1 hour, stirring from time to time. There will be quite a bit of liquid at the end of the cooking time, but once the chutney has cooled, the consistency will be perfect.

Either bottle in hot, sterilized jars, or put in a bowl to serve (*see* page 368 for sterilizing instructions). Store in a cool, dark place.

Sweet and Sour Grape Pickle

There is nothing better than reaching for a jar of your own pickle to add that extra kick to your meal! Pickles can be sweet, sour, or spicy.

MAKES 4 CUPS

1 lb 10 oz (750 g) seedless white grapes

10 sprigs fresh tarragon

generous 2 cups champagne vinegar or white wine vinegar

3/4 cup honey

1 tsp salt

Wash and dry the grapes. Put them in a large sterilized preserving jar with the sprigs of tarragon (*see* page 368 for sterilizing instructions).

Boil the vinegar and honey together for 2 minutes, then add the salt and pour the mixture over the grapes. Seal the jar immediately.

For the best results, store the pickle in a cool dark place for up to a month before opening.

Not everyone likes pickles and chutneys, but they are a must in a book on British food. Together with jams and marmalades, they are staples for so many of us, but very few of us try making them. This is an old recipe that I first used while at college. It takes a while to make, but it's worth it. My dad loves mustard pickle with pork pie. I like it with some cold sliced meat, such as ham, and bread, and cheese. But whatever you decide to serve it with, try. Come back the pickle, I say.

Mustard Pickle

MAKES 2¼ LB (1 KG)

¾ cup table salt

1 lb 2 oz (500 g) pearl onions

9 oz (250 g) cherry tomatoes

5 cups cauliflower florets

1 lb 2 oz (500 g) cucumbers, seeded and cut into large dice

1 tbsp capers

1 tsp celery seeds

generous ½ cup butter

3 tbsp all-purpose flour

generous 2 cups malt vinegar

⅔ cup superfine sugar

1 tbsp ground turmeric

2½ tsp mustard powder

black pepper, to taste

Dissolve the salt in a large pan or bowl in about 4 quarts (4 liters) of water and add the onions, tomatoes, and cauliflower. Cover with plastic wrap and keep in the refrigerator or in a cool place for 24 hours.

Drain, then add the diced cucumber, the capers, and celery seeds and put in a pan. Cover with 8 cups (2 liters) of water and bring to a boil. Boil for 10 minutes.

Drain again and put the vegetables into a bowl.

In a separate pan, melt the butter, then add the flour and stir well over the heat to make a roux. Slowly add the vinegar, stirring all the time, and cook for a few minutes.

Add the sugar, turmeric, and mustard powder, and season with black pepper before pouring over the vegetables. Put the vegetables into sterilized jars and seal (*see* page 368 for sterilizing instructions).

Let stand for at least five days in a cool, dark place before eating, so that the vegetables can absorb all the flavors.

Every month as a child, I was woken by the smell of vinegar boiling on a hot stove below my bedroom. It was pickled onion day, and my father was pickling tons of onions. Left in a jar for just a week, they're fabulous. Love them or hate them, we used to eat them all the time with pork pie—a must. I had to stop eating them, though, when I started on the girl front, but hey—you can't have everything!

Hot or Cold Pickled Onions

SERVES 4

COLD

3/4 cup table salt

10 cups water

2 1/4 lb (1 kg) shallots or pearl onions

2 1/2 cups malt vinegar

HOT

2 1/4 lb (1 kg) shallots or pearl onions

1/3 cup table salt

3 1/2 cups malt vinegar

For cold—or uncooked—pickled onions, mix half the salt with half the water and add the shallots or pearl onions. Let stand overnight.

Drain and peel the onions and make up the same brine with the remaining salt and water. Let the onions stand in this mixture for about three days.

Drain the shallots again, and place them in pickling jars that have been sterilized (*see* page 368 for sterilizing instructions), then pour over the vinegar. Cover, seal, and label, then let stand for 3 months before eating.

For hot—or cooked—pickled onions, put the shallots or pearl onions in a saucepan of water and bring to a boil. Boil for 3–4 minutes. Drain and peel the onions and place on a baking sheet. Dust all over with the salt and let stand for a day.

Wash the onions well and simmer in a pan in the vinegar for 8 minutes before placing them in sterilized jars (*see* page 368), covered in vinegar. Cover, seal, and label, then let stand for three weeks in a cool, dark place before eating.

Cranberry jelly or sauce is now traditional with our Christmas turkey, although cranberries are indigenous to North America. This jelly is also good with other cold meats, particularly ham. For more detailed intructions on jelly-making, see the next recipe.

Spiced Cranberry Jelly

MAKES 4 CUPS

2 1/4 lb (1 kg) Granny Smith apples

2 1/4 lb (1 kg) fresh cranberries

1 tsp ground cinnamon

granulated sugar

Peel and chop the apples. Put the cranberries into a large pan as they are with the apples, cinnamon, and enough water to just cover. Bring to the boil and simmer until the cranberries are soft.

Pass the mixture through a strainer or colander lined with a cheesecloth (*see* next page) into a measuring pitcher. This may take some time: be patient—and never push it through. For every 2 1/2 cups of liquid, add 2 1/2 cups of granulated sugar.

Pour the mixture back into a clean pan and cook gently until it reaches 220°F/105°C on a sugar thermometer (or when a few drops on a cold saucer begin to set within a minute or two).

Pour into sterilized jars, cover while still hot, and let cool and set (*see* page 368 for sterilizing instructions). Store in a cool, dark place.

Mint Jelly

My grandmother was never a lover of mint jelly: she couldn't understand why you put apples in it, and her mint sauce was simply some malt vinegar, a little sugar, some salt, and chopped mint from the yard. But for me, mint jelly is a classic, great with any number of dishes. It needs to be made with apples to let it set, but it's simple to make.

MAKES 2 LB (900 KG)

4 lb (1.8 kg) cooking apples

generous 1/2 cup chopped fresh mint, including stalks, plus 2 tbsp finely chopped mint leaves

juice and finely grated zest of 1 lemon

1 tbsp white wine vinegar

approx. 3 1/2 cups superfine sugar

Chop the apples coarsely, including the cores, and put them in a pan with the chopped mint, including stalks, the lemon zest and juice, and the vinegar. Barely cover with about 5 cups of cold water. Bring to a boil, turn down the heat, and simmer gently for 45 minutes.

The proper piece of equipment for the next stage is a jelly bag, but if you don't have one you can improvise. Line a colander with a double thickness of fine cheesecloth and scald with boiling water to sterilize. Put this over a bowl, pour the contents of the pan into it, and let it drip through overnight. Don't try to hurry this process by pushing with a spoon or squeezing the bag, because this will force solids through and make the jelly cloudy.

The next day, measure the juice and put it into a pan with 2 1/4 cups superfine sugar per 2 1/2 cups of apple juice. Bring to a boil slowly, then increase the heat and boil rapidly for about 8 minutes. Continue to boil for another 2 minutes, when the right amount of water will have evaporated and the frothing boil will have changed to a thicker rolling boil, with fat bubbles plopping noisily to the surface. At this stage, the setting point should have been reached.

Remove from the heat, pour through a strainer into a warmed pitcher and then stir in the remaining finely chopped mint leaves. Test by putting a spoonful of the mix on a cold plate. The surface should set as it cools and will wrinkle when prodded. Pour immediately into warm sterilized jars (see page 368 for sterilizing instructions). Don't tilt them until set. Put on sterilized lids and keep in a cool cupboard. Once opened, keep in the refrigerator.

Chicory and Orange Jam

This is my all-time favorite relish, which I make in batches ready to liven up quick pan-fries. It goes really well with thick, large scallops or plump free-range chicken breasts.

MAKES ENOUGH FOR 1 LARGE JAR

1 onion, chopped

1 fat clove garlic, chopped

2 tbsp butter

1 tbsp olive oil

5 heads fresh Belgian endive, thinly sliced

finely grated zest and juice of 2 oranges

2 sprigs fresh thyme

generous 1/2 cup superfine sugar

generous 1 cup dry white wine

Place the onion, garlic, butter, and oil in a large heavy saucepan and heat until it starts to sizzle. Gently sauté for about 5 minutes, until softened.

Add the remaining ingredients and bring to a boil, stirring. Reduce the heat and simmer gently, uncovered, for 30–40 minutes, until the Belgian endive becomes transparent and wilted right down.

Once cooked, let the relish cool slightly before spooning into a warmed, sterilized jar (*see* page 368 for sterilizing instructions). Seal immediately and let cool completely. Use within a month.

Orange Marmalade

Thought to be English, orange marmalade was first made in Dundoo in Scotland in about 1770. The Keiller Company there is one of the oldest producers of this fantastic product, but if you want to try making it, here's an old recipe my grandmother and aunt once used. You must, however, use bitter, or Seville, oranges to give it that real "just-like-granny-used-to-make" taste.

MAKES ABOUT
900G (2LB)

1 1/4 lb (550 g) Seville oranges

juice of 1 lemon

5 1/2 cups water

5 1/2 cups granulated sugar

Halve the oranges and, with a spoon, scoop out the insides, leaving the pith behind.

Place the orange juice, membrane, and seeds in a food processor and blend. Once the mixture is smooth, pass through a strainer into a large pan.

Using a tablespoon, scoop out as much of the pith from the orange peel as possible and then cut the peel into very thin strips. Add to the juice, then add the lemon juice and water. Bring to a boil and simmer for about 1–1 1/2 hours, until the peel is tender and the mixture has reduced by half.

Add the sugar and mix over a low heat until it has dissolved. Boil for about 10 minutes, removing any froth from the surface with a large spoon.

After 10 minutes, spoon a little of the marmalade onto a cold plate— it should be like jelly. If it is still runny, cook for another 5–10 minutes.

Let cool slightly before filling, sealing, and labeling the sterilized jars (*see* page 368 for sterilizing instructions). Keep in a cool place until ready to use. Once opened, store in the refrigerator.

Onion Marmalade

This is in season around winter, and what could be better than a jar of onion marmalade given away as a gift? It goes wonderfully with melted cheese on toast, steak, roast fish, and a huge variety of other things, either hot or cold.

MAKES 2 LB (900 KG)

4 lb (1.8 kg) brown onions, thinly sliced

generous 1/3 cup olive oil, plus extra to cover the marmalade

1 tbsp chopped fresh thyme

generous 3/4 cup superfine sugar

2/3 cup red wine

6 tbsp red wine vinegar

salt and pepper, to taste

Place the onions in a large, heavy saucepan with the olive oil and thyme, and cook over a moderate heat for 5 minutes. It is important not to let the onions brown at this stage or they will become bitter. Lower the heat, cover with a lid, and cook for 20 minutes.

Remove the lid and add the sugar, wine, vinegar, and some seasoning. Continue to cook, stirring from time to time, for about 20–30 minutes.

Once the marmalade is sticky, spoon it into sterilized jars (*see* page 368 for sterilizing instructions). Lightly cover the surface with olive oil and put on the lids. Keep in a cool place until ready to use. Once opened, store in the refrigerator.

Chunky Strawberry Jam

I find making a preserve one of the most rewarding things you can do, because you get to use the fruit at its best when it is in season and you reap the rewards throughout the rest of the year. That is, if you make enough— I never seem to because I keep deciding it makes a nice gift for someone!

MAKES ABOUT
1 1/2 LB (675 G)

3 cups sugar

juice and finely grated zest of 1 lemon

2 1/4 lb (1 kg) fresh strawberries, hulled and cut in half if large

Place the sugar and the juice and zest of the lemon in a large pan and heat slowly until the sugar has melted.

Add the strawberries and stir gently. Bring to a boil and cook for 3–4 minutes, or 10 minutes if you prefer a thicker style of preserve.

Let cool slightly, skimming off any froth with a clean spoon. Spoon into sterilized jars, seal, and label (see page 368 for sterilizing instructions). When cold, store in a cool, dark place.

Raspberry Jam

This is one of my favorite preserves.

MAKES ABOUT
1 1/2 LB (675 G)

3 cups jam sugar

juice and finely grated zest of 1 lemon

2 1/4 lb (1 kg) fresh raspberries, picked over carefully

Make this preserve exactly as the one above, merely substituting raspberries for the strawberries.

sweets & treats

Chocolate Truffles

Dark-chocolate truffles, like these, are the quickest and simplest to make. Milk and white chocolate truffles need different chocolate, because dark sets more solidly—increase the amount by 4 ounces (115 g). Mine are coated in cocoa powder. You can use confectioners' sugar, coconut, or grated chocolate, but if you do, roll the truffles in the coating while the chocolate is wet.

MAKES 20–30 TRUFFLES

1¹/₄ cups heavy cream

10 ¹/₂ oz (300 g) dark chocolate (70 percent cocoa solids)

1 tbsp rum or brandy (optional)

COATING

7 oz (200 g) dark chocolate (70 percent cocoa solids), broken into small pieces

¹/₂ cup good cocoa powder

Place the cream in a pan and heat until hot, but do not boil.

Break the chocolate into small even pieces and place in a bowl. When the cream is hot, pour it slowly on to the chocolate and, using a whisk, mix well until all the cream is combined and the chocolate has melted.

Before you set this mix, add the rum or brandy, if using, then let it set for about 2 hours in the refrigerator.

Using a melon scoop dipped in hot water, spoon the mixture into balls. Place them onto a baking sheet and put them back into the refrigerator.

Melt the chocolate for the coating in a bowl over a pan of hot water. Then stab each truffle with a fork, using it to dip the truffle in the chocolate and roll it in the cocoa. Place it on a plate and, once you have coated all the truffles, put them back in the refrigerator to set.

Festive Marrons Glacés

Marrons glacés are French crystallized chestnuts, but we Brits buy them enthusiastically at Christmas now, too. If you don't want to just devour them out of the jar, here is something to do with them for a party dessert.

SERVES 4

1¹/₄ cups heavy cream

a dash of whiskey

a dash of Grand Marnier

2 tbsp vanilla sugar (*see* page 393)

12 marrons glacés in syrup

1 oz (25 g) dark chocolate, grated

4 fresh mint sprigs

Whip the heavy cream until almost stiff. Add the whiskey, Grand Marnier, and a little of the vanilla sugar to taste.

Using 2 tablespoons dipped in hot water, spoon the cream onto the plates in football shapes, three per plate. Place the marrons glacés on the side, three per plate, and drizzle over some of the syrup.

Drizzle the remaining sugar over the top along with the grated chocolate, garnish with a sprig of mint, and serve.

Why do people buy marshmallows when they are simple to make—just a sort of royal icing with gelatin in it? The sugar must be at the right temperature before you add it to the whipped egg whites. What a fantastic way of finishing a Halloween party: having a pile of these with some sticks or skewers so that you can toast them over an open fire.

Marshmallows

MAKES 1¹/₂ LB (675 G)

3¹/₂ cups granulated sugar

1¹/₂ tbsp liquid glucose

14 gelatin leaves

3 medium free-range egg whites

vegetable oil

confectioners' sugar, for dusting

cornstarch, for dusting

1¹/₂ tsp vanilla extract

Put the sugar, glucose, and scant 1 cup of water in a heavy saucepan. Add a sugar thermometer. Bring to a boil and cook until it reaches 260°F/127°C.

Meanwhile, soak the gelatin in ²/₃ cup of cold water and beat the egg whites until stiff. Lightly oil a shallow baking sheet, about 12 x 18 inches (30 x 20 cm). Dust it with sifted confectioners' sugar and cornstarch.

When the syrup is up to temperature, carefully slide in the softened gelatin sheets and their soaking water. The syrup will bubble up, so be careful not to burn yourself. Pour the syrup into a metal pitcher.

Continue to beat the egg whites—preferably with an electric handheld mixer—while pouring in the hot syrup from the pitcher. Do this very slowly, or the heat will cook the egg whites too much. The mixture will become shiny and start to thicken. Add the vanilla extract and continue whisking for about 5–10 minutes, until the mixture is thick enough to hold its shape on the whisk.

Spoon the mixture into the prepared baking sheet, and smooth it with a wet palette knife if necessary. Let stand for at least an hour to set.

Dust the work surface with more confectioners' sugar and cornstarch. Loosen the marshmallow around the sides of the baking sheet with a palette knife, then turn it out onto the dusted surface. Cut into squares and roll in the sugar and cornstarch. Let dry a little on a wire rack, then pack into an airtight container.

Bloody Mary

The ultimate hangover cure! Make your own tomato juice or use watered down tomato sauce. The only other things you need are plenty of Tabasco sauce, a good wedge of lemon, and, most importantly, loads of ice cubes. That way you get the Bloody Mary chilled right down, which is perfect for those mornings after the night before.

SERVES 1 (IF YOU
LIKE IT STRONG!)

1/4 cup vodka

1/3 cup tomato juice
(*see* above)

juice of 1/2 lemon

2–4 dashes Tabasco sauce

3 dashes Worcestershire sauce

freshly ground black pepper

ice cubes

1 lemon wedge

Place the vodka, tomato and lemon juices, and Tabasco and Worcestershire sauces in a blender or a cocktail shaker and mix. Taste and season with black pepper and/or more of either sauce if needed.

Pour into a tall glass full of ice, and serve with the wedge of lemon on top of the glass.

Sweet Kir Royale

This is one of the best predinner drinks around. It's this drink and Parma ham wrapped around thin, homemade bread sticks that I remember most about my vacation in Italy. A much cheaper option is to drink this while watching television!

SERVES 6

6 tbsp crème de cassis

6 brown sugar cubes

1 bottle champagne or sparkling wine

Place a tablespoon of crème de cassis in each of the champagne glasses along with a brown sugar cube.

Open the champagne carefully and pour it into the glasses at a 45-degree angle. Serve immediately.

Mulled Wine

Mulled wine is great served anywhere, especially when the nights are drawing in and you want something to really knock that sore throat on the head.

SERVES 8–10

3 bottles red wine

2 oranges, zest peeled with a peeler, then juiced

2 lemons, zest peeled with a peeler

2 vanilla beans, split

1 cinnamon stick

4 1/2 cups superfine sugar

3 cloves

4 juniper berries

1 bay leaf

Simply chuck everything into a saucepan with 4 cups of water, bring it to a boil over a medium heat, and let steep for 10 minutes.

Serve warm.

My aunt used to make toffee, which she served in a waxed bag. This was really popular with all the kids! I think she learned the recipe from my great-great-grandmother, who had a corner store selling toffee and fudge. My aunt would make a variety of toffees—some with raisins or golden raisins, some plain, some with syrup, and some, of course, with black treacle. To break it up, she used an old toffee hammer that she got from Terry's Chocolates when my father was manager of their restaurant in York (now sadly shut down). She always made it nice and soft, probably because she never refrigerated it. The toffee was kept in the cookie container with the commemorative plaque of Queen Elizabeth II from when she got married, a container that I treasure to this day. My aunt sadly passed away several years ago, but the legacy of her toffee remains.

Treacle Toffee

MAKES 1 3/4 LB (800 G)

2 1/4 cups raw brown sugar

6 tbsp unsalted butter, softened

1/2 tsp cream of tartar

scant 1/3 cup blackstrap molasses

scant 1/3 cup golden syrup

a handful of golden raisins

Place the sugar in a heavy saucepan with 2/3 cup of water and heat until all the sugar has dissolved. Add the rest of the ingredients, apart from the raisins, and put in a sugar thermometer.

Bring to the a, brushing the sides of the pan down with a pastry brush dipped in water to stop crystals from forming. Do not stir. When the sugar reaches 270°F/132°C, quickly and carefully fold in the raisins. Pour the mixture into a 7 inch (18 cm) tin lined with wax paper and let cool. When set, break into pieces and store in a jar.

Toffee Apples

The first secret of good toffee apples is to get a nice apple. Make sure the apples are dry, or else the caramel won't stick. It's also important to add enough butter to your caramel.

MAKES 8

8 small, dry apples

toffee (as on page 390, but replacing the molasses with another golden syrup, increase the butter to 1/2 cup and omitting the raisins)

Make the toffee as on page 390. When you reach the raisin stage (omitting the raisins), stick a fork in each apple (forks are much better than sticks) and dip the apple into the caramel.

Immediately put the apple on a lightly oiled work surface or nonstick baking sheet. Repeat with all the apples. Let stand until cool and the toffee has set.

Vanilla Sugar

I can never understand, when walking around supermarkets, why people would want to buy prepared vanilla sugar, because it is so simple to make. You can easily sell it at a farmers' market—or, if you are more charitable, you can give it as a present. Otherwise use it in desserts, and it's great in coffee.

MAKES 3 1/2 CUPS

3 vanilla beans

3 1/2 cups superfine sugar

Chop the vanilla into pieces with a knife, and place in a blender with 1/2 cup of the sugar. Blend to break up the pieces.

Add the rest of the sugar and store in glass jars.

Coffee 'Mushrooms'

I invented this dish while working as a pastry chef at Chewton Glen. The guests there used to go on mushroom hunts, and bring back their treasure, which was a great way of stocking the refrigerators and freezers with mushrooms—and the hotel guests had done all the work! This dessert seemed to suit the occasion!

SERVES 4

1¼ cups good coffee ice cream, slightly softened

9 oz (250 g) dark chocolate (50–70 percent cocoa solids)

good cocoa powder

confectioners' sugar, sifted

TUILES

½ cup unsalted butter, softened

1¼ cups confectioners' sugar

3 medium free-range egg whites

¾ cup all-purpose flour

COFFEE SAUCE

1 tbsp instant coffee

2 tbsp superfine sugar

½ cup heavy cream

Preheat the oven to 400°F/200°C.

To start the "stalks" of the mushrooms, take four large and four small dariole molds and line them with plastic wrap. Fill with the softened ice cream and refreeze until set hard again.

Prepare templates for the tuiles using two margarine tub lids. Cut a large circular hole in one lid and a small circular hole in the other. Cream the butter and sugar together. Slowly add the egg whites to the mix, then fold in the flour. Place the templates on a baking sheet, spread the tuile mix over the holes with a palette knife, then lift off the templates, leaving perfect circles. You need four of each size.

Bake for 2–3 minutes, until lightly colored around the edges. Remove and place each disk of tuile over an eggcup or similar until cold. The soft tuiles will fold over into mushroom-cap shapes and become crisp.

To make the sauce, place the coffee and sugar in a teacup and add a little boiling water to dissolve to a very heavy syrup. Pour the cream into a bowl, then pour coffee onto it to color and flavor it.

Grate the chocolate and scatter the gratings in a circle around the edges of the plates. Spoon the coffee sauce into the middle. Unmold the ice creams, removing the plastic wrap, and stand these "stalks" upright, one of each size on each plate, in the center of the pool of sauce.

Turn the tuiles dome-side up, dust with the cocoa powder and confectioners' sugar in a small strainer, and place the small mushroom "caps" on the small mushroom "stalks"; the large "caps" on the large "stalks".

Serve the coffee mushrooms immediately.

Pork Scratchings
It's nice to offer your own scratchings with predinner drinks, or you can even use them as an appetizer for a meal.

MAKES AS MANY AS YOU LIKE!

pork rind (preferably from the loin)

fine salt

Cut any excess fat from underneath the pork rind.

Preheat the oven to 400°F/200°C/400°F.

Instead of scoring the rind, cut into 1/4-inch (5-mm) strips, then sprinkle with salt. Bake for 30–40 minutes (or longer for thicker pieces), until the pieces become crunchy.

Hot Spiced Nuts
My sister once picked up some nuts in a pub, chewed on them for about half an hour, then spat them out, only to discover they were olive pits. (Sorry, sis!)

SERVES 4–6

4 tbsp unsalted butter

1 1/2 cups mixed nuts

1/2 tsp each of dried chili flakes, medium curry powder, cayenne pepper, and ground ginger

5 tbsp brown sugar

salt, to taste

2 tbsp chopped fresh parsley

Preheat the oven to 425°F/220°C.

Melt the butter in a large sauté pan and sauté the nuts over a gentle heat for 3–4 minutes. Add the chili flakes, curry powder, cayenne, ginger, and sugar and cook for another 3–4 minutes.

Pour the nut mixture into a baking tray and dust with salt to taste. Stir, then roast for 5 minutes. Stir in the parsley and serve warm.

I like these with anchovies inside, but you can leave them out if you want. If you are going to add anchovies, buy those preserved in olive oil—these have less salt in them, and will taste much better inside the straw.

Cheese Straws

MAKES 24

13 oz (375 g) prepared puff pastry

4 tbsp unsalted butter, melted

10 anchovies, drained and blended to a paste

2 tbsp sun-dried tomato paste

1/2 cup freshly grated Parmesan cheese

2 tbsp chopped fresh flat-leaf parsley

salt, to taste

1 free-range egg yolk, beaten with 1 tbsp water

Preheat the oven to 425°F/220°C. Place the pastry on a floured work surface, roll out slightly, then cut to create two squares. Using a large, sharp knife, trim the edges of the pastry so that the straws cook uniformly. Brush the pastry lightly with the melted butter.

Spread the first pastry half with the anchovies. Spread the other piece of pastry with the sun-dried tomato paste. Sprinkle both with Parmesan, parsley, and some salt. Fold the bottom half of each piece over the top half, and gently press down. Roll out a little to compress the filling. Brush the pastry with the beaten egg.

With a large, sharp knife, cut the pastry, lengthwise, into 1/2-inch (1-cm) strips. Hold the ends between your fingers and carefully stretch and twist the strips in opposite directions.

Place the twisted strips onto lightly oiled baking sheets, spacing them evenly apart. Bake for 10–12 minutes, or until crisp and golden.

Remove the cheese straws from the oven and let cool on the baking sheet for 5 minutes to firm up. Using a spatula, carefully transfer the cheese straws to a wire rack or serving plate.

index